Pervez Musharraf has been the President of Pakistan since 1999. As a four-year old, he moved to Karachi upon the partition of India and creation of Pakistan, and his lifespan and career has been tied to the life of his country ever since. After attending Pakistan's military academy he became a commando in the elite Special Services Brigade, fighting in the wars with India in 1965 and 1971. He rose through the ranks to become General and Chief of Army Staff in 1998. He became President in a dramatic confrontation with Prime Minister Nawaz Sharif, and has remained in office despite two assassination attempts.

Pervez Musharraf

15 Sep '10

D0281175

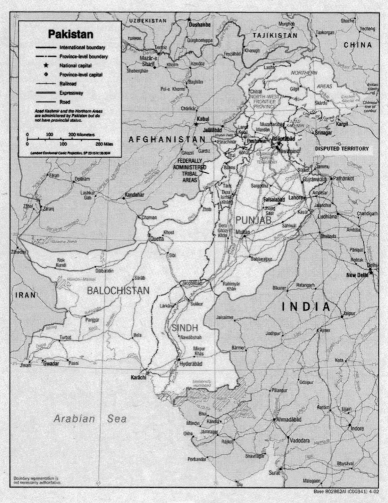

Map of Pakistan

IN THE LINE OF FIRE

A MEMOIR

PERVEZ MUSHARRAF

POCKET
BOOKS

LONDON • SYDNEY • NEW YORK • TORONTO

First published in Great Britain by Simon & Schuster UK Ltd, 2006
This edition first published by Pocket Books, 2008
An imprint of Simon & Schuster UK Ltd
A CBS COMPANY

Copyright © 2006 by President Pervez Musharraf

This book is copyright under the Berne Convention.
No reproduction without permission.
All rights reserved.

The right of President Pervez Musharraf to be identified as author
of this work has been asserted in accordance with sections 77 and 78
of the Copyright, Designs and Patents Act, 1988.

1 3 5 7 9 10 8 6 4 2

Simon & Schuster UK Ltd
Africa House
64–78 Kingsway
London WC2B 6AH

www.simonsays.co.uk

Simon & Schuster Australia
Sydney

A CIP catalogue record for this book is
available from the British Library.

ISBN: 978-1-4165-2778-7

Designed by Erich Hobbing

Printed and bound in Great Britain by
Cox & Wyman Ltd, Reading, Berks

I dedicate this book to the people of Pakistan—
those who toil, sacrifice, and pray for their country
and who wait patiently for a better future.
They deserve a committed, selfless leadership,
which can help them realize their boundless potential.

AND

To my mother,
whose unwavering faith in me
has been the driving force in my life—
her unconditional love and prayers
remain my unremitting source
of strength.

CONTENTS

PART THREE

THE HIJACKING DRAMA

PART FOUR

REBUILDING THE NATION

PART FIVE

THE WAR ON TERROR

PART SIX

PAKISTAN AT HOME AND ABROAD

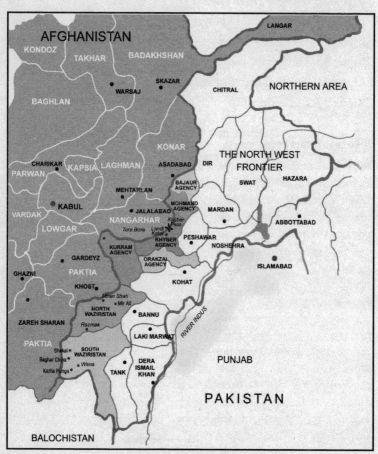

Map of the Federally Administered Tribal Areas

PREFACE

This book is a window into contemporary Pakistan and my role in shaping it. I have lived a passionate life, perhaps an impetuous one in my early years, but always I have focused on self-improvement and the betterment of my country. Often I have been chastised for being too forthright and candid, and I trust you will find these qualities reflected here. I do not shy away from sensitive issues, circumscribed only by certain dictates of national security.

I decided to write my autobiography after Pakistan took center stage in the world's conflicts, including the war on terror. There has been intense curiosity about me and the country I lead. I want the world to learn the truth.

Pakistan is a nation of many parts, rural and urban, rich and poor, highly educated and illiterate. Our 160 million people speak several different languages. Moderation collides with fanatical extremism, and westernization squares off against a conservative traditional culture. Governing Pakistan has been labeled by some as one of the most difficult jobs in the world. September 11, 2001, multiplied Pakistan's challenges many times over, amplifying domestic issues, and reshaping our international relations.

Our nation plays a key role in the developing story of the twenty-first century. What happens in Pakistan—socially, politically, and economically—in the coming years not only will help decide the outcome of the global war on terror, it will also shape what the future will look like for both Islam and the West. I am determined that that future be peaceful and prosperous—not just for Pakistan but for the entire international community. That vision is possible only if the Muslim world and the West, led by the United States, strive together toward resolving the issues before us.

My wife Sehba and other close family members, Hidayat Khaishgi, Huma, Aftab, and Shabnam have encouraged me throughout the process of writing this book. They gave me the confidence to persevere in spite of my otherwise busy schedule. My personal thanks are also due to Humayun Gauhar and Bruce Nichols for their editing contributions. Humayun has burned much midnight oil to help with the checking of my scripts. Most of all I would be remiss if I did not express special gratitude to my staff officer, Brigadier Asim Bajwa, for his painstaking and laborious efforts of both recording my thoughts and then transcribing them. Without his efficiency and devotion to me, the arduous task of completing the book would have been difficult to achieve.

My autobiography is my contribution to the history of our era. It is also of course my own story, expressed in my own way, about an eventful, turbulent life in which both luck and destiny played leading roles.

Pervez Musharraf
August 1, 2006
Islambad, Pakistan

PROLOGUE

FACE-TO-FACE WITH TERROR

Suddenly, there was a huge explosion and my car was airborne. I was face-to-face with terror. It was December 14, 2003, and I was on my way home to Army House after having landed in Islamabad a few minutes earlier. Religious extremists had struck right in my midst, and it was only by the grace of God that I was saved and no precious lives were lost.

I have confronted death and defied it several times in the past because destiny and fate have always smiled on me. I only pray that I have more than the proverbial nine lives of a cat.

I first avoided death as a teenager in 1961, when I was hanging upside down from the branch of a mango tree and it broke. When I hit the ground, my friends thought I was dead.

In 1972, when I was leading a company of commandos as a major in the mountainous Northern Areas, I should have been on a plane of Pakistan International Airlines that crashed into a glacier up in the Himalayas on a flight from Gilgit to Islamabad. At the last minute, I hadn't boarded it, because the bodies of two of my men who had been killed by an avalanche had been found, and my commanding officer and I opted to give up our seats to make the weight available for the conveyance of the bodies. The plane has still not been found.

I should have been on President Zia ul-Haq's C-130 airplane that crashed on August 17, 1988. I had been selected to become military secretary to the president, but as luck would have it, another brigadier was appointed to the post at the last minute. That poor man went to a fiery death instead of me. The United States ambassador, Arnold Lewis

1

Raphael, was also among the unfortunate passengers. The crash was never fully explained and remains a mystery in the modern history of Pakistan.

My closest call was in 1998, when, as a lieutenant general commanding the Mangla Corps, I was called to army headquarters in Rawalpindi for a conference. After finishing my official commitments, I went off with a friend, Lieutenant Colonel Aslam Cheema, to play bridge in his office, which was at a remote location. My commander of aviation, who was flying a helicopter back to Mangla started looking for me. He wanted to take me back to Mangla by the chopper to avoid the two-hour road journey. I would have readily flown with him. But he didn't know where I was, gave up looking, and left. The helicopter crashed and he died. A simple game of bridge with a friend saved me.

On October 12, 1999, I was chief of the army staff, the highest military position in Pakistan. My plane was about to land at Karachi from Colombo, when the prime minister effectively hijacked it from the ground, blocking the runway and closing all airports in Pakistan. He ordered my plane to leave Pakistan air space. Our fuel was so low that we would have crashed had the army not taken control of Karachi Airport before it was too late. We landed with only seven minutes of fuel to spare. The nearly fatal confrontation with the prime minister brought me to power—a story that I will relate fully in this book.

I also had two brushes with death in the India-Pakistan war of 1965.

As if these real risks were not enough, in 2001, when I took off from New York to Pakistan after the United Nations Summit, the pilot alarmed me by relaying a message that air traffic control claimed there might be a bomb on the plane. We returned to New York to find, after hours of search, that the warning was a hoax.

But the events of December 2003 put me in the front line of the war on terror and are part of my reason for writing this book now, while I am still fighting. On December 14, 2003, I landed from Karachi at Chaklala Air Force Base, about 2.5 miles (four kilometers) from Army House in Rawalpindi, and six miles (ten kilometers) from Islamabad. My aide-de-camp met me with two pieces of news: Pakistan had beaten India in a polo match, and Saddam Hussein had been caught. I made my way home to Army House. I was talking to my military secretary,

Major General Nadeem Taj, seated to my right, when I heard a loud, though muffled, thud behind us. As my car became airborne I immediately realized what was happening—I was staring terrorism in the face. I thought ruefully that while leaders of other countries only visit scenes of carnage later or see it on a television screen, I was personally in the midst of it. Not only that—I was the target. But unlike most leaders, I am also a soldier, chief of the army staff, and supreme commander of my country's armed forces. I am cut out to be in the midst of battle—trained, prepared, and equipped. Fate and the confluence of events have seen to it that Pakistan and I are in the thick of the fight against terrorism. My training has made me constantly ready for the assignment.

I had just crossed a bridge very near Army House when it happened. All four wheels of my car left the road and we shot quite some distance up in the air. Though the sound of the explosion was muffled by the armor plating of the car, I knew instinctively that it was a bomb. So did my military secretary. I knew too that it was a huge bomb, because it had lifted the three-ton Mercedes clean off the road. I looked back and saw a pall of smoke, dust, and debris on the bridge that we had just sped over. When we reached Army House, about 500 yards (400 meters) away, my deputy military secretary, Lieutenant Colonel Asim Bajwa, who had been traveling in another vehicle in my motorcade, confirmed that the explosion was an assassination attempt.

I entered the house to find my wife, Sehba, and my mother sitting in the family lounge. Sehba has been with me through thick and thin— avalanches, hijacked flights, risky road journeys. She had heard the explosion because Army House is so close to the bridge. She saw me enter and started to ask what the explosion had been about. My mother's back was to the door, and she didn't realize that I had arrived. I put my finger to my lips and motioned to Sehba to come out of the room, lest my mother hear and become terribly upset, as any mother would. In the corridor, I told Sehba that it had been a bomb meant to kill me, but that everything was all right now. After comforting her I drove back to the bridge to get a firsthand look at the situation. The bridge had literally been ripped apart—so if the explosion had occurred a second before my car reached the spot, we would have crashed twenty-five feet (7.5 meters) to the ground through the gap. There was still chaos at the bridge, and the people there were utterly surprised to see me.

Keeping the news from my mother was impossible, of course. She soon discovered what had happened as concerned colleagues, relatives, and friends started calling or dropping in. The story was all over television and on the front pages of newspapers the next day. I had overshadowed both Saddam and polo, at least in Pakistan.

That evening Sehba and I were to attend a wedding at the Serena Hotel in Islamabad. We did not hesitate. Both of us went. Our decision caused no little consternation among the guests, as they thought that I had good reason to remain in the safety of my house only a few hours after terrorists had tried to assassinate me. I am sure that my escape, and my not breaking my schedule, must have caused disappointment and dismay among the terrorists. Sticking to the schedule may have caused some concern among my security personnel, but they are trained to take such things in stride. It certainly did cause some inconvenience to motorists, as the traffic along the route was blocked.

Before the assassination attempt, I would flow with the normal traffic, stopping at every red light. Now things started changing. The police started blocking all traffic in either direction along the route that I was to take. There were new escort vehicles on either side of my car. And, of course, my exact schedule would not be known to anyone except those closest to me.

People had barely stopped chattering about this assassination attempt when—on December 25, 2003, a holiday—there was yet another one. After addressing a conference at Islamabad's Convention Center, I left for Army House at about one fifteen PM. My chief security officer, Colonel Ilyas, and my aide-de-camp, Major Tanveer, were in the lead car of my newly expanded motorcade. Next came the escort car. I was in the third car with my military secretary.

We crossed the fateful bridge, which was still under repair after the bomb blast, and reached a gasoline pump on the right. In front of the pump there was an opening in the median of the two-way road for U-turns. The oncoming traffic had been blocked. There was a policeman standing at the opening. I noticed that though all the oncoming traffic was facing straight toward us, a Suzuki van was standing obliquely, as if to drive into the opening to get to my side of the road. Reflexively, I turned and looked over my right shoulder at the van, as one does when one sees something odd. Then I looked straight ahead. It all took a split second. Hardly had I turned my head back when there was a deafening bang and my car was up in the air again.

All hell broke loose. There was smoke; there was debris; there were body parts and pieces of cars. Vehicles had been blown to smithereens, human beings ripped to pieces. It turned dark, and we couldn't see anything. It was the middle of the afternoon, but it seemed like dusk.

Jan Mohammad, my admirable driver, reflexively put his foot on the brake. I took out my Glock pistol, which is always with me, and shouted to Jan Mohammad in Urdu, *"Dabaa, dabaa"*—"drive, drive." He floored the accelerator but had gone only about 100 yards (90 meters) when we came to another gasoline pump. Again there was a horrendous bang. Again all hell broke loose. The first explosion had come from our right rear; this one came straight on from the immediate right front. Something big and very heavy hit the windshield. I don't know what it was, but it made a big dent in the bulletproof glass—which, however, did not break. It came from such an angle that any broken glass would have gotten either my driver or me.

Once again my car took off. Again there were human parts, car parts, debris, smoke, and dust—and a lot of noise. Again it went dark—very dark. It seemed as if midnight had come at noon.

My car's tires had blown. We were on the rims now, but such cars are designed to go on their rims for thirty-five miles or so (fifty or sixty kilometers). Again Jan Mohammad hit the brakes, and again I shouted, *"Dabaa, dabaa.* Hit the accelerator. Let's get out of here." The car lurched forward on its rims, making a lot of noise, like a rattletrap, and got us to Army House.

Sehba, of course, had heard the horrific explosions and had run out to the porch. When she saw the first car roll in on its rims—spewing smoke, filled with holes, and plastered with human flesh—she started screaming. She screamed and screamed. I had never seen her do that before. She is always calm in the face of danger and during horrific events, then she has a delayed reaction the next day, when tears come. But now she was screaming uncontrollably, hysterically. She wouldn't look at me. She started running toward the gate. I asked her, "What are you doing? Where are you going?" But she just went on screaming. I couldn't understand what she was saying, except, "What is going on? What is happening?" It was understandable hysteria, and it helped her to get the shock out of her system. It also diverted my mind and the minds of others with me from our own shock. I got hold of her and took her inside the house. I sat with her and told her, "Look at me, I am all right, everything is all right." When she finally calmed down I went out again.

I looked at the cars and saw that the lead car was the most badly damaged, especially its right rear door. It too had sunk down to its rims. Tanveer's hair was standing straight up, I suppose because the blasts had created static. Any normal car would have been blown to bits, destroyed beyond recognition. As it was, human flesh and blood were all over the cars. They were a gruesome sight.

The squad car that had been behind me was also very badly damaged. All in all, I was told, fourteen people had been killed. Three of our people had been injured. The poor policeman standing at the gap between the two roads had come in front of the first suicide van and been blown to bits. A police van had stopped the second suicide bomber from hitting my car by ramming into his vehicle. The van had blown up, killing all five policemen in it, including an inspector. It was heartrending. The first suicide bomber had hit the nine-inch-high (22.5-centimeter) divider between the roads and rolled back, probably because he had made a cold start with a heavy, bomb-laden vehicle. If the police hadn't blocked the oncoming traffic, God alone knows how many more would have been killed or mutilated.

We later discovered that there was supposed to be a third suicide bomber to attack me frontally where the road had no median divider. For some reason he didn't materialize. At the time I thought that either he had lost his nerve after seeing what had happened to his two co-terrorists, or he thought that they must have gotten me, and ran away to save himself and come back to kill another day. If he had not abandoned the job he would almost certainly have succeeded in killing me, for by then my car was in very bad shape and was "naked," without protection. Such are the ways of the Almighty.

The investigation into my would-be assassins led us to some of al Qaeda's top people in Pakistan. The full story of that investigation needs to be told, because it represents one of our greatest victories in the war on terror. I will relate it in full in these pages. But first, you need to know how I came to be the man the assassins were targeting. The story of my life coincides almost from the beginning with the story of my country—so the chapters that follow are a biography not only of a man, but of Pakistan as well.

PART ONE

IN THE BEGINNING

CHAPTER 1

TRAIN TO PAKISTAN

Date: August 14, 1947

Place: India and Pakistan

Event: The twilight of the British Empire, with the independence of India and the creation of the nation-state of Pakistan.

These were troubled times. These were momentous times. There was the light of freedom; there was the darkness of genocide. It was the dawn of hope; it was the twilight of empire. It was a tale of two countries in the making.

On a hot and humid summer day, a train hurtled down the dusty plains from Delhi to Karachi. Hundreds of people were piled into its compartments, stuffed in its corridors, hanging from the sides, and sitting on the roof. There was not an inch to spare. But the heat and dust were the least of the passengers' worries. The tracks were littered with dead bodies—men, women, and children, many hideously mutilated. The passengers held fast to the hope of a new life, a new beginning in a new country—Pakistan—that they had won after great struggle and sacrifice.

Thousands of Muslim families left their homes and hearths in India that August, taking only the barest of necessities with them. Train after train transported them into the unknown. Many did not make it—they were tortured, raped, and killed along the way by vengeful Sikhs and

Hindus. Many Hindus and Sikhs heading in the opposite direction, leaving Pakistan for India, were butchered in turn by Muslims. Many a train left India swarming with passengers only to arrive in Pakistan carrying nothing but the deafening silence of death. All those who made this journey and lived have a tale to tell.

This is the story of a middle-class family, a husband and wife who left Delhi with their three sons. Their second-born boy was then four years and three days old. All that he remembered of the train journey was his mother's tension. She feared massacre by the Sikhs. Her tension increased every time the train stopped at a station and she saw dead bodies lying along the tracks and on the platforms. The train had to pass through the whole of the Punjab, where a lot of killings were taking place.

The little boy also remembered his father's anxiety about a box that he was guarding closely. It was with him all the time. He protected it with his life, even sleeping with it under his head, like a pillow. There were 700,000 rupees in it, a princely sum in those days. The money was destined for the foreign office of their new country.

The little boy also remembered arriving in Karachi on August 15. He remembered, too, the swarm of thankful people who greeted them. There was food, there was joy, there were tears, there was laughter, and there was a lot of hugging and kissing. There were thanksgiving prayers too. People ate their fill.

I have started my narration in the third person because the story of that August train is something I have been told by my elders, not something I remember in detail. I have little memory of my early years. I was born in the old Mughal part of Delhi on August 11, 1943, in my paternal family home, called Nehar Wali Haveli—"House Next to the Canal." A *haveli* is a typical Asian-style home built around a central courtyard. *Nehar* means canal.

My brother Javed, who is something of a genius, was born one year before me. When my younger brother Naved arrived later, our family was complete.

Nehar Wali Haveli belonged to my great-grandfather, Khan Bahadur Qazi Mohtashim ud din, who was the deputy collector of revenue in Delhi. He arranged for his daughter Amna Khatoon, my paternal grandmother, to be married to Syed Sharfuddin. The honorific *Syed* denotes a family that is descended directly from the Holy Prophet Muhammad, peace be upon him. I am told that generations ago my father's family came from Saudi Arabia.

My grandfather was said to be an exceptionally handsome man and was a landlord of some stature from Panipat, in northern India. He left my grandmother, Amna Khatoon, and married a second time, leaving their two sons, Syed Musharrafuddin (my father) and Syed Ashrafuddin, to their mother. She moved with her sons to her father's home, where I would be born.

My father, Syed Musharrafuddin, and his elder brother graduated from the famous Aligarh Muslim University, now in India. My father then joined the foreign office as an accountant. He ultimately rose to the position of director. He died just a few months after I took the reins of my country.

Khan Bahadur Qazi Fazle Ilahi, my mother's father, was a judge— the word *qazi* means judge. He was progressive, very enlightened in thought, and quite well off. He spent liberally on the education of all his sons and daughters. My mother, Zarin, graduated from Delhi University and earned a master's degree from Lucknow University at a time when few Indian Muslim women ventured out to get even a basic education. After graduation, she married my father and shifted to Nehar Wali Haveli.

My parents were not very well off, and both had to work to make ends meet, especially to give their three sons the best education they could afford. The house was sold in 1946, and my parents moved to an austere government home built in a hollow square at Baron Road, New Delhi. We stayed in this house until we migrated to Pakistan in 1947.

My mother became a schoolteacher to augment the family income. My parents were close, and their shared passion was to give their children the best possible upbringing—our diet, our education, and our values. My mother walked two miles (more than three kilometers) to school and two miles back, not taking a tonga (a horse-drawn carriage), to save money to buy fruit for us. We always looked forward to that fruit.

Providing a good education to our children has always remained the focus of our family, a value that both my parents took from their parents and instilled in us. Though we were not by any means rich, we always studied in the top schools. In Delhi, Javed and I joined Church High School, but I have no memory of it. Neither do I have any memory of friends or neighbors.

CHAPTER 2

SETTLING IN KARACHI

Karachi is a very old city; like most of our cities, it dates back to antiquity. It started off as a fishing village on the coast of the Arabian Sea. In 1947 it became the capital of Pakistan. The capital has since been shifted to Islamabad, a picturesque new city nestled in the foothills of the Himalayas.

On our arrival in Karachi, my father was allotted two rooms in a long barracks of ten two-room units in a place called Jacob Lines. There was a kitchen and an old-style toilet that had no flush mechanism. Along one side of the building ran a veranda covered by a green wooden trellis. Other uprooted members of our family—assorted aunts and uncles and cousins—came to live with us. At one time there were eighteen of us living in those two rooms. But we were all happy. I now realize that we accepted all this discomfort because our morale was supremely high—as were our spirit of sacrifice and our sense of accommodation. Actually, we could have filed a claim to get a house in place of the huge home that my maternal grandfather had owned in Delhi. Left behind, it had become "enemy property." But for some reason no one pursued this.

One night I saw a thief hiding behind the sofa in our apartment. Though I was only a little boy, I was bold enough to quietly slip out to my mother, who was sleeping on the veranda (my father had left for Turkey). I told her that there was a thief inside, and she started screaming. Our neighbours assembled. The thief was caught with the only thing of value we had—a bundle of clothes. While he was being thrashed, he cried out that he was poor and very hungry. This evoked

15

such sympathy that when the police came to take him away, my mother declared that he was not a thief and served him a hearty meal instead. It was a sign of the sense of accommodation and of helping each other that we shared in those days.

Our cook, Shaukat, who had come with my mother when she got married—in her dowry, so to speak—also came with us from Delhi. He was an excellent cook. He now lives in Hyderabad, Sindh, and I last met him when I was a major general.

My brother Javed and I were enrolled in St. Patrick's School, run by Catholic missionaries, but I don't remember much about it at this time, except that we had to walk a mile to it and a mile back (about 1.5 kilometers each way).

My father started working at the new foreign office, which was then located in a building called Mohatta Palace. It was later to become the residence of Miss Fatima Jinnah, sister of Pakistan's founding father, Mohammad Ali Jinnah, whom we respectfully call Quaid-e-Azam, "great leader." It is now a museum. We would visit him there sometimes. I remember that the facilities were so sparse that he didn't even have a chair to sit on. He used a wooden crate instead. Often the office ran short of paper clips, thumbtacks, and even pens. My father would use the thorns of a desert bush that grows everywhere in Karachi to pin his papers together. He would also sometimes write with a thorn by dipping it in ink. This was the state of affairs in the new Pakistan, not least because India was stalling and raising all sorts of hurdles rather than sending us our portion of the pre-Partition assets. Actually, the British had decided to quit India—"grant freedom," as they arrogantly called it—in June 1948. But Lord Louis Mountbatten, the last viceroy, persuaded London that Britain could not hold on till then and had the date moved forward to August 1947. This was announced in April 1947. In the frenetic four months before Partition, one of the many decisions made mutually by the representatives of Pakistan, India, and the British government was the allocation of assets to the two new countries. Now free and no longer under the dictates of the British government, India was not honoring its commitment.

My father was a very honest man, not rich at all, but he would give money to the poor—"because their need is greater." This was a point of contention with my mother, who was always struggling to make ends meet. "First meet your own needs before meeting the needs of others," she would tell him. Like most Asian mothers, despite their demure public demeanor, my mother was the dominant influence on our family. But on the issue of giving to the needy my father always got his way, because he wouldn't talk about it.

My mother had to continue working to support us. Instead of becoming a schoolteacher again, she joined the customs service. I remember her in her crisp white uniform going to Korangi Creek for the arrival of the seaplane, which she would inspect. I also remember that she once seized a cargo of smuggled goods and was given a big reward for it.

One sad event that I remember vividly was the death of our founder, the Quaid-e-Azam, on September 11, 1948. It was akin to a thirteen-month-old baby losing its only parent. Quaid-e-Azam Mohammad Ali Jinnah has best been described by his biographer, the American writer Stanley Wolpert: "Few individuals significantly alter the course of history. Fewer still modify the map of the world. Hardly anyone can be credited with creating a nation-state. Mohammad Ali Jinnah did all three." His death shook the confidence and exuberance of the infant nation. The funeral procession had to pass through Bundar Road—the main avenue of Karachi—very close to our house. I remember sitting on a wall along the road for hours waiting for the funeral cortège, with friends from our locality. When it came, everyone cried. I could not hold back my tears. It was a day of the greatest national loss and mourning. The nation felt a sense of hopelessness and uncertainty. It is to the credit of the Quaid's successor, Liaqat Ali Khan, our first prime minister, that he ably pulled the nation out of its depression.

Those were happy years in Karachi. Hardship was overcome by hope and the excitement of being in our new country and playing one's part in building it. This excitement and hope infused the young too. The thrill that comes from the memory of hope to be fulfilled, the excitement of great things to come, often returns to me. Once again I am transported back to being a little boy on the train to Pakistan. Those years in Karachi were an important time for me, as indeed they were for all of us who had taken such a risk by migrating to our new country.

Gradually, as we settled down, the initial exuberance wore off, and the uncertainties of our present and future began to weigh on my parents.

A metamorphosis took place in me in the first months and years after Partition. An uprooted little boy found earth that was natural to him. He took root in it forever. I would protect that earth with my life.

CHAPTER 3

TURKEY: THE FORMATIVE YEARS

Two years after arriving in Karachi, my father was posted to our embassy in Ankara, Turkey, as superintendent of the accounts department. My brothers and I were very excited by the idea of going to another country. Our seven-year stay there would prove to have a huge influence on my worldview.

Turkey and Pakistan have many things in common—first and foremost, Islam. Just as Pakistan was a new country in 1947, Atatürk's country was a "New Turkey." With the fall of the Ottoman caliphate, Mustafa Kemal had saved Turkey from balkanization and modernized it by dragging it out of dogma and obscurantism. His grateful people call him Atatürk, "father of the turks." As a victorious commander he was perhaps inevitably also called *pasha*, "general." In fact, even his second name, Kemal, which means "wonderful," was given to him by a teacher because he was quite remarkable as a young boy. Thus, Mustafa Kemal Pasha Atatürk.

Much of Pakistan's cuisine originated in Turkey. So does Urdu, our national language—my parents' tongue. *Ordu* is a Turkish word meaning "army." Two characteristics of the Turkish people have made a special imprint on my mind. One is their deep sense of patriotism and pride in everything Turkish. The other is their very visible love and affection for Pakistan and Pakistanis.

For three young boys, the journey to Turkey was filled with wonder. First, we sailed on HMS *Dwarka* from Karachi to Basra in Iraq. Traveling by ship was a unique experience for us. Then we took a train to Ankara, a journey of about three or four days, but very enjoyable compared with the fateful train to Pakistan in 1947, a trip fraught with fear and danger.

We found a house in Ankara and stayed in it for a year. We would move to three more houses, staying for a year each in the second and third, before settling in the fourth for the remainder of our time in Turkey. These were only medium-size houses, but comfortable and adequate for our needs—certainly a far cry from the two-room apartment we had left behind.

As a working woman, my mother joined the Pakistani embassy as a typist. She was a very good typist and won an embassy competition for speed. Perhaps that is why she is also a good harmonium player. She had a good voice too. Both my parents loved music and dancing, especially ballroom dancing. My father was a very elegant, very graceful dancer. During the coronation of the queen of England, there was a dance competition in which many of our embassy people participated. After a process of elimination, my parents won the first prize in ballroom dancing.

Naturally, the embassy staff did their utmost to help us settle down, but it was really our Turkish relatives who made us feel at home. One of my mother's brothers, Ghazi Ghulam Haider, who became the first English-language newscaster on Radio Pakistan, was—how shall I put it?—a great romantic. He was always falling in love, and every so often we would discover that he had married again. Uncle Haider's first wife was a half-Turkish woman whose mother was a full Turk. Her brother, Hikmet, left India for Turkey and settled down there.

On reaching Ankara my father tried to locate Hikmet, even placing an advertisement in the newspapers, without success. Then, as luck would have it, a Turkish woman who knew Hikmet joined the Pakistani embassy as a typist. Her name was Mehershan. Hikmet was in Istanbul. She telephoned him, and he came to Ankara to meet us. He introduced us to our other relatives. We would meet every so often, and we were always in and out of each other's homes. One of those relatives was Colonel Kadri Bey. He was married to Leman Khanum. Of their two sons, Metin was extremely handsome, with a golden-brown moustache and curly hair, and Chetin is a wonderful man. I am still in contact with them.

For the first six or eight months of our stay, my brothers and I were enrolled in a Turkish school. The English taught there was rudimentary, but the school helped us to learn very good Turkish, which went a long way in enabling us to become good friends with Turkish boys. Children at that age learn very fast and very well, and our accent and pronunciation became perfect. Soon, we were so fluent that our Turkish friends couldn't tell we were foreigners. Even now, when I speak Turkish in Pakistan, it is very different from that of our interpreters. But we needed English as our medium of instruction. My parents discovered a German woman who had a private school attended by a number of foreign boys and girls. We were admitted to her school and studied there for the rest of our time in Turkey. She was Madame Kudret—Kudret being her Turkish husband's surname. She laid great emphasis on mathematics and geography, and that is why Javed and I became very good in both subjects; we were especially good at making calculations in our heads. Madame Kudret had a unique ability to make us enjoy mathematics, and she taught us easy methods for mental calculations. She honed our skills by making the children compete with one another. My later marks were always the best in mathematics and geography, thanks to Madame Kudret. Even in class ten (the equivalent of tenth grade in the United States), when my grades dropped dramatically for reasons that I shall explain, I earned a perfect score in mathematics. Madame Kudret also taught us world geography; we learned how to draw and read maps and how to identify countries, capitals, oceans, rivers, deserts, and mountains. This knowledge helped me immensely when I joined the Pakistan Army.

Since Madame Kudret's school was coeducational, there were non-Turkish girls there too. All three of us brothers were very shy around girls. They would invite us to their homes and parties, but we would invariably feel very awkward. I think they realized this and found it very amusing: ten-year-old girls are far more mature than ten-year-old boys, and they could run circles around us.

It was in Turkey, too, that I developed my lifelong fondness for sport. I trained in gymnastics and played volleyball, badminton, and football. Badminton is not a Turkish sport, but it was played in our embassy. Turkey is a soccer-crazed nation. Of course we also played marbles, as little boys do the world over, but this made my mother very angry. Our hands would be chapped in winter, sometimes to the point of bleeding, making it obvious that I had been playing marbles. I would bandage my hands and hide the marbles from my mother by putting them in socks.

I was a precocious but naughty little boy, always good at my studies, but not brilliant like Javed. I was not very studious; Javed was. Those who are familiar with Mark Twain's works will understand when I say that I was something of a Tom Sawyer, with the difference that I went to school happily.

The orchard in the Lebanese embassy in front of our house had many fruit trees. I observed the guard there and noticed that he would take a short round of the embassy building in one direction, and then a much longer round coming back. It was on the longer round that I would get into the embassy compound and pluck fruit from the trees.

Since I got involved in boyish games and pranks and often did things that other boys wouldn't or couldn't do, I became very popular in my neighborhood. Sometimes my mother would discover my antics and get very angry. She would even get angry with my friends when they came to collect me. "Go away," she would say, "let him study." This would upset me, but there was little I could do except bide my time and wait for an opportune moment to steal out to play with them.

One outdoor activity that my mother could not keep me from was accompanying my father on duck shoots. He would go with the embassy staff to a lake called Gol Bashi, which is now in a crowded part of Ankara. I found these shoots most enjoyable and adventurous. The most exciting part was the silent, motionless wait when the ducks would fly in, and it was even more exciting when occasionally I was allowed to shoot. I can never forget my first successful shot, when I got a duck in the water. I must admit that I never succeeded with flying shots.

Like neighborhoods the world over, ours had boys' gangs. We would fight, but the fighting was nothing serious. We threw stones at each other and made shields with which to protect ourselves. Each gang had its own flag. Even at that age I was very good at making strategies and planning tactics to ambush and trap other gangs. We would lure them into an area, ambush them, and run off with their flag to the top of a hill. It was defeat for them and victory for us!

Being the outdoors type, I suffered torture when I was forced to stay indoors. I had more than my fair share of energy, and it had to be expended somehow. It had to find outlets outside the house; burning it up inside was impossible. Of course, in those days there was no television, which has turned many of today's boys into couch potatoes.

Javed was very fond of books, but I read them only when I had to. We became members of the British Council Library and would take out our weekly quota of two books each. Being a voracious reader, Javed would finish his books in a couple of days and then read my books in the next two—if not sooner! Before the week was up he would want to return to the library and take out four more books. I had perhaps read one, or not even that. So I would insist that we wait until the end of the week, after which I would want to renew one of the books and take out only one new one. This would upset Javed and lead to arguments.

We had a Turkish maid named Fatima whom we respectfully called Hanim, meaning "madame"—thus, Fatima Hanim. Our parents made it a point that we show respect to elders regardless of their station in life. We were not allowed to call our domestic staff "servants"—they were employees who earned an honest living and deserved respect.

Fatima Hanim was an old, uneducated woman, quite a simpleton really, but extremely hardworking. We would tell her that the earth is flat and that Pakistan is at its edge and when you look down you can see paradise. Either she really believed us or she went along with our game, because she always insisted that we take her to Pakistan so that she could look down and see paradise.

There were two military attachés at our embassy—colonels Mustafa and Ismail—whose smart ceremonial uniforms attracted me to the army at a very young age. But a man who had a greater impact on me was Hameed, their personal assistant. Hameed was a junior commissioned officer, a very smart and handsome young man from Kashmir. He was very fond of our family and would take me and Javed out on long treks in the hills. There was a zoo very far away, and we would trek up to it and then return on foot. Hameed was very good at games and would coach us. It was he who taught me badminton and volleyball.

Across the road from our embassy was the house of a retired Turkish general who had become a big industrialist. He had a beautiful daughter named Reyan. She could see Hameed sitting in his office from her window. One day he was called and invited to have tea at their house.

Much to Hameed's consternation, the old general offered him his beautiful daughter's hand in marriage. They married, and it caused quite a stir. When Hameed was transferred back to Pakistan, she went along with him. He was so bright that he advanced in rank and retired as a major. He started his own business and did quite well. The last time I met him was when I was a brigade major in Karachi. Sadly, he suffered a heart attack and died suddenly. On one of my foreign trips as president of Pakistan my wife and I met Reyan in London.

My love of dogs began in Turkey. We had a beautiful brown dog named Whiskey. I loved him. He was killed in a road accident but left with me a lifelong love of dogs. I prefer small dogs, though, not the huge ones. This surprises my friends, for they expect a commando to have something like a rottweiler. I think people who keep rottweilers, and similar dogs, have a need to cultivate a macho image.

Our seven years in Turkey passed in a flash. We departed with very heavy hearts, saying good-bye to a country that we had come to love, to our relatives, and to our many good friends. We were all crying. Those were among the most enjoyable and formative years of my life. Our journey back was filled with wonder, too, for my father drove his small Austin Mini up to Basra. We drove through Turkey, Syria, and Lebanon. We crossed Jordan into Iraq, ending at the port city of Basra. From there our car was put into the hold of a ship and we returned to Karachi by sea, just as we had left it seven years earlier.

CHAPTER 4

HOME

In October 1956, when I was thirteen years old, we arrived back in Karachi. The sheer hassle of settling down dulled much of the pain of leaving Turkey and our many friends and relatives there. Coming home has its own charm, too, of course, even though our home was very different now. In the seven years that we had been away, Karachi had exploded into a large and vibrant cosmopolitan metropolis. The city was humming with life.

My father reported back to the foreign office, still located in Mohatta Palace. We soon found a house in Nazimabad Block 3, one of many new settlements that had mushroomed after independence to accommodate the millions who had fled India. It was well planned, with wide roads and boulevards. Most of its neighborhoods were middle-class or lower-middle-class. Ours was one of the few families on the street to own a car.

My mother soon found another job. My parents were friendly with a Dutch couple, Mr. and Mrs. Brink. Mr. Brink was the general manager of the Philips factory, located in a new industrial area called SITE, and my mother became his secretary. Her pay was good, and one of the perks of the job was that she got a Philips radio at a discount. She worked there for a long time. Years later, I stayed for three days with the Brinks in the Netherlands.

That fall, Javed and I took the entrance examination for classes nine and eight, respectively, at St. Patrick's, the old and highly regarded Catholic missionary school for boys that we had attended earlier. Both of us did very badly in Urdu, not having studied that language in Turkey. Javed got in anyway, because of his excellent showing in every other subject. I didn't, and was temporarily admitted to a school called Mary Colaco. My parents immediately worked to bring our Urdu up to scratch. We picked it up quickly; it was, after all, their tongue. They both taught it to us, and they also hired a tutor. I became good enough to get into St. Patrick's after three or four months, though I suspect that my swift admission may also have had something to do with Javed's high score on the first quarterly examination he took. They must have thought that the brother of such a bright boy couldn't be a completely hopeless case.

My younger brother, Naved, joined St. Patrick's School later, in class six, in 1957. He was a steady boy who earned average grades.

In Ankara we had walked to school through beautiful fields. In Karachi our school was too far for walking, and the route wasn't pretty either. Sometimes my father dropped us off in his car; usually we went by bus. The bus was always brimming with people, with hardly ever any vacant seats. To return home, Javed and I walked from school to the Regal Cinema nearby, where the bus had to slow down at a turning. There, we would both jump onto the moving bus, thanks to our gymnastics—a dangerous practice, but boys at that age normally throw caution to the wind. It would take us half an hour to get home, dead beat from the heat and the humidity.

Our neighborhood, Nazimabad, was a tough place to live, and it has become tougher since. I would not call it the Harlem of Karachi, but perhaps it was the South Bronx. A boy had to be street-smart to survive. There were the inevitable street gangs, and needless to say, I joined one. Needless to say, too, I was one of the tough boys.

Flying kites is a favorite sport in Pakistan, but it is done with a difference. Here, as in Afghanistan, people dip the string in glue filled with crushed glass. There are kite fights, with one flier trying to cut the string of the other to make him lose his kite. The flyers' fingers always get cut, and bleed. The cuts are very painful, much worse than paper cuts. The severed kite floats slowly to the ground and, in an unspoken tradition, the boy who catches it gets to keep it.

A recent popular American novel set in Afghanistan, *The Kite Runner,* brings this tradition to life, and my own experience included a variation of a key moment in that story. There was a bully in our area who would walk up to the boy who had caught a kite and demand that he hand it over, or else. Most boys would oblige. One day my older brother got hold of some string from a cut kite. The bully, accompanied by two other boys, rudely asked him to hand it over. I held my brother's hand and said, "Why should we give you the string?" Then, without thinking, I punched the bully hard. A fight ensued, and I really thrashed him. After that people recognized me as a sort of boxer, and I became known as a *dada geer*—an untranslatable term that means, roughly, a tough guy whom you don't mess with. The lesson I learned was that if you call a bully's bluff, he crumbles. The secret is to stand your ground for a few seconds, and your initial fright vanishes. This lesson later stood me in good stead as a commando.

I remember St. Patrick's with great affection. I learned a lot there, and not only from books. Of course I couldn't help being naughty, and I would get punished, especially by one teacher, Mr. De Lima. I think that at the back of their minds, my teachers compared me unfavourably with my brother, who continued to get superb grades. Sometimes I was made to kneel in a corner; sometimes I had to stand outside the classroom. Once when I was standing outside, I saw my father coming to meet with the principal. I sneaked behind the building so that he wouldn't see that I was being punished.

The punishment I remember best happened when Father Todd caught me throwing chalk at another boy in class and gave me six of the choicest blows on my posterior with a sturdy cane. It stung like hell. When, as president of Pakistan, I returned to St. Patrick's for a reunion, I reminded Father Todd of the caning. "I felt like sitting on ice, Father," I told him during my speech. An old classmate of mine came to the microphone and said, "Father, did you know at that time that you were caning the presidential seat?" Everyone laughed. Father Todd is a good soul and I have great regard for him, as I do for all my teachers.

One teacher was Mr. Mendis. He was very good and worked on building our character. I can never forget how he would try to inculcate in us the attributes that make a gentleman. He himself personified the qualities of a gentleman.

•   •   •

Of course my pranks weren't limited to school. My romantic uncle Ghazi Ghulam Haider, the one who married the half-Turkish woman, was great at mixing with youngsters and would take the lead in many practical jokes. He would pile eight or ten of us boys into his car—a German Opel Rekord—and go looking for mischief.

One day, he took us to Frere Gardens, where people go to relax in the evenings. He spotted a man who was as bald as a golf ball, sitting on a bench. For some reason, the man had oiled his bald pate, making matters worse, for it was shining like a mirror and inviting trouble. "I'll give five rupees to the boy who slaps that man on the head," announced Uncle Haider. We all shrank back, asking him how we could do such a thing and get away with it. "Watch me," said my redoubtable uncle. He walked right up behind the man and gave him a tight smack right in the middle of his shiny head, saying, "Bashir, there you are. I've been searching for you." It must have stung like hell. The baldy spun around in shock, but before he could say anything my uncle apologized profusely. "I am so extremely sorry, my brother. You are a carbon copy of a good friend of mine and I mistook you for him. He was supposed to be here." The poor man, still in shock, shifted to another bench some distance away, looking sheepishly this way and that. We were aghast but also relieved: that was the end of that, we hoped, and Uncle Haider would think up something less dangerous and embarrassing next. Lo and behold, he raised the stakes. "Now I will give ten rupees," our disbelieving ears heard him saying, "to the boy who smacks his bald head again." We were appalled. To get away with it once was a miracle. To get away with it twice was asking for very serious trouble. When we demurred, Uncle Haider said, "Watch me." He stole up behind the man again and smacked him even harder on the head, saying, "O Bashir, there you are. I just saw a man who looks exactly like you and smacked him on the head." The poor man spun around again in utter consternation, his eyes wild with disbelief. His mouth gaped like a goldfish. Before he could get a word out, Uncle Haider started acting contrite. He apologized even more profusely, asking in mock dismay, "How was I to know that you had shifted seats?" Without giving the stunned man a chance to say anything, he walked away. We all rolled on the grass with laughter.

Don't get Uncle Haider wrong, though. He was in the air force and had won the sword in the Indian Air Force before Partition.

Before I reached class ten, at the age of fifteen, I had been an above-average student, usually among the first four in my class. That year, however, my grades dropped dramatically. The cause: my first romance. A first crush is a distraction that all young people must suffer sooner or later, but different people handle it differently. The later a man gets it, the more of an ass he makes of himself. I let it become the focus of my life, not least because it came out of the blue. Truth to tell, she made the first move. I was still too shy to initiate a romance, let alone woo a girl.

She was a neighbor, about my age, perhaps a year older. I found it far more convenient to be wooed than to have to court a girl myself. Anyway, I could think of nothing else except her. She didn't know English, and I wasn't brilliant in Urdu. A friend would read her letters to me in Urdu, and I would dictate my reply to him in Urdu. The person who would deliver the letters was my younger brother's friend. He was slightly built and could squeeze in and out of most places. He would deliver my letters and pick up hers, by quietly sneaking into her house.

I went so far as to get my Nani Amma, my maternal grandmother, into the act without her realizing it. She was a lovely woman who used to wear a burka, as conservative Muslim women do. I would tell Nani Amma that she must visit the neighbors, and then direct her to the girl's house. Before she went, I would hide a letter in a pocket of her burka and pass a message to the girl explaining where to find it. Poor Nani Amma would go to the girl's house as an unwitting courier with a romantic letter in her pocket. Had she known, she would have been quite upset, to put it mildly. Certainly my mother would have come to know of it.

This girl was very beautiful. It was puppy love, really, just an infatuation, and it lasted only until my parents moved to another house, far away on Garden Road, near the Karachi Zoo with its beautiful gardens.

On Garden Road, I fell straight into my next romance. She was a beautiful Bengali girl from East Pakistan (now Bangladesh). This crush was somewhat less frivolous than my first. She is happily married now, and lives in Bangladesh. I think my mother suspected all along, because I suddenly slipped in my studies. She wasn't sure, but she became very annoyed with me for my poor results. I did well enough on my finals for class ten, ranking in the second division and missing the first by just four points. I earned the first prize in mathematics.

At that point, my mother decided that Javed would go into the civil service of Pakistan (CSP), the most prestigious branch of our bureaucracy. Her youngest son, Naved, she decreed, would become a medical doctor. With my excess energy and mischievousness, I would go into the army. And so it came to pass.

CHAPTER 5

LEAVING THE NEST

I could not get into the army right away. First I had to go to college to get through classes eleven and twelve, which we call freshman of arts (FA) or, if you take science, freshman of science (FSc). This is unlike the American and British systems, where grades eleven and twelve are part of high school. I chose nonmedical science. Only after doing my FSc would I be eligible to join the army, provided I passed the military's highly exacting entrance examinations and arduous physical tests.

Frankly, none of the colleges in Karachi were good enough at the time, so my parents sent me to the famous Forman Christian College in Lahore, better known as FC College, which is run by American missionaries. Lahore was the obvious choice. It has long been a center of learning, art, culture, poetry, and literature, not just of Pakistan but of the entire subcontinent. The college principal was a wonderful American gentleman who mixed with all the students. Another American I remember there was our director of physical education, Mr. Mumby. He was very good at organizing athletic tournaments.

Javed went to Government College—now a university—in Lahore, a school for the brightest students. Yet another of Lahore's famous colleges is Islamia College, which among other things produced most of our international cricketers in the early years of Pakistan.

Forman Christian College was known as a college for anglicized "modern" students; Government College attracted the more studious types, and Islamia the more earthy types. All three have produced many leaders for Pakistan in various fields because they keep their students grounded in native culture and history, quite unlike those boys who went to foreign universities, which have mostly produced political leaders disconnected from Pakistan's culture and history, leaders who have damaged the country, not only with their corruption but also with their alien political and economic philosophies.

I was keenly aware of never having lived away from home on my own. I didn't realize then that I would never return to live with my parents as a dependent. A time would come, as it naturally does in life's course, when roles would be reversed and my parents would come and live with me. But for now, I was on my own and terribly homesick. However, I soon got into the swing of things and made good friends.

I was assigned room and board in Kennedy Hall. Its warden, Mr. Dutta, was also our English teacher. He was a good man, tough but fair. Forman Christian is a beautiful college and has fine facilities for studies and sport, the latter being compulsory. You had to play at least one game. Athletically I became a jack-of-all-trades, competing in gymnastics, cross-country running, bodybuilding, and athletics. I was fourth in cross-country, was the top gymnast, and was third in the "Mr. FC College" bodybuilding competition. All in all I earned the most certificates. Muhammad Iqbal Butt, who had competed creditably in the Mr. Universe competition, told me at the time that I had a most muscular physique.

Campus life taught me independence. I interacted with boys from all backgrounds, even from abroad. Some were rich, some not; some were modern, some religious. There were quite a few East Africans. There were female students, too. I got along with all of them. I made friends with boys from the Niazi tribe, especially Amanullah Niazi, who was senior to me and was later to become a brigadier. They persuaded me to run in the elections for first-year representative. That is when I gave my first public speech. They made me stand on a table. Trembling with nervousness, I managed to tell the listeners that if they elected me I would look after their interests. I didn't enjoy it a bit. The students from Karachi, the Niazis, and the East Africans supported me, and I won. Tariq Aziz, who was my principal secretary after I became president and was later appointed secretary to the national security council, was there too. He was senior to me and we were not that friendly, probably because he was a "good boy," reluctant to join me in mischief-making.

My pranks continued. As early as seven or eight in the evening the hostel gates would shut, and no student could go out, nor could any visitor come in. However, there was a mango tree next to a hedge at the hostel periphery, and thanks to my gymnastics, I could climb the tree and jump over and across the high hedge. So would some of my friends. We would take in a movie from nine PM to midnight, usually at the Regal Cinema, and return to college on foot because tonga drivers refused to go that far at night. Obviously, we couldn't get back in, but just outside the main gate of the college there was a mosque, and no one could stop us from sleeping there, as mosques have traditionally been a haven for wayfarers. Early in the morning, when the college gates opened, we would sneak back in.

It was in FC College that I learned how to make a time bomb, which I later used as a commando to good effect. In today's age of terror, this is hardly the thing to say, but those were relatively innocent times, and the only kind of homemade bomb then known was the Molotov cocktail. I discovered that if you take a normal firecracker and attach a filterless cigarette to its fuse, it becomes a timed fuse, depending on the length of unsmoked cigarette. One day, three or four of us decided to give Mr. Datta, the warden, a scare. We left a timed firecracker in a big steel trash can outside his house so that it would make an awful bang. We placed another outside the assistant warden's house, and a third inside a mailbox at the entrance. Then I went back to my room. The firecracker in Mr. Datta's trash can went off first, with a deafening bang, just like a small bomb. The trash can made it worse, for it amplified the sound. Everyone started running toward the warden's house. I did, too. As soon as we got there, the "bomb" in the assistant warden's trash can exploded. We all ran there, at which point the firecracker in the mailbox exploded. There was utter confusion. It was terrible.

A few days later Mr. Datta got hold of one of my friends, Hameed, and asked him for the name of the boy behind the bombs. If he didn't reveal it, he was told, he would be either suspended or expelled. Hameed, who was from Hyderabad, Sindh, told me about the sword hanging over his head. I knew it would be unconscionable if he were punished so severely for something that I had done, so I told him to tell Mr. Datta the truth. He said that Pervez Musharraf was the culprit.

Mr. Datta called me to his house that evening. On the way, I wondered what I would tell my parents if I were thrown out. Mr. Datta began by asking me who was behind the "bombing episode." I confessed. "Pervez, you are the block monitor, and you did this?" he said, visibly disappointed. I really felt ashamed of myself. I said that I was very sorry and it would not happen again. He did not do anything. All he said was, "OK, never do this again," and let me go. That is when I learned the power of truth, a lesson that has never left me.

My first brush with death, as silly as it was, happened at FC College, thanks to a mango tree. It was laden with fruit. My friends told me to use my skill as a gymnast and climb the tree to pluck some mangoes. I shimmied up. Hanging high up from a branch, I would swing upward and pluck the fruit with my feet. Things went fine and I had plucked quite a few mangoes when on a high swing the branch in my hands broke. I came crashing down, hit the ground very hard, and passed out. My friends thought that I was dead. I opened my eyes quite some time later in Mr. Dutta's house, under a doctor's care. I was young and strong and soon recovered.

I was always getting into scrapes. Lahore's most famous girls' college is Kinnaird, and you invariably see a lot of boys hanging around outside it, especially in the evenings. One day there was a debate at FC College in which some girls from Kinnaird had been invited to participate. A boy sitting behind me kept hitting my chair with his foot, really irritating me. I repeatedly told him to stop, but he would not. With girls from Kinnaird there, my testosterone level had probably shot up, so I told him to step outside. He did, and a big fight ensued, but soon the other boys separated us. They told me that he belonged to a club of wrestlers headed by Badi Pehalwan and they would return to beat me up. But they never did.

If, from all this, you have concluded that I was not intensely focused on my studies, you would not be far wrong. I was more involved in extracurricular activities, both healthy and naughty. Lahore is a great city, with numerous attractions, particularly for a young boy free of direct parental supervision, but in reality my mother and father were always with me through the values that they had inculcated in their sons. Those values were always present to stop me from crossing the line between right and wrong. Of course, my parents were very concerned about my studies, but I had already appeared before the Inter Services Selection Board and been selected for the prestigious Pakistan Military Academy as a cadet before my final examinations for FA. After a three-year course, if successful, I would get my commission as an officer of the Pakistan Army. So I took my FSc finals somewhat nonchalantly and managed to get through, because the actual result had no bearing on my selection by the army, as long as I passed. My life as a carefree teenager was over. The longest chapter of my story was about to begin, a chapter that would define my life and career as soldier and statesman.

PART TWO

LIFE IN THE ARMY

CHAPTER 6

THE POTTER'S WHEEL

Have you ever seen a potter going about his work? First he carefully chooses the clay, poking it, pushing it, feeling it between thumb and forefinger. After making his choice he wets it just so, with the exact amount of clean water, kneading it into fine dough with just the correct consistency. He then puts it on his potter's wheel and spins it at the right speed, then fastidiously fashions it into shape. Next he places it in the kiln, heated to the correct temperature. After the exact amount of time—not a moment before, not a moment later—he takes it out of the oven. Now the piece is ready.

This is exactly how a soldier is made. How good he is depends on how good the potter is, how good his choice of clay was, and how good his hand was on the wheel. A cadet in a military academy is like clay on the wheel. When he is shaped, he is let loose in the oven of army life. How good a soldier he becomes depends on the fire that bakes him every day of his life in the army.

I was only eighteen when I entered the Pakistan Military Academy (PMA) in 1961. Winning a spot was a cinch for an athletic, intelligent boy. To begin with, there was a written test in Karachi. I was selected for further tests and went up to Rawalpindi by train and then on to Kohat in the North-West Frontier. The tests were physical, mental, psychological, and medical. At one stage during the psychological tests I was told to write whatever I was imagining at the time, whatever came to mind as I looked at a blank picture frame. There were socioeconomic discussions. I was put in command of five people and given a task, like clearing a minefield. I was pretty good at all that. I completed the obstacle course nearly twice in the time allotted. Finally, we were interviewed by a commandant. I didn't find the interview difficult. I know I did well.

During the testing process I shared a room with P. Q. Mehdi, who later became an air marshal and our air chief. I remember we saw a movie called *Savera,* which means "Dawn." I was selected and we reported to the PMA.

The PMA is a historic place. It has verdant lawns and beautiful red-shingled colonial buildings in the lap of the Himalayas in a place called Kakul, near the town of Abbotabad, named after a British commissioner called Abbot. Imagine our excitement—a batch of fresh-faced young cadets in their new civilian clothes and immaculate haircuts—as our truck rolled in. The senior cadets were waiting for us like predators. Now imagine our shock when our smiles were met with deafening commands—"Crawl under the truck; now climb over it." Again and again came the orders, over and under the truck, over and under. "So this is the army," I thought to myself when I was on one of my crawling "expeditions" under the truck. "I will go along. They can't break me." When our clothes were completely soiled, we were made to do somersaults in the mud, down a slope, and then back up. If our mothers had seen us they would have been horrified.

The senior cadets let us have dinner; then they crowded us into an anteroom and made all seventy or eighty of us squeeze into the fireplace, one on top of another. We should have made the *Guinness Book of World Records.* Next we were taken for haircuts, army-style. They simply sheared us like sheep. We looked extremely odd. They made us do all sorts of indescribably silly things, like balancing a metallic tub of ice-cold water on our heads in the dead of winter, which in Kakul is very cold. If the tub falls, not only do you get drenched and freeze, you are given another equally terrible punishment. I had been told to expect hazing—or "ragging" as we call it in Pakistan—and was prepared for it, but it was a terrible experience nevertheless.

That first night I fell onto my bed and was out like a light, overcome by conflicting emotions—from excitement to incredulity to exhaustion.

I dreamed of my parents' comfortable home in Karachi, St. Patrick's, FC College, and the Bengali girl.

Not many boys break down under ragging, and I took it in stride. It lasts for only the first ten days. I learned to outsmart the 'raggers.' I would do whatever they said—like front rolls—slowly, so as to exert myself as little as possible; or I would simply hide in the bathroom until the ragging was over. I knew that they were not allowed to touch us. I knew too that when I became a senior I would be ragging the new cadets myself. When my turn finally came, I didn't rag much, and I was never cruel. I ragged with a purpose: to instill discipline and respect for authority in soldiers-to-be. Soldiers become a breed apart, a breed that willingly dies for its country without question.

It was in the PMA that I actually started studying seriously. Fortunately, I learned that if I applied myself, I could excel. We were taught all kinds of subjects—science, mathematics, geography, military tactics, map reading, and of course, weapons training and drill. We were also taught how to command men and get the best out of them. We learned how to absorb psychological pressure and develop physical endurance. Above all, we learned about making decisions in a crunch, and no ordinary crunch: the kind that could mean the difference between life and death—yours and others'. If the men under you don't trust your decisions, they will not have the confidence to go into battle under your command. A military academy is a great place to learn how to be a man who can deal with a crisis, provided it is a good military academy. The PMA is the best in the world.

I did well in the PMA and was one of the top cadets in my course, one of the ten sword carriers. If not for my nonchalant attitude and my tendency to react badly to irrational authority, I would have done even better. Frankly, I was quite an ill-disciplined young man—quarrelsome and irresponsible. I was one of four candidates short-listed to go to Sandhurst, England, to complete my training, but another cadet, Ali Kuli Khan Khattak, was selected. He retired as a lieutenant general and chief of general staff when I became army chief, but I suspect that his retirement, which was optional, had more to do with disappointment at not becoming chief himself, which is perfectly understandable.

I was sometimes careless. Once during an outdoor exercise my platoon commander asked me to look at the other cadets and tell him what was missing from my uniform. I looked, but could not figure out what they had that I lacked. He asked me to touch my "damn head." It was bare, without a helmet. I was marched in the next day, for punishment. "Quick march, right turn, right turn, halt, salute," screamed the drill sergeant. The platoon commander was so impressed by my drill that without imposing any punishment he ordered the sergeant, "Good drill; march him off."

In fact, my physical bearing and drill were so good that I passed my "saluting test" on the first try with a special commendation from the adjutant. "Which cadet college do you come from?" he asked. When I told him I was from Forman Christian College and not from a cadet college, he was quite surprised. Later, during a parade rehearsal, he singled me out for a drill demonstration to the whole battalion of senior cadets. This got me into immense trouble with my seniors for "having the audacity to show them proper drill." It became the cause of many punishments at their hands whenever they saw me.

On another occasion, however, I was nearly thrown out of the PMA. In our final term, just before we were to graduate, there was a drill competition of the first-term cadets in which the senior cadets, as spectators, were expected to wear black socks. Some of the seniors wore the wrong color. The battalion commander called me and ordered me to note down all their names and serial numbers—"and put your name at the top," he thundered. Our punishment was to run nine miles. When we came to a loop in the road some of us cleverly decided to take a shortcut and save about 200 yards (180 meters). Unknown to us, we were being closely watched through binoculars. About fifteen of us were caught. Inquiries started, and the whole thing became quite serious. Academy officials were determined that we should be thrown out for taking the shortcut—even though six of us who had done so were sword carriers who were to lead the graduation parade! Luckily, good sense prevailed and we were spared expulsion. Instead, our course grade was lowered. I was the battalion junior under-officer, and my position in the class would have been very high on merit, but as punishment we were pushed down six positions. So even though I ranked fourth in my course, I was placed tenth. Other junior under-officers got moved up six positions and thus graduated above us.

The experience at PMA was akin to an overhaul—being taken apart and put back together differently. Gaining acceptance into the school was like being chosen as the right clay. The PMA wet us—the clay— and placed us on the potter's wheel, ready for fashioning by the potter's hand. Once fashioned, we were all set to be baked and hardened in the kiln. I was now ready for the army, guided by the maker's hand.

CHAPTER 7

INTO THE FIRE

O n graduation from the academy, I was a second lieutenant. Without giving it much thought, I opted for the Thirty-sixth Light Antiaircraft Regiment, because its training, firing, and courses were all in Karachi. Why my fixation on Karachi? The reason was not my family—it was that my Bengali girlfriend was there. I suppose the army can change many things, but it cannot change primeval instinct. No matter where I was stationed, I reckoned, I would still have to go to Karachi twice a year for a course or for practice in firing.

My plans came to naught when that year it was decided that after graduation no one could go directly into antiaircraft without first going into artillery. So after six months I was posted to the Sixteenth Self-Propelled Artillery Regiment. Worse, my romance came to an abrupt end when the girl's family returned to East Pakistan.

I never did go into air defense. I stayed in artillery. From then on my entire career would be dedicated to the army and the defense of my country.

I was still more of an officer than a gentleman. It didn't take long for me to get into trouble. In mid-1965, with clouds of war with India gathering, my unit was moved into the Changa Manga forest near Lahore, a train ride of about twenty-four hours from Karachi. The rest of the young officers belonged mostly to the Punjab, and it took them only a few hours to get home to see their families. I applied for six days' leave to go to Karachi, and with a Sunday at both ends it would be effectively an eight-day leave. My commanding officer would have none of it—it

44

was too long, he said. I thought he was being irrational and insensitive. I defied his decision, bought a train ticket, boarded the Karachi Express, and went home for the eight days. One of the officers slightly senior to me, Javed Ashraf Qazi, who retired as a lieutenant general and later became my minister for railways and then for education, phoned me and told me to return immediately. Otherwise, I would be in a lot of trouble on disciplinary grounds for being absent without leave. I refused, and took the full eight days off that I had "granted" myself. On my return, my commanding officer went ballistic and initiated court-martial proceedings against me.

What saved me was the war of 1965, when India attacked Pakistan on all fronts and strafed a passenger train, killing many civilians. The Indian attack came on September 6. The war lasted seventeen days and ended in a cease-fire sponsored by the UN Security Council, but Pakistan gave India a fright and a bloody nose to go with it. There was no strategic gain on either side. Still, Pakistan certainly achieved a tactical victory in the sense that we conquered more territory, inflicted more casualties, took more prisoners, and almost blew the Indian Air Force out of the air. My performance in the war earned me recognition and an award for gallantry. The commanding officer had little choice but to change his opinion about the "fiery young officer all out of control." In fact, it is precisely because I was a fiery young officer that I did well in the war.

My artillery regiment was a part of the only elite armored division of the Pakistan Army equipped with American-made Patton tanks. We were launched into an offensive in the Kasur–Khem Karan sector on September 7, 1965. We established a bridgehead across the Roohi Nullah (a water drain) and quickly seized enemy territory up to fifteen miles deep, capturing the sizable town of Khem Karan. My artillery battery was deployed just ahead of the town. During a lull in the firing, I took a quick tour of the deserted streets of Khem Karan, and felt very proud. Only dogs were barking: there was no sign of human life. I wrote my first letter during the war to my mother, proudly saying that I was writing from India.

After three days of battle my division was ordered to move to the critical Lahore sector, which was under enemy threat. We stabilized our position there after two days of intense fighting. This was the only time in my entire military career that I have seen a gun barrel go red-hot from firing.

Having stabilized the Lahore front, we were ordered to move again to the Sialkot front. This was the front where the famous tank battles of Chawinda were fought. At the end of the war this sector was to become a graveyard of Indian tanks.

My next confrontation with death came on the night of September 16, 1965. I was detailed as an artillery observer attached to an infantry company that had been ordered to attack and capture a village called Jassoran, situated on a mound. The company commander was my best friend, Lieutenant Bilal. We were to attack at midnight. After preparatory movement in the dark, we went into a "forming-up place" 800 yards (about 730 meters) from our objective, where the company lined up in a formation for the final assault. Bilal and I impulsively embraced each other. This could be our last embrace, we thought.

I brought the whole weight of our division's artillery fire on the village. Under cover of this fire we advanced, and finally charged the village crying *Allah o' Akbar* ("God is the greatest"). The artillery fire was very accurate and effective, keeping the enemy's head down. We braved the enemy's counterfire and forced them to beat a hasty retreat. We had accomplished our task. I felt great.

Another significant action took place on the night of September 22. Our guns were positioned in a graveyard. An enemy shell hit one of our self-propelled artillery guns and set its rear compartment on fire. The flames leaped up toward the sky in the darkness of the night. The ready-to-fire shells on the gun were in danger of catching fire and bursting, setting off a chain reaction with all the other guns. It was a very dangerous situation. "Hell!" I thought. "My gun battery could be blown to pieces, taking all of us along." I had to act immediately; there was no time to lose.

While everybody took cover, a lesson that I had learned on the streets of Nazimabad came into play. I stood my ground, dashed to the blazing gun, and climbed into it. One brave soldier followed me. We saw three men of the crew lying in a pool of blood. Instinctively, I ignored them, in order to save the shells first. We took off our shirts and wound them around our hands for protection from the hot shells. One by one we took the shells off the gun and threw them to safety on the ground, hoping that they would not burst on impact. God saved us from that disaster. In the meantime, seeing me facing all this danger, all my men who had run for cover returned. Together we first put the fire out and then, sorrowfully, pulled out the three crewmen. I noticed that one of them was still alive. I took his head in my arms, but while I was trying to put a field bandage on his wound, he died. I will never forget it. Such are the brutalities of war; they leave a permanent imprint on the mind. I received an award for gallantry for saving lives and equipment. The brave soldier who helped me was also decorated for gallantry. I can never forget that night.

These two actions changed the commanding officer's opinion about me. I should have been decorated with two awards for gallantry, but instead I received one award and the dismissal of the court-martial proceedings. The war ended on September 23, 1965, and I was promoted to the rank of captain soon after.

In 1966 I opted for and was assigned to the Special Services Group (SSG), our elite commando outfit, the world's best. Commando training demands tremendous physical and mental stamina, so it was exactly the right kind of environment for me. Commandos have to undergo survival training in jungles, mountains, and deserts, and learn to make it on their own. Eating delicacies like snakes, frogs' legs, and the local lizards (which are like iguanas) is not infrequent. I learned that one can eat anything except plants with white sap. Ever since then I have not been finicky about food—I can eat anything, though I do appreciate good food. You learn to really appreciate food and water when you are hungry or thirsty for a long time. Then you thank God for anything that He provides.

The training was physically exacting. There was very tough physical exercise for an hour every day, starting with a warm-up run of two miles (about three kilometers). We ran four miles (nearly 6.5 kilometers) with a weapon in forty minutes once a week; twelve miles (nineteen kilometers) with a weapon in two hours; and thirty-six miles (58 kilometers) with a thirty-pound pack and weapon in ten hours. In addition, there were several tactical exercises involving hundreds of miles of route marches. Then there was watermanship in lakes and fast-flowing canals, as well as parachute training in which one had to qualify in six jumps. I was considered very good at these tests. I ended the course among the top three, getting the highest grade. The course gave me confidence in my physical and mental abilities. It taught me that enduring extreme hardship has more to do with mental resilience than physical stamina.

After my initial training I served in the SSG for two periods of four and a half and two and a half years, respectively, first as a captain and then as a major. When I look back on my service with the SSG, I feel that my self-confidence and my qualities as a soldier and a leader were all honed there. I felt physically very tough, mentally alert, and able to handle tough assignments with ease. The SSG provided me with ample opportunities to develop initiative and drive because it encouraged so much independence of training and operation.

I developed my own, very innovative style of training the men under my command. I expected them to undergo several confidence-building and nerve-testing actions.

One test was to hold a self-made grenade of plastic explosive with holes made at three-second intervals in the time fuse. A new SSG volunteer was expected to throw the bomb when the spark of the ignited time fuse came out of the last hole just three seconds before exploding. Some got jittery and threw it prematurely.

A second test was to run on a yard-wide iron beam 300 feet (90 meters) high, spanning the top of the side structure of a metal bridge about 150 yards (136 meters) in length. The distance had to be covered in forty seconds. It might sound easy, but when one reached the middle of the length, with a fast river flowing underneath, it became dangerous. You could get dizzy if you looked down.

Another improvised test was to lie flat on one's stomach in a railway culvert, looking toward a train hurtling at full speed that would pass one or two feet (about one-third to one-half meter) away. Closing the eyes was not allowed.

Then I would make my men sit a couple of yards to the side of a target being fired at from 200 or 300 yards (180 to 270 meters). The whizzing and thud of the bullets helped inoculate them against the stress of battle.

I have always believed in leading from the front by setting a personal example. Never ask your men to do what you would not. So I made sure that I demonstrated each training assignment before expecting others to follow suit. I became an exceptionally good shot with a rifle and a submachine gun. I was also a good runner. I would compete with my men in everything and would treat them to a cold drink if I lost; a few did beat me, but not many. All this endeared me to my men, who started looking up to me. They loved me because I was just and compassionate. I would share their worries and help them with their problems. My seniors recognized me as an exceptional leader, but also as a bluntly outspoken, ill-disciplined officer. I was given a number of punishments on different occasions for fighting, insubordination, and lack of discipline. When I became army chief, my military secretary showed me my service dossier and naughtily asked me to look at my discipline record. It was shocking indeed. Entries in red ink were overflowing the total allocated space. The consolation, however, was that I was never punished for any lapse of character or for moral turpitude. My annual confidential reports were always very good—only my lack of discipline held me back.

On the whole, life in the SSG was tough, active, thrilling, dangerous, and very fulfilling. I shall never forget it. It made me what I am today.

You might think that a person like me would have had a passionate affair and married for love. But I was hitched in the traditional fashion—an arranged marriage. An aunt of mine knew the parents of an eligible girl named Sehba Farid, and suggested that we would be a good match. My parents initiated the proposal. On the day that I was supposed to go to Sehba's house and meet her family, I arrived in a shirt and trousers wearing a pair of open-toed sandals called Peshawari chappals, the kind favored by Pathans and army personnel when they are in civilian clothes. Our salaries were hardly enough to buy designer shoes! Not being an army girl, Sehba was appalled that a fashion disaster had come for her hand. She had received many proposals before and rejected them all for one reason or another—either the suitor's hair was no good or his dress sense was wanting, or whatever. She certainly didn't like mustaches. Yet for some reason, she didn't reject me, despite my mustache (which I refused to shave off) and my attire. At least she approved of my hair and face!

Sehba was extremely beautiful, and I fell for her immediately. Any man of that age who tells you he has anything except looks on his mind is not being truthful. It is my good fortune that, apart from being beautiful, Sehba also turned out to be a wonderful human being, a terrific mother, and a perfect homemaker. She smoothed my rough edges and managed to mellow me, little by little. "Quarrelling with superiors, even if they are being stupid, will affect your career," she would chide me. Gradually, her advice started sinking in, but it took me some time to calm down.

Sehba told me later that of all her family, it was her father, Ghulam Ghaus Farid, who worked in the ministry of information and broadcasting, who was the most enthusiastic about me. "He is a very good officer and will go places," he told her, though I'm sure that he had no idea of the places I would go. Neither had I, nor anyone else.

Love came gradually, because after we were formally engaged I was posted for two years to Chittagong in East Pakistan. We exchanged letters. I would correct her spelling mistakes (this was neither very romantic nor very chivalrous of me, considering that Sehba's English is far better than mine) and in retaliation she would correct my mistakes. Whenever I was in Karachi we would go out on dates—innocent little forays to parties or to a movie or to the disco at the old Metropole Hotel.

Sehba Farid and I were married on December 27, 1968. I was then a captain. Immediately afterward, I was posted to Cherat, high up in the mountains. A day or two after we got there, I was due to make a parachute jump with about sixty-four other men, as part of a training exercise. I decided to be romantic and asked a friend to take Sehba to the place where we would drop. I told Sehba I would wave a white handkerchief as I came down, so that she could identify me. I suppose there was an element of machismo too, as I wanted to show off my bravery to my new wife. The whole scheme was well coordinated and executed. I carried my largest handkerchief and waved it vigorously. Sehba did see me, and I loved seeing her wave back at me.

Cherat is on a ridge. The tin-roofed houses and buildings on the ridge are 50 to 100 yards (45 to 90 meters) apart from each other. It is full of snakes and wild animals—hardly a place for a new bride to begin married life. But that is what young army wives have to suffer.

I had to go out one evening, and returned at about one in the morning to find the front door locked. I knocked and knocked, but Sehba wouldn't open the door. I became worried, and broke a window to enter. Our bedroom door was locked too. I started banging on it. Finally, she opened it, with a petrified expression on her face. There had been all sorts of scary noises coming from the tin roof creaking in the wind, so she had switched on the radio at full volume. Unfortunately, there was a horror program going on, which terrified her even more.

At the time I was probably not as sensitive to her fears as I should have been. Becoming a father changed my happy-go-lucky attitude toward life. Suddenly I was responsible for a little human being—our first child, our daughter Ayla, born on February 18, 1970. Our son, Bilal, was born a year and a half later, on October 17, 1971. Having two children so close together made for sleepless nights and disturbed routines. You can imagine how busy they kept us, particularly their mother.

They say that behind every successful man is a greater woman. In my case I happily married Sehba because I was attracted by her beauty, dignity, and poise. She deserves the credit for sobering my outlook towards life in general and my profession in particular. She significantly helped transform me from a carefree, brash, and abrasive officer to a more balanced and responsible individual. She developed in me the urge to do my best. I certainly owe the improvement in my written and spoken English to her, She has always been more articulate than me. Even now, whenever I get stuck for a word or a sentence, I approach her instead of spending time with a thesaurus. Sehba has taken on the role of First Lady admirably and has created a positive impact on everyone with whom she has come in contact. She has been a wonderful wife.

Both children, from a very early age, have given us great comfort and have been a very real source of satisfaction. Their cooperation and focus in matters of academics, diet, and even sleeping patterns were amazing. They seemed to have an innate sense of the commitment and devotion that their parents felt toward them. They have never let us down. As adults, Bilal and Ayla have well-rounded, wholesome personalities. Their hallmark is humility and poise, coupled with maturity and a good sense of humor.

Bilal's name carries a special significance for me. He was originally named Sheharyar, but when my best friend, Bilal, was killed in the war of 1971 against India, I was so distraught that I phoned Sehba and told

her to change our son's name to Bilal in memory of my martyred
friend. Bilal and I were coursemates; we had fought the war of 1965
together and then joined the SSG together. We were extremely close. I
can never think of my friend Bilal without a pang of pain, but then I can
never think of my son Bilal without a surge of joy.

Grandchildren are a source of great delight, too—you get all the
joy but none of the responsibility; when they get tiresome or fidget, as
children always do, you just hand them back to their parents. Ayla's
daughters—Maryam (born on June 23, 1997) and Zainab (born on July
16, 2000)—are beyond infancy. However, Bilal and his wife, Erum, are
having periods of disturbed sleep with young Hamza (born on September 18, 2003) and with their daughter, Zoya, born on July 31, 2005.

I will turn now to political developments in Pakistan. In 1970, before
elections could be held, there was a devastating cyclone in East Pakistan,
with winds of 120 miles (190 kilometers) an hour. It was accompanied
by a huge tidal wave, or tsunami, the worst of the twentieth century and
left 200,000 people dead. The response of President Yahya Khan and his
government was callous in the extreme. It took him quite some time to
react. He did not even visit the devastated province for many days, and
then only under pressure. The people of East Pakistan felt angry,
alienated, and badly let down, as if they were a colony instead of part of
the country. I am convinced that the government's attitude during this
disaster reinforced the impression among the East Pakistanis that the
western wing didn't care for them, and that this brought many more
voters behind Sheikh Mujibur Rahman's Awami League.

Pakistan's elections of December 7, 1970, were among the most
fateful in its history. The country still included East Pakistan (now
Bangladesh), where more than half of our population lived. The actual
winner of the voting was Sheikh Mujibur Rahman and his Awami
League, with all its seats coming from East Pakistan. They got 160 of the
162 seats for the National Assembly from East Pakistan, out of a total of
307. The two largest provinces of Pakistan's western wing, Punjab and
Sindh, voted for Zulfikar Ali Bhutto and his PPP (Pakistan People's
Party), which got 82 of the 138 seats allocated to the four provinces in
west Pakistan. Neither of them was represented in the other wing.

Immediately after the elections Bhutto more or less declared himself prime minister, suggesting such bizarre ideas as two constitutions, one for East Pakistan and the other for "West Pakistan," with a prime minister for each wing, forgetting that now the latter was no longer one but four provinces and there was no such thing as "West Pakistan" except in the geographic sense. He played on the fears of the west Pakistanis that the Awami League would use its majority to foist a constitution on Pakistan on the basis of its campaign promise to give maximum autonomy to the provinces, leaving only defense, currency, and foreign affairs with the center. He conjured up visions of everlasting domination by the Bengalis, forgetting that they too were Pakistanis and the Awami League had won the elections perfectly legitimately through democratic means. Bhutto even threatened members elected to the Constituent Assembly from west Pakistan that he would break their legs if they attended its inaugural session in Dhaka, East Pakistan, and that if they insisted on attending they should buy a one-way ticket. The Constituent Assembly was supposed to make a new constitution for Pakistan in three months, but it never met, not least because of Bhutto's threat. It was a nexus between Bhutto and a small coterie of military rulers that destroyed Pakistan. The myopic and rigid attitude of Sheikh Mujibur Rahman didn't help matters, and he played into Bhutto's and Yahya's hands by remaining rooted in East Pakistan, forgetting that now he was prime minister–elect of the whole of Pakistan and needed to tour the four provinces of the western wing in order to reassure the people there and allay their fears.

Under pressure from the wily Bhutto, and no doubt because he didn't want to lose power, Yahya Khan postponed the meeting of the Constituent Assembly indefinitely on March 25, 1971. He did not stop there. The very next day he outlawed the Awami League and arrested its leader, Sheikh Mujibur Rahman, the clear winner of the election. This act infuriated the Bengali masses of East Pakistan, who were already agitating and had a sense of deprivation and alienation. Tempers rose so high with the arrest of the undisputed Bengali leader that an open insurgency was launched by the populace. This was massively supported by the Indians from across the border. With the army completely bogged down in quelling the insurgency, India stabbed

Pakistan in the back by blatantly attacking it across its border on several fronts in East Pakistan on November 21, 1971. All-out war between India and Pakistan commenced on December 3, 1971.

My assignments during this crucial period were directly linked to events in East Pakistan. I was posted out of the Special Services Group (SSG) to an artillery regiment in December 1970, after serving this elite commando outfit for a mandatory period of four years. With war clouds on the horizon and insurgency in East Pakistan, the army decided to beef up the SSG.

I was recalled in October 1971 to raise a new SSG company at Cherat. It took me a month and a half to raise the company, but when we were ready to be airlifted to East Pakistan, war broke out and all flights between Pakistan's two wings were suspended. My company was then placed under the command of an SSG battalion in the Punjab sector.

My SSG company was ordered to prepare to seize a bridge about twenty miles (thirty-two kilometers) deep inside enemy territory in West Pakistan and hold it till a linkup force of an armored brigade reached us. I war-gamed and practiced the offensive with my troops. I even planned for the worst contingency: if, after taking the bridge, we failed to meet the linkup forces, we were to exfiltrate back home through the desert in the south on commandeered buses and trucks.

My troops were brimming with confidence, and we were all set to go when the cease-fire was announced and East Pakistan was forcibly torn away from us to form the separate state of Bangladesh. It was a terrible day. When I was telling my troops about the cease-fire, the surrender of our 90,000 personnel (military and civilian), and the end of our plan to seize the bridge, I broke down and cried. All my brave soldiers cried with me. It remains the saddest and most painful day of my life. My anger at the generals who had taken charge of government, and at some of the politicians of the time, still makes me see red.

What happened in East Pakistan is the saddest episode in Pakistan's history. The loss of our eastern wing and the creation of Bangladesh were all a result of inept political handling ever since our independence. Blame ultimately fell on the army. As events developed, the army was confronted with an impossible situation—a mass popular uprising within and an invasion from without by India, supposedly nonaligned but now being helped overtly by the Soviet Union under a treaty of peace and friendship. It was actually an alliance of war. On the other hand, our longtime ally, the United States of America, apart from making sympathetic noises and wringing its hands, was nowhere to be seen. No army in the world can sustain such a multidimensional threat. Nonetheless, the operational handling of the troops by the army's senior leadership was simply incompetent. It brought avoidable disgrace to the army. A cease-fire was declared on December 17, 1971, and Pakistan was cut in half.

CHAPTER 8

LIFE IN THE FIRE

After the cease-fire of 1971, the entire SSG was withdrawn to recoup. My company was moved to Kamri in the mountainous Northern Areas, deep in the Himalayas, to check on reported incursions of Indian troops. It took me over a month to complete the move through a most rugged terrain, and the experience offers a hint of how difficult it can be to guard borders among the highest mountains in the world. We first drove 250 miles (400 kilometers) to Gilgit in jeeps on the famous Karakorum Highway—our mountain link with China. This was the time when it was under construction and was called the "eighth wonder of the world." We took ten days to get there after navigating through innumerable roadblocks and landslides along the way. From Gilgit onward we went some distance in jeeps. Then we proceeded on mules, trekking across the Burzil Pass at 14,500 feet (about 4,400 meters); descending into the Minimarg valley, at 9,000 feet (2,700 meters); and making the final ascent on foot to reach Kamri, high up at 13,000 feet (nearly 4,000 meters). This was a beautifully green pine-forested area. It was an experience of a lifetime.

One has to adjust to the low oxygen in the atmosphere at these elevations. In winter, snow falls by the yard. It was a tough assignment, but we acquitted ourselves very well. I stayed almost a year in the harshest of conditions, but I really enjoyed being there and emerged more self-confident. In the winter, I used to move around to various valleys and peaks, where at times few dared to go. My theory was to keep busy and active to overcome the feeling of isolation and loneliness. My movement also contributed to a show of force to the enemy, who stay put in their bunkers throughout the winter.

One of the treks I undertook in November 1972 became a real adventure. I decided to move from my location, Kamri, to Muzaffarabad, the capital of Azad (Independent) Kashmir, reconnoitering the Line of Control between India and Pakistan all along the way. This meant covering a total distance of 175 miles (280 kilometers), of which the first 130 miles (208 kilometers) to Athmoqam were done on foot. I set out from Kamri with six of my soldiers and a guide. Our first destination was Nekrun, about forty miles (64 kilometers) away. We crossed the Kamri Pass at about 13,500 feet (4,100 meters) went across several features at heights of over 12,000 feet (3,600 meters), finally descending into Nekrun valley. During the three-day trek we did not come across a single human being. We could move only from first light until eleven AM, and then from about three in the afternoon to last light, because avalanches generally occur between eleven and three, when the sun is brightest and the snow melts. Not that our timing was a guarantee against avalanches. Movement was hazardous at any time, because at some stretches even talking loudly could suddenly initiate an avalanche. Beyond Nekrun our trip took us through the most picturesque sites. The Kishinganga River from Indian-occupied Kashmir enters Pakistan at Nekrun, where its name becomes the Neelum River. Our movement from Nekrun to Kel and finally to Athmoqam was all along the Neelum. It was heaven on earth.

With East Pakistan gone, to become Bangladesh, Bhutto's largest number of seats in what was left of Pakistan gave him a dubious legitimacy. He became president of Pakistan, but he also used the absence of a basic law as a pretext to become chief martial law administrator. There was nothing to stop Bhutto from reverting to the constitution of 1956, with amendments to the clauses that pertained to East Pakistan, but he chose raw power instead.

At first I admired Bhutto. He was young, educated, articulate, and dynamic. He had eight years' experience in government under President Ayub Khan. But as time passed, my opinion of Bhutto started to change. My brother Javed, who was principal secretary to the chief minister of the North-West Frontier province, told me that Bhutto was no good and would ruin the country. My brother was right. I saw how the country, and particularly its economy, was ravaged by mindless nationalization. Its institutions were destroyed under his brand of so-called Islamic socialism. Bhutto took control of virtually all the nation's industries—steel, chemicals, cement, shipping, banking, insurance, engineering, gas and power distribution, and even small industries like flour milling, cotton ginning, and rice husking, as well as private schools and colleges—the start of the destruction of our educational system. Mercifully, he did not touch textiles, our largest industry. Bhutto ruled not like a democrat but like a despotic dictator. He threw many of his opponents, including editors, journalists, and even cartoonists, into prison. He was really a fascist—using the most progressive rhetoric to promote regressive ends, the first of which was to stay in power forever. It was a tragedy, because a man of his undoubted capability could have done a lot of good for his country. By the time his regime ended, I had come to the conclusion that Bhutto was the worst thing that had yet happened to Pakistan. I still maintain that he did more damage to the country than anyone else, damage from which we have still not fully recovered. Among other things, he was the first to try to appease the religious right. He banned liquor and gambling and declared Friday a holiday instead of Sunday. This was hypocrisy at its peak, because everyone knew that he did not believe in any one of these actions.

Still a major, I was selected for the prestigious staff course in the Command and Staff College in 1974. I finished the course with flying colors, ending with the top grade. I was posted as a brigade major in 206 Brigade, Karachi—the most coveted assignment for a major. The brigade later saw action against revolting tribesmen in Sui and Kohlu in Balochistan. I gained tremendous experience during this difficult assignment, particularly in practical planning and staff work. As a staff officer in Kohlu, I developed good relations with some tribal chiefs, and won over a few of them. I had to take some risks, though, to do this. Once a chief of a subgroup of the ferocious Marri tribe invited me for lunch to his house in the mountains, about thirty-five miles (fifty-six kilometers) away from our camp. I accepted and went in a jeep with my driver and a radio operator. The only weapon I carried was a pistol. This was in violation of orders, which stipulated that whenever an officer is on the move in dangerous territory he must be accompanied by a strong armed escort in the front and rear. My behavior was "reckless" because I knew that the Balochi tribes admire and respect bravery. The gamble paid off. Pirdadani, my host, had lined the entire route with his armed tribesmen for the protection of his guest. From then on Pirdadani became my friend and a frequent visitor to my brigade headquarters. He became entirely cooperative.

Balochistan is Pakistan's largest province in area but the smallest in population. It is also the most backward. Its inhabitants are 40 percent Pashtun, settlers of generations ago from the North-West Frontier; and 60 percent native Balochi. The Baloch are mainly a tribal society, comprising about seventy-seven tribes. A few among them have always been antigovernment. Ninety-five percent of Balochistan is administratively a "B area," where the government does not exercise total authority and the local tribal sirdar or chief plays an important role. Only 5 percent is an "A area," which comes under the regular government. A few of the sirdars in the B areas have been manipulating and blackmailing every Pakistani government for decades, using the militant mercenaries that they maintain as their local militia force. They have also kept their own tribes suppressed under their iron grip through indiscriminate use of force. I have taken on myself to convert all the B areas into A areas and establish the government writ there. So far we have managed to convert fourteen of the twenty-six districts into A areas.

Another memorable experience was my brigade's assistance in flood relief operations. Pakistan was hit by one of its worst floods in 1976, when the melting snow and glaciers combined with unprecedented rains caused all rivers, especially the Indus, to overflow. Sindh was worst affected. Our brigade was moved to Sukkur, which faced the most devastation. My brigade commander detailed me to take charge of filling a breach in a canal. This was beyond the purview of my responsibilities as a staff officer, but understanding the confidence that was vested in me, as well as the challenge the task posed, I accepted readily. The command placed under me was unique. Other than the army engineers, I was given about 200 Hurs (members of the fabled warrior tribe of Sindh) and 250 shackled prisoners from Sukkur jail. I managed this disparate force, gelled them into a team, and worked the whole night to plug the breach by morning. When the brigade commander came to inspect the situation in the morning, he was surprised and pleased. He commended me for my performance.

My brigade commander found me to be not only an efficient staff officer but also a bold leader, willing to stick my neck out beyond the call of duty. My career was now well on course, given all my qualifications and achievements.

Throughout this period the political scene became more and more murky. Bhutto's despotic, dictatorial, suppressive rule led to nationwide political discontent. He set up a Gestapo-like force called the Federal Security Force (FSF) that was much hated and feared. His interpersonal dealings with friends, colleagues, and foes were so arrogant and degrading that people hated him but were too frightened to express their feelings openly. He set up a concentration camp in a place called Dalai, where opponents were "fixed." The situation was something like Iran under the shah or Iraq under Saddam. Bhutto is said to have adopted a mocking, belittling attitude even toward his own appointee as army chief, General Zia ul-Haq. Such an attitude led to unity among all the opposition forces.

In this environment Bhutto ventured into his first election, in 1977, to prove his legitimacy. The opposition formalized its unity into a political alliance called the Pakistan National Alliance (PNA). Either Bhutto became unnerved during the election campaign or he was bent on winning two-thirds of seats in the National Assembly to enable him to change from the parliamentary system to a presidential system by making a constitutional amendment, as some of his former colleagues now assert. The ballot was grossly rigged—so rigged, in fact, that the people lost their fear and came out in the streets to protest, often violently. The PNA, of course, led the protest demonstrations. The army was called out in Lahore to quell the disturbance. Bhutto imposed martial law in Lahore, but the high court struck it down. On one occasion the situation got so far out of control that the army was ordered to fire at the demonstrating civilians. Three brigadiers commanding the troops were bold enough to refuse the orders to fire and opted to resign their commissions instead. These honorable and principled officers were brigadiers Ashfaq Gondal, Niaz Ahmed, and Ishtiaq Ali Khan, who were then retired from service.

Finally, the situation came to a head. General Zia ul-Haq removed Zulfikar Ali Bhutto's government in July 1977. He imposed martial law after suspending the constitution. I was still a major, posted at Kharian as second in command of the Forty-fourth Self-Propelled Artillery Regiment. Rafi Alam, who was then a major general and our general officer commanding (GOC) in Kharian, was appointed deputy martial law administrator of the Rawalpindi Division. He had developed a liking for my professional qualities, and he chose me along with two other officers to establish the deputy martial law administrator's headquarters in Rawalpindi. It was a very unusual situation. While we were carrying out our duties related to martial law, we were also expected to devote time to our units, discharging our normal peacetime duties.

I was promoted to lieutenant colonel in 1978 and given command of the Forty-fourth Self-Propelled Artillery Regiment, part of the armored division. Initially, I was offered the command of the First Self-Propelled Regiment. "You will have a comfortable time there," I was told, because it was a well-established old unit. I refused. Instead, I preferred the challenge of going to the Forty-fourth, called the "Men of Crisis," and raising its standards. In my two years in command, I melded the men and officers into one team and motivated them to a very high level, instilling in them confidence and the will to win.

The unit was particularly weak in sports. In a soccer match against a rival team we lost nine to zero. We performed just as poorly in other sports. We were jeered at by other units. It was humiliating. I moved quickly to hunt for talent, organize teams, and launch an intense training program with newly hired coaches. I also concentrated on the training, operational preparedness, and administration of the unit, enhancing its all-around caliber. My men responded admirably. The result was that the next year we won many sporting events and were declared champions in training. Our administration was always highly commended by the GOC. I felt proud to turn around our average unit, in one year, into possibly the best all-around unit of the armored division. I had made the right choice of assignments: it is better to turn an underperforming group around than to coast along atop an already successful one.

Achieving the turnaround did not come easily. It requires real, down-to-earth leadership to motivate your men to achieve. You have to lead from the front, and be better than your men (at least most of them) at anything you want them to do—especially if it's something physical. A leader has to be just, firm, compassionate, and considerate toward his men. He has to look after their welfare and help them even with their domestic problems. That is when he starts earning their deepest respect and unquestioning obedience. I feel proud to say that I have always been loved by those under my command and therefore I could move them to achieve anything I desired. In the morning, I ran with them in physical training (normally in the lead); I played football, hockey, basketball, and volleyball with them; I ran on the track with them; I fired small arms with them (they normally found me a better shot than most of them); and I ran grueling obstacle courses with them. Through personal demonstration I taught them how to cross obstacles faster than ever. This is how I earned their respect. They always looked up to me. On a few occasions when there was an accident and my men were injured, I was the first to reach the hospital to donate blood for them. Giving blood is no big deal for a young, healthy man, but when soldiers see their commander giving blood, it means a lot. They knew they could count on me on any occasion. On the whole, my command of the regiment was most fulfilling. It developed more confidence in me, and I came to be known as a good leader of men. I have always believed that leadership is an art, not a science. It can be developed to some extent, but mostly it is inborn.

My command was successful because I enjoyed it, and I enjoyed it in no small measure because I was lucky to have a boss as outstanding as Major General Rafi Alam. I think he considered me his best commanding officer. This was evident from the reports that he wrote about me as well as from the fact that he selected me—out of his entire division and outside his own staff—to be taken to the martial law headquarters. It meant an appointment one rank higher than the one I actually held, lieutenant colonel. He appointed me as colonel martial law and allowed me almost total liberty in running affairs related to martial law. Such was the trust he had in me that once when I entered his office, I overheard him on the phone saying, "If my colonel martial law has given the instructions, I know he must have done the right thing." He did not even ask me about the complaint of the man at the other end, then or later. I could not restrain myself, and told him bluntly, "Sir, you trust people too much; you could be taken for a ride." He shot back, "I know who I can trust."

Major General Rafi Alam taught me some of the finer elements of leadership. I tried to develop many of his attributes. Once, after a long test exercise with troops in the field in the heat of summer, with a temperature of over 110 degrees Fahrenheit, he called me to a mound from where he was observing us. When I reached him, a waiter was bringing him a cold drink. Just as the general was about to take a sip, his glance fell on me, looking at him thirstily. He immediately stopped and offered the drink to me. He insisted, "Come on, bugger, you need it and deserve it much more than I do." I gulped it down.

Working at martial law headquarters was a totally different (and unnatural, I might add) assignment, compared with the command of troops, which I relished. However, here I learned that one could contribute immensely toward establishing justice and improving governance. I contributed my humble bit in a limited way within the confines of the Rawalpindi division, which was one of the five divisions of the Punjab province. My stint there gave me an insight into the functioning of civil government and taught me how to interact with the civilian bureaucracy. There were both negatives and positives in this experience, all of which would come in handy when I was thrust into a situation of authority in the country.

A terrible punishment during General Zia's martial law was lashing people who had committed a crime. I noticed that only the poor were given this punishment—those who were involved in petty crimes. The rich and the influential involved in large-scale crime and corruption managed to avoid this particular form of "justice." One day I decided to go to the Rawalpindi jail to observe a lashing for myself. It was an ordeal just to be present at such a distasteful event, the most inhuman and humiliating that I have ever witnessed. The jailer set out a sofa for me, and a table laden with cakes and pastries for my pleasure. The image of the Roman Colosseum sprang to mind. The least I could do was order him to remove the cakes and pastries immediately.

The wretched man, who was to get five lashes, was in underpants and was tied to a wooden X frame with his arms and legs so firmly stretched out that he could not move a muscle. The lasher was in trunks, like a wrestler. The lasher began by drawing a line with a marker across the buttocks of the criminal, indicating the exact spot where the lashes were to be delivered. The lasher then lined up his cane along the prisoner's bottom with his arm stretched out. He drew a line on the ground to mark his spot, and then moved away about five steps. He came running and gave the first lash as hard as he could. The man tightened his muscles on the first lash, squirmed on the second, and screamed on the third. I could barely look at the fourth and fifth. I think he fainted. They untied him and he fell on the ground facedown. I could see red fleshy pulp on his bottom. A crude doctor appeared, checked the miserable man, and then did the stupidest thing. He started pressing the man's bottom with his feet, with all his weight on it. Seldom have I heard a man scream louder. I have never been more disgusted, not just at the inhuman treatment but also at the unfairness of it all.

I related this episode to Major General Rafi Alam and asked him to have this inhumanity stopped, at least within his jurisdiction. Bless the man's kind heart—he listened to me and told the courts not to sentence poor people to lashing any more.

I got another taste of martial law when we ordered the police to round up known miscreants to improve law and order. They very obediently arrested everyone in two categories in their records. I was told that these included pimps, madams, and musicians of Rawalpindi's red-light area. I cursed the police and ordered their release. To my great embarrassment, they all came to martial law headquarters and started shouting slogans in my favor—"Long live Colonel Musharraf." I had to tell them that if they didn't leave I would have them rearrested.

On one occasion, we ordered all drug cases to be tried in military courts. This order soon turned into a farce, as the police started arresting and trying poor people who were peddling or using just a few grams of drugs. The military courts were flooded, and we had to rescind the order.

This, in brief, was my experience with martial law. I learned a few lessons. First, whenever the army gets involved with martial law, it gets distracted from its vital military duties. Military training and operational readiness suffer. Second, when we superimpose martial law and place the military over the civilian government, the latter ceases functioning. When martial law is later lifted, the civilian functionaries remain ineffective. Their growth is stunted. Last, I learned that whatever the law, civil or military, the poor are always victims of oppression. The rich and the powerful generally remain above the law. During my tenure at martial law headquarters I tried my best to give comfort to the poor or go soft on them and to be firm against the privileged. I believe that a poor, hungry man may have a reason to steal, because the state has not provided for him, but a rich man taking bribes deserves the harshest treatment, because he already has plenty.

In July 1978, I took two months' leave to go abroad on a holiday with my wife. We flew to London and stayed with a relative. We then went to Chicago to visit my brother Naved, who had moved to America in 1974 to become a doctor. We spent about ten days with him, after which we returned to London and purchased a Toyota hatchback for the long drive to Pakistan. It was a great experience. We stuffed the car with canned food, a gas stove, a tent, an air mattress, and two air pillows, and off we went. The route that we mapped was ideal from a tourist's point of view. We followed the Rhine River through Germany, ending at the picturesque Rhine Falls in Switzerland. From Lucerne we drove to Italy and stayed at Lake Como, which I knew from my study of the Napoleonic campaigns in the area. Then we went across Italy from Milan to Venice, staying two days in Venice. From that point on, we kept the sea on our flank. Through Yugoslavia we traveled all along the Adriatic coast, then through Greece along the Aegean coast, and through Turkey along the Black Sea coast. We stopped and stayed a day or two at any place that we found interesting, often at campsites on the beach. This journey of a month and seven days was inexpensive and is one whose memory we fondly cherish.

In 1979 I was posted to the Command and Staff College as an instructor. This is a highly prized appointment awarded to all top lieutenant colonels, and it is where I developed my public speaking skills. Normally, instructors "inherit" lecture notes, which we call pinks because they are written on pink paper. After trying this system for a while, I decided to lecture without the pinks and to add my own thoughts and ideas from practical experience. I was a successful instructor and quite a popular one. The two years I spent there, from 1979 to 1981, were extremely rewarding professionally. They were also very enjoyable socially, as we were a small and close-knit community. Sehba and our children enjoyed these years greatly.

Staff College had its own distinct life and culture, with students from about fifteen countries. I was in charge of the foreign students, and enjoyed my interaction with them, especially when I took them on a tour around Pakistan.

I was also responsible for extracurricular activities at the college. That assignment had its hazards. In 1980 we were to celebrate our platinum jubilee—the Staff College having been erected in 1905. President Zia was to grace the occasion. I was therefore to arrange a special program in the evening. I did so by getting Pakistan's cultural troupe to perform. This troupe included the most prominent male and female musicians and dancers, and had showcased Pakistani culture abroad. Two days before the event, however, when the artists were on a train from Lahore to Quetta, I received an urgent call from the commandant. He told me, to my utter consternation, that the president did not want any song or dance performed, least of all by women. He shocked me further by saying that the president did not even want the troupe to land in Quetta, lest the fundos (slang for "fundamentalists") got wind of it. Despite my protests, I was told to execute the order.

The train had already left Lahore; how could I stop the artists from reaching Quetta? I telephoned the sub–martial law administrator (a brigadier) at Sukkur (a town in the middle of Sindh province) at midnight and told him about the crisis. I asked him to intercept the train, detach the compartment of the artists, and attach it to any Lahore-bound train. The brigadier's first response was quite unfriendly and offensive—how dare a lieutenant colonel wake him up in the middle of the night and ask him to undertake this task? I had to drive home to him the point that both his reputation and mine were at stake with the president. As his groggy mind awoke, he jumped into action and performed the task beautifully, with military precision. The mission was accomplished by two AM. I wish I had been there to see the artists' expressions the next morning, thinking that they were getting off at Quetta, only to discover that they were back where they started!

President Zia, in the 1980s, completed what Bhutto had started in the dying phase of his regime—the total appeasement of the religious lobby. Zia did not have a political base or lobby. By hanging Bhutto, he turned Bhutto into a martyr and his political party—the PPP—into a greater force. Zia found it convenient to align himself with the religious right and create a supportive constituency for himself. He started overemphasizing and overparticipating in religious rituals to show his alignment with the religious lobby. Even music and entertainment became officially taboo, whereas I am told that in private he personally enjoyed good semiclassical music.

From being an instructor I went back to being a student. I was sent to the National Defense College (NDC) in Islamabad, for the armed forces war course. This is considered a landmark progression in an army officer's career, because if you haven't done a war course at the NDC, you will not make it to general. Military history, military strategy, political and border geography, and—most of all—operational strategy are the main ingredients of this course. Operational strategy is taught through several very realistic war games and map exercises.

I think my strength in mathematics facilitated my comprehension of the main elements of war—time, space, and relative strength. I did very well in the course and was graded among the top students. My planning and execution of military operations and my confidence during presentations were highly commended. The course was most useful in grooming me for the highest command or staff or instructional appointments. I came out of the course a much more self-confident officer, prepared for higher ranks. I knew now that if all went smoothly I would make it to general.

After the war course I was back in Kharian, this time in command of the Sixteenth Self-Propelled Regiment, with which I had fought the war of 1965. I was still a lieutenant colonel and was again detailed as the colonel martial law in Rawalpindi. This time my tenure was not as pleasant as it had been under Rafi Alam. My new boss was rough-hewn and known for keeping subordinates under pressure. Adapting myself to him was not easy. We clashed on several occasions. Once I asked the police to remove an obstruction on a road, caused by construction. Instead, I was very harshly admonished by my commander, on the phone. The next day, when he came from Kharian to Rawalpindi's martial law headquarters, I went to his office in a very somber mood and asked him to relieve me of my appointment and allow me to go back to the command of my regiment. "Because," I said, "if I have to be ticked off for doing the right thing, I will not know how to make decisions in the future." This came as a shock to him. He pacified me by praising my overall performance. I continued with martial law duties, and fortunately he became much more careful in dealing with me.

From 1983 to the middle of 1984 I was posted to the Military Operations Directorate as deputy director military operations (DDMO). I was also approved for promotion to the rank of brigadier general, but had to settle temporarily for full colonel because there were no vacancies at the brigadier level.

My short time at the Military Operations Directorate was not as rewarding as it should have been, mainly because my boss lacked the ability to inspire and teach. However, I did witness operational planning at the highest level of the Pakistan Army. When the Siachen Glacier conflict between India and Pakistan erupted, I was part of all that happened. The conflict persists to this day.

Siachen is a long glacier almost at the junction of India, Pakistan, and China, in the Karakoram Range. From the Pakistan side the approach to it is blocked by the Saltoro Range, with passes from 17,000 to 21,000 feet (5,200 to nearly 6,400 meters) high. In 1983 we had learned that India quite frequently intruded into the Siachen Glacier, which belonged to us. We dispatched a team from the Special Services Group (SSG) to confirm the reports. They confirmed the intrusions, because they came across telltale evidence of a hurriedly abandoned camp on the glacier, left by some Indian personnel.

At general headquarters (GHQ) we began planning to occupy the passes on the watershed of the Saltoro Range that dominated the Siachen Glacier. Winter had set in, and we had no experience of operating at such heights, over 16,000 feet (4,800 meters), or at temperatures that could fall to fifty degrees below zero Celsius (−50 C.) with wind chill. The key decision was when to occupy the passes. Time was critical because we assumed that the Indians would try to occupy the same passes, now that they already knew that our SSG team had crossed into the glacier from the Saltoro Range. We suggested early March, to ensure that our forces got to the passes first, just as the worst of winter had passed. We were opposed by the general officer commanding the Northern Areas, who had jurisdiction over this area. He felt that the harshness of the terrain, and the low temperatures, would not allow our troops to reach there in March. He proposed May 1 instead. His opinion prevailed, because he was the commander on the spot. This proved to be a mistake: when we went there we found the Indians already in occupation of most of the dominating features on the Saltro Range, beyond the Siachen Glacier. Still, our troops moved up and performed the challenging task of occupying heights and features around the Indian positions. The result was a series of positions by both sides, at great heights, within shooting range of each other.

Many precious lives have been lost to enemy fire and to hazardous weather and terrain. The Indians suffer far more than we do. It takes them three to seven days of trekking over the Siachen Glacier with all its crevices to occupy the passes. On the Pakistan side a gravel road reaches close to the Saltoro Range. Troops can climb to any of the passes in one day after traveling by jeep. Innumerable small skirmishes have taken place at various locations along the entire front whenever either side has attempted to readjust or occupy new heights. In the initial stages the Indians undertook several such endeavors only to realize very quickly that the attempts were futile. They suffered very heavy losses. Later, we were amused to see a change in their "strategy." Their troops would transmit stories and communications about what can best be called "fake encounters" with the enemy while nothing actually was happening on the ground. Several times, when we picked up such intercepts, our GHQ would get worried and initiate a flurry of signals asking for clarification of the operational situation from the forward posts, only to be told that all was quiet. India has the largest film industry in the world and is rightly famous for making highly romanticized and unrealistic movies, so it came as no surprise to us when we intercepted the Indians' communications about the fake skirmishes and encounters that they were regularly having with the Pakistan Army in their fertile imagination. We actually started enjoying listening in on their make-believe actions; the imaginative details included "enemy" attacks and the "gallantry" of their defense. Later, our amusement turned to hilarity when these fake encounters became the basis for recommendations and nominations for awards for gallantry. Now, much later, it appears that the Indian top brass has discovered the tricks that their forward troops have played. There have been several courts-martial against defaulting officers and commanders for such serious lapses of character.

On several occasions we also intercepted messages about casualties on the Indian side and the inability of the Indian troops to evacuate them because of bad weather and harsh terrain. The dead would lie for days before being evacuated by helicopter. The snow and freezing temperatures created a natural mortuary.

The confrontation at Siachen is one of the major skirmishes we have had with the Indians on the roof of the world. The other serious, nearly full-scale conflict we had was the Kargil episode, which I shall discuss later. Other than these two, the Line of Control that separates Azad (Independent) Kashmir from Indian-occupied Kashmir has always remained volatile. Exchanges of fire, artillery duels, and sniper activity have been an almost daily occurrence. All this goes to show that when two neighbors are hostile, extreme terrain or extreme weather is no obstacle to their engaging each other.

CHAPTER 9

LIVING THROUGH
THE DREADFUL DECADE

From 1985 to 1998, my army career took me from lieutenant colonel to chief of the army. There were several steps along the way, and quite a few lessons in the high politics of Pakistan. The pattern in my country has been repetitive: elected officials have been vulnerable to corruption and create conditions that lead to an army takeover, while those in opposition and many from other walks of life, particularly the intelligentsia, frequently appeal to the army to take power or change the government. In this period, which includes what I call the "dreadful decade of democracy," beginning in 1988, I saw many changeovers in Islamabad and more tension with India, and I had yet one more brush with death. I was no longer on the front lines, but I still felt that way.

In 1985 I was promoted to brigadier and sent back to the National Defense College as an instructor. There are three categories of appointment within which an officer of the Pakistan Army gets rotated—command, staff, and instructional. This is done in accordance with merit, depending on the officer's qualities. Officers having potential for all three are considered top of the line. I have been considered an all-rounder and therefore was regularly rotated among all three categories.

Being an instructor at the NDC—the highest seat of learning of the armed forces—was a great experience. Not only does one have to do a lot of reading and research to remain up-to-date with the latest knowledge regarding strategy, tactics, operations, and management; one also gets a chance to crystallize one's own ideas.

After two years as an instructor at NDC—1985 and 1986—I became commander, artillery, of the armored division in Kharian. It is odd, but in every rank I have been posted back to Kharian. This was the first posting where I was authorized to fly a flag on my staff car or jeep—a source of great pride to me.

During this command, more tension with India arose. It all started with the conduct of a major war game by India involving several corps—especially offensive corps close to Pakistan's border in the southern desert front. Pakistan took this seriously, because Indian army formations were made to carry all their ammunition with them, which is not the normal practice in exercises. This exercise was code-named Brass Tacks and was the brainchild of the volatile and vitriolic Indian army chief General Sundarji.

We decided to give a strong and strategically superior response. Our armored division, with other strike corps elements, was moved to the Sialkot sector in northern Punjab, posing a direct threat to India's line of communication to the part of Kashmir that is under its occupation and which we call Indian-occupied Kashmir. With that deployment, Pakistan enjoyed what is known as "superiority of strategic orientation": we could threaten more sensitive objectives of the enemy than they could of ours, and in less time. This move deterred India from any misadventures. The standoff continued for several months until good sense prevailed on the Indian side and disengagement was negotiated. During this confrontation the morale of the Pakistan Army remained at a peak. I motivated my brigade to the highest pitch. My troops were itching for a chance to avenge what had happened in 1971 in East Pakistan.

It was also during this command that I was selected as military secretary to President General Zia ul-Haq. My name was suggested by President Zia's former military secretary, Brigadier (later Major General) Mahmood Ali Durrani, fondly nicknamed "MAD," who came to Kharian to command a brigade. (He was appointed Ambassador to Washington in 2006.) I was told to be prepared to move at short notice. I told my wife, Sehba, that I would leave with a suitcase and she should close up the house and join me later. Five days passed, but there was no official word. Then news came that Brigadier Najeeb had been given the post. I was disappointed. My commanding officer, Major General Farrakh, later told me, that President Zia had phoned to say he had selected me, but Farrakh had said to the president that I was on an upward career path and becoming military secretary would be a spoiler because I had not yet commanded an infantry brigade. If an officer is one of the front-runners and wants to make it to higher ranks, he has to command an infantry brigade at some stage, no matter what arm of the fighting force he comes from.

This is how not only my career but also my life was saved. I was given the prized appointment of commander of the Twenty-fifth Infantry Brigade in Bahawalpur, and poor Najeeb became Zia's military secretary. I remained there for about eight months, and left just a month before President Zia's C-130 crashed in Bahawalpur on August 17, 1988, with some of the top officers of the Pakistan Army, including the chairman of the Joint Chiefs of Staff Committee, General Akhtar Abdur Rahman. Also killed were an American brigadier general; the American ambassador, Arnold Raphael; and Najeeb. I was saved by the grace of God and thanks to Major General Farrakh's intervention.

The cause of the accident still remains shrouded in mystery. The report did note that the investigators found traces of potassium, chlorine, antimony, phosphorous, and sodium at the crash site. Since these elements are generally not associated with the structure of an aircraft, the inquiry concluded that internal sabotage of the plane was the most likely cause of the accident. Mysteriously, the case was not pursued further. The black box was recovered but gave no indication of a problem. It seems likely that the gases were used to disable the pilots. But who unleashed them, we don't know. I have my suspicions, though.

My next assignment was back in Rawalpindi as deputy military secretary to the GHQ, a staff appointment. My job here was to deal with the career management of all majors and lower ranks of the army. I became their "godfather." The assignment put great demands on my sense of compassion and justice.

One day, out of the blue, a friend of Benazir Bhutto's husband Asif Zardari came to call on me. Benazir was prime minister at the time. The friend's name was Javed Pasha. I had never seen him before.

Pasha suggested that I become Benazir's military secretary. I do not know whether this was Pasha's personal initiative, or if it had the backing of the prime minster. I asked for time to think about it.

The next day, I broached the subject with my boss, Major General Farrakh. He rejected Pasha's suggestion outright, saying, "You are a professional soldier and should continue with your professional work." This was yet another time my career was saved. Had I become her military secretary I would have gone down with her and her government.

In 1990 I was selected for the prestigious one-year course at the Royal College of Defence Studies in London. It was another great experience, both for my family and myself. There were civilian and military officers from many countries at the college, and I made good friends with several of them. The course was a "mini UN," as the commandant remarked. Here, I learned how to be flexible and accommodating of differing views. Any issue has different perspectives when seen from different parts of the world. Competing views often sound equally logical. Also, I utilized my weekends and holidays to travel extensively in England, Wales, Scotland, Europe, and even the United States.

On returning home I was promoted to major general and appointed general officer, commanding (GOC), of the Fortieth Division. This was a strike division within an offensive corps. It needed an aggressive spirit. I relished this part of it. A GOC does not directly command troops; his commanding officers do that for him. But I led from the front. I would go out to meet a platoon on exercise, even if it consisted of only thirty people. This made an impact and instilled confidence in the men. I would do physical training exercises or even the obstacle course with the troops in one battalion or the other. If someone did badly, I would give a demonstration of how to get over an obstacle. I walked on long marches with them. While crossing a canal during training exercises, I would frequently swim with the leading wave, even in the cold of winter or in the darkness of night. This gave me the moral authority to check and reprimand the men for any weakness.

• • •

In 1993 I was appointed director general of military operations (DGMO), the most highly coveted post for a major general. This was the first time that I got involved in almost everything having to do with the nation in which the army is involved. The Military Operations Directorate is the core think tank of the army and is involved in whatever is on the army chief's mind, be it military or political.

My tenure as DGMO was quite eventful because this was also the time when Pakistan became the largest contributor to UN peacekeeping missions around the world. We already had a brigade in Somalia and were now requested to provide another brigade in Bosnia. Somalia and Bosnia were both tough and challenging assignments for the Pakistani troops.

We had initially dispatched an infantry battalion to Somalia in mid-1992, and later built up its strength to a brigade group in early 1993. The warlord Farah Aideed then reigned supreme, and no other forces dared to go to Somalia. Pakistan, under a special request of the UN, decided to help the UN in its time of need. Our brigade moved in and deployed efficiently. Tragedy struck in June 1993, when one of our battalions—the Tenth Baloch Regiment—was ambushed while returning from a routine search operation in a built-up area. The hail of fire from surrounding buildings inflicted heavy casualties: twenty-eight dead and several wounded. I went to Mogadishu after this incident, to shore up the morale of our troops. Traveling around the countryside by chopper, I saw how Somalis had completely destroyed their own country. Hardly any houses were in a livable state. It was distressing, especially because I knew that Somalia had once been an attractive posting for members of Pakistan's military advisory mission.

However, I was glad to be briefed and to see firsthand that the Pakistani troops were in high spirits and were very highly regarded by the United Nations Operation in Somalia commanders. Our force acquitted itself admirably. In fact, when the UN decided to pull out its force from Somalia, the rearguard action was given to U.S. and Pakistani troops to execute. It was a Pakistani battalion that threw a security cordon around Mogadishu, under cover of which all UN contingents withdrew into waiting ships at the port. It was this battalion along with a U.S. contingent that executed a tactical withdrawal under fire.

The outstanding performance of the Pakistani troops under adverse conditions is very well known at the UN. Regrettably, the film *Black Hawk Down* ignores the role of Pakistan in Somalia. When U.S. troops were trapped in the thickly populated Madina Bazaar area of Mogadishu, it was the Seventh Frontier Force Regiment of the Pakistan Army that reached out and extricated them. The bravery of the U.S. troops notwithstanding, we deserved equal, if not more, credit; but the filmmakers depicted the incident as involving only Americans.

The mission in Bosnia was even more serious than the one in Somalia. I was detailed to go to Bosnia to decide on the commitment and deployment of the Pakistani Brigade. I flew in with a small team of four officers. We reached Sarajevo in a UN helicopter. From Saravejo we were driven in an armored fighting vehicle, winding up and down hilly terrain for about forty miles (sixty-four kilometers) to Kisiljak. The winter Olympics had been held there a few years earlier, but now the area was desolate. We were put up at a hotel that had been built for the Olympic games and was now occupied by UN officers. I was given a briefing on the prevailing conditions in Bosnia and the likely deployment areas of the "Pakbats," as the Pakistani battalions were to be called.

I was conscious of the fact that many Europeans were not eager to have a Pakistani force "intruding" in their domain of influence. This was manifest in the briefing I was given. The brigadier briefing me tried to change my mind about our involvement, by overemphasizing the difficult conditions in the zones of operation. "Living conditions are very tough," he said. "You have to operate at heights exceeding 8,000 feet [about 2,400 meters] and in subzero temperatures." He must not have relished my reply: I told him that our troops belonged to the Azad Kashmir Regiment, most of whom were born in the Himalayas and had seen action at heights of over 18,000 feet (5,400 meters) in temperatures of minus fifty degrees Celsius (−50 C.). I assured him that they would be at home in Bosnia, and would consider the mountains to be molehills.

Kisiljak is a beautiful and picturesque place. What a pity that it was now a scene of battle instead of the winter Olympics. From Kisiljak I was driven back in the same armored fighting vehicle to Saravejo. I stayed a night there with an Egyptian battalion, housed in a grand palace. I can never forget that day and night. During the day I asked to be driven around the streets of the city. This was arranged in an armored fighting vehicle for protection against the sporadic fire coming from the Serbs occupying the hills around the city. Saravejo was under siege. The population was hungry and cold, with no power supply and only subsistence-level food. The streets were deserted except for old men and women braving the firing from the hills to dig out the roots of trees that they had already cut down and burned for warmth. I was, however, extremely moved when people peering out of their doors and windows cheered me all along the route as they noticed the Pakistani flag insignia on my uniform.

That night, while I was strolling around the compound of the palace with the commanding officer, a colonel, of my host Egyptian battalion, I heard a distinct sound of whining from outside. I asked what it could be. The colonel knew what it was and said it was quite a regular feature every night. He took me to the main entrance gate. There were some dozen or two dozen children, begging and crying for food. My eyes swelled with tears, both at their misery and at my helplessness to assist them. I gave them all the dollars I was carrying and turned back, full of pain and sorrow. When the Pakistani Brigade group of three battalions finally came, all its personnel fasted one day of every week, and distributed the food they had saved among the more needy Bosnians. It was taken as a noble gesture by the populace.

At this point in my career, I began to observe, and sometimes get indirectly involved in, affairs of state, over and above purely military commitments. In 1995 I was promoted to lieutenant general and posted to Mangla to command the elite strike corps of the Pakistan Army. As a corps commander I was automatically part of the army's highest decision-making body—the Corps Commanders' Conference. I saw then how national personalities from all professions—including opposition politicians—regularly visited the army chief to encourage him to oppose the sitting government. I also came to know of many peoples' political agendas. Whenever any government was performing poorly (unfortunately, that was the norm in the "democratic" decade of the 1990s) or was in political trouble, all roads led to the army GHQ. During this decade, whenever there was acrimony between the president and the prime minister, which was more often than not, the army chief would be sucked into the fray. He was expected by all and sundry, including the antagonists, to act as an arbitrator. The Pakistan Army has always been held in high esteem as the only powerful stabilizing factor in the nation. In the other direction, I also saw how the unrelenting pressure of what I can only call "influence wielders" made the army chief visit the prime minister and "advise" him or her on how to govern. In the absence of institutional checks and balances over government leaders, the only recourse to those out of power was the commander of the army.

After the fatal crash of the C-130 and President Zia's death in 1988, Benazir Bhutto formed a coalition government and became prime minister in November 1988. During the period from November 1988 to October 1999, a span of nearly eleven years, no national or provincial assembly completed its term. The office of prime minister changed four times. We had three different presidents. We even saw political workers, parliamentarians, and officeholders of one prime minister physically assault the Supreme Court of Pakistan. Presidents and prime ministers began each regime harmoniously but ended at each other's throats. The presidents used their discretionary constitutional authority to dissolve the assemblies and order fresh elections. There were four national elections in nine years.

The four changes of prime minister involved two cycles of alteration between Benazir Bhutto and Nawaz Sharif. Never in the history of Pakistan had we seen such a combination of the worst kind of governance—or rather, a nearly total lack of governance—along with corruption and the plunder of national wealth. During these eleven years, every army chief—there were four of them—eventually clashed with the prime minister. The head of the government invariably got on the wrong side of the president and the army chief. Advice to Nawaz Sharif or Benazir Bhutto fell on deaf ears, leading every time to a confrontation.

The army always tried to play a reconciliatory role, avoiding a military takeover. It is our misfortune that the nation plummeted to the depths of economic bankruptcy. Because this was coupled with an absence of governance, we came near to being declared a failed or defaulted state. This was the period that I have always called "sham democracy."

Politics aside, my tenures as DGMO and corps commander went very smoothly. I enjoyed my command because I managed to raise the morale and spirit of the corps to a level where the troops felt confident of delivery on the offensive missions expected of them. For recreational purposes I opened a water sports club in Mangla Lake, which is near the corps headquarters. We introduced sailing with different categories of boats, water skiing, parasailing, and all categories of rowing. I enjoyed participating in each. I even managed to learn canoeing, sailing, and some water skiing, beyond the rowing and parasailing that I already knew. The facility has now been developed into an excellent lakeside resort.

In 1997, when General Jehangir Karamat was the army chief, a new chief of general staff (CGS) was to be selected. Most army officers felt that I would—or should—get the job. I knew that General Jahangir Karamat regarded me very highly as a commander and as a staff officer. He had been my instructor in the war course, my corps commander when I was commanding a division, and my boss as the chief of general staff. He had always given me high grades. Yet instead of me, he selected Lieutenant General Ali Kuli Khan Khattak, who I felt was a mediocre officer. I must confess I was quite surprised and disappointed.

I reconciled myself to retiring from the army as a lieutenant general, and told Sehba that we should be grateful to God that we had come so far. I was third in seniority of lieutenant generals, though this happened because of some manipulation by the former army chief General Waheed Kakar to give the advantage of first position to Ali Kuli, whom he wanted to promote. If not for this unfair manipulation, I would have been first in line and Ali Kuli would have retired before the promotion of the next chief was considered. The appointment of Ali Kuli to the prized position of CGS indicated that General Jahangir Karamat preferred him as the next Chief after Karamat retired. It was also well known that the president of Pakistan, Farooq Leghari, who had the authority to appoint the chief, was a college classmate of Ali Kuli. I was more of a commoner—a soldier's man at that—who was not at all into such social links and maneuvering.

One night when I was corps commander I was sitting in my house in Mangla, past midnight, in a very pensive mood. Suddenly a thought came to my mind in the form of a prayer. I jotted it down on my official letterhead. I still keep it in my personal file.

> *O Allah! The only thing I can promise my Army and my Nation is*
> *sincerity, honesty, integrity, and unflinching loyalty.*
> *You give me the vision to see and perceive the truth from the false.*
> *The wisdom to comprehend the problem and find a solution.*
> *The courage to speak and project and the clarity to express the right.*
> *The chance to serve the Nation as I deserve.*

It was August 11, 1998, my fifty-fifth birthday. I did not know at that time that my prayer to serve my country was soon to be answered. The little boy who journeyed on that fateful train to Pakistan had come a long way. Little did he know that the most difficult stage of his life was about to begin.

CHAPTER 10

FROM CHIEF TO CHIEF EXECUTIVE

O ne night after dinner, on October 7, 1998, around seven-thirty PM, I was watching television with my wife in my house in Mangla when I got a call that Prime Minister Nawaz Sharif wished to see me. I said that I would get to Islamabad the next morning.

"No, sir, he wants to see you now, as soon as possible, tonight," insisted the prime minister's military secretary. My back tightened. It is not normal for a prime minister to call a lieutenant general like that, and at night, when the army chief is available next door to sort anything out.

"OK," I said. "Let me inform the chief."

"No," said the military secretary. "This is highly confidential. You just come without telling anyone."

I sensed that there was something abnormal afoot.

"In what connection am I being summoned?" I asked.

"Sir, you will find out for yourself once you get here. Don't talk to the chief."

"Should I come in uniform?" I asked.

"Yes," I was told, "and get here as fast as you can."

I got into my uniform, summoned a military police escort, strapped on my favorite Glock 17 pistol (out of abundant caution), and started off for Islamabad, a good ninety minutes drive away. I had been told not to call anyone. I had no idea what was happening.

Just as my car was entering Islamabad, I received a call from Brigadier Ijaz Shah, a friend who was the ISI's (Inter Sevices Intelligence) detachment commander in Lahore.

"Congratulations," he said. "You are being made chief."

"What nonsense are you talking?" I said. "Karamat's term is not yet up. How can I become chief?"

"The chief has resigned," said my friend. "It is all over the news."

My mind raced back to the Corps Commanders' Conference in GHQ some months ago, when General Karamat had announced that through a constitutional amendment Prime Minister Nawaz Sharif had taken away the power of the president to dissolve the National Assembly and dismiss the government. He had also taken on himself the power to appoint the three service chiefs and the chairman of the Joint Chiefs of Staff Committee. I remembered that the color had drained from Lieutenant General Ali Kuli's face. He was friendly with President Farooq Leghari, and it was more or less a foregone conclusion that he would be selected as the next chief. But if Nawaz Sharif were to make the decision, all bets were off. Some generals told me that my chance of becoming chief had returned, but I brushed the idea aside because I felt that before retirement the outgoing chief would propose Ali Kuli's name. Despite the constitutional amendment, the president still had to sign the order of the appointment of the next chief, and so President Leghari still had some input in the matter.

After this there was open and utterly unseemly conflict between the prime minister on the one hand, and the president and chief justice of the Supreme Court of Pakistan on the other. As had become the norm, both sides dragged in the army chief to arbitrate. President Farooq Leghari tried to get the chief justice to claim that the constitutional amendment was unconstitutional. If the chief justice had done this, the president would have dissolved the National Assembly and dismissed the government of the errant Prime Minister Sharif.

The prime minister convinced certain judges to take his side, and they passed a resolution against their own chief justice. Then the prime minister got his party goons to storm the Supreme Court building while the court was in session. Their lordships had to hide in their chambers to avoid a thrashing, or worse. This was, to put it mildly, a very low point in Pakistani political history.

General Jahangir Karamat called a conference of the corps commanders to discuss the situation, since both the president and the prime minister had asked him to enter the fray as arbiter. The ISI confirmed that the president and the chief justice were in collusion to throw out the National Assembly and with it their real target, Prime Minister Nawaz Sharif.

We considered our options. One was to send the chief justice a message asking him to behave himself and remain neutral, neutrality being an imperative in his job. Some felt that Nawaz Sharif was using his brute majority in the National Assembly to bend the constitution to his will and was really damaging the country. Best to let him be thrown out before it went too far. Ali Kuli, for obvious reasons, said that in case the president lost the battle and was thrown out, so should Nawaz Sharif be—both must go and we should impose martial law. But I argued that what the president and the chief justice were doing was very wrong, that Nawaz Sharif had been elected and we must let his term take its course if democracy was to take root and mature. I was the strongest proponent of maintaining the prime minister in his position, and keeping the National Assembly in place. If there had to be a human political sacrifice, I felt, it should be the president and the chief justice. I remember that I gave a rather long analysis.

The next day General Karamat called a meeting of the principal staff officers. I was not there, but Ali Kuli was. I was later informed that Ali Kuli said a great deal, the import of which was that General Karamat should take over and impose martial law.

After a few days the army chief called another meeting in Army House, at which some corps commanders including myself were also present. Ali again repeated that the army should take over, and send both the president and the prime minister packing. I had a small run-in with Ali then, because this was not fair play; it was self-promotion. Once again we considered sending a message to the chief justice to behave himself, but finally it was decided that the only way to break the impasse was that both the president and the chief justice must be advised to go. The army supported the elected prime minister. Then we dispersed.

The next day, with none of us present, a desperate Ali Kuli played his last card and insisted that Nawaz Sharif must go if the president went, and that the army must take over the country. General Karamat did not agree, and he threw his weight behind the prime minister. President Farooq Leghari decided to resign. The chief justice followed soon after, having lost the support of many of his fellow judges. And so the "battle for the Supreme Court" came to an ignoble end. The army chief had been dragged into it, as usual, by the politicians, but this time he did the right thing.

I was in some turmoil as I entered the prime minister's office. He was sitting on a sofa and smiling a victorious smile. He told me that the chief of the army staff had resigned and that he had appointed me instead.

I asked him what had happened. "I demanded his resignation and he gave it to me," said the prime minister. I was taken aback. General Karamat's "mistake" had been to make some suggestions during a speech at the Naval Staff College, about how to improve the governance of the country, including setting up a national security council. Nawaz Sharif had taken his scalp for it. What shocked me even more was the meek manner in which General Karamat resigned. It caused great resentment in the army, as soldiers and officers alike felt humiliated.

I know that in western democracies, military personnel on active duty, especially the chiefs, are not supposed to make political statements. But then, in western democracies neither do the heads of government and state perennially drag army chiefs into politics. In a country where such a practice is rampant, an army chief cannot be blamed for getting involved, if he acts sensibly.

I thanked the prime minister for reposing confidence in me. While pinning on my badges of rank he said, "One of the reasons why I have selected you is that you are the only lieutenant general who never approached me, directly or indirectly, for this job." I saluted the prime minister and left.

The first thing I did was to drive straight to Army House and meet General Jahangir Karamat, now my predecessor. "Sir, what happened?" I asked him. He didn't tell me anything. Not to this day has he told me why he resigned. He only congratulated me. What could I say? "Sir, I'm sorry for you and happy for myself"? I was with him for only about ten or fifteen minutes and then left.

I went to the Armored Corps mess for the night. Obviously, the first people I called were my wife and my parents. Needless to say, they were thrilled. A short while later I got a call from Ali Kuli, who was now my chief of general staff (CGS) and would be looking after my appointment ceremony the next morning. Imagine my surprise and pain when, after Ali expressed some lackluster congratulations—"Pervez, congratulations"—he informed me in the same breath, "I have to go to Peshawar tomorrow for a wedding."

I said, "OK, go if you must."

Then Ali added, "Maybe I won't come back."

"Ali, it is entirely your choice," I replied, trying to hide the disappointment in my voice. "I want you to continue to come to the office, but if you don't want to, it's up to you." Ali never did come back. He retired from the army. He even stopped talking to me. He also refused to respond to my dinner invitation for all my army course mates. His behavior was odd, to say the least. After all, he was a lieutenant general, the chief of general staff, and, above all, my friend and course mate. If nothing else, he should have been glad that his friend had become the chief and that he was my CGS. Obviously, our friendship soured. He needed to remember the old adage, "Man proposes and God disposes."

There was even greater resentment in the army than I had imagined over General Jahangir Karamat's forced resignation. An overbearing prime minister with a huge parliamentary majority, he had been busy gathering all powers in his office. Through constitutional amendments he had silenced dissent, not only within his party but in parliament as well. His party goons had physically attacked the Supreme Court, and the whole sordid episode had been caught on film by the security cameras. He had bribed and coerced judges. He had also tried to muzzle the press and had arrested and mistreated a number of journalists and editors. By reducing the president to a mere figurehead, he had removed the safety valve that could get rid of corrupt and inept governments without intervention by the army. With that safety valve gone there was nothing to stand between a prime minister on the rampage and the army. Nawaz Sharif had axed the army chief simply for speaking up.

One of the first things I did was to tell the army that our job was to assist the government in all possible ways, particularly in areas where it asked us to help. We should stop brooding over the forced resignation of General Karamat and get on with our jobs. We would not allow another humiliation to befall us in case the prime minister tried something like this again, but we would only react, never act unilaterally.

I was army chief for only a year before the army had to react against Nawaz Sharif. My working relationship with him was perfectly good in the beginning, with some minor disagreements over the sacking of two major generals, the appointment of two lieutenant generals, and his request to me to court-martial a journalist for treason. I must say that I was quite amused by his style of working: I never saw him reading or writing anything.

Our relationship soured only with the Kargil episode and Nawaz Sharif's sudden capitulation before President Bill Clinton in Washington on July 4, 1999. That episode was so fraught with tension, and so dangerous—the first clash of India and Pakistan since we both had detonated nuclear weapons—that it demands its own chapter in this account.

CHAPTER 11

THE KARGIL CONFLICT

The year 1999 may have been the most momentous of my life, assassination attempts notwithstanding. The events of 1999, and the fall of 1998, dramatically catapulted me from soldiering to leading the destiny of the nation. They also brought two nuclear powers to the brink of war. It is time to lay bare what has been shrouded in mystery.

As a backup to understanding the Kargil conflict it needs to be stressed that Kargil was not a one-off operation, but the latest in a series of moves and countermoves at a tactical level by India and Pakistan along the Line of Control in the inaccessible, snowbound Northern Areas. India would capture a location where they felt that our presence was thin, and vice-versa. This is how they managed to occupy Siachen (ostensibly without clearance from the Indian government). This is how the Kashmiri freedom fighting mujahideen occupied the Kargil heights that the Indian army had vacated for the winter.

In October 1998, India claimed it had beaten back two Pakistani attacks in the area of the Siachen Glacier, on October 16 and 18. My own staff insisted that no such attacks had taken place. Nonetheless, I summoned the commander of Force Command Northern Areas (FCNA) to understand what was really going on in his area of responsibility. He, too, reassured me that no official incursions were under way. He dismissed the Indian reports as false, and added that India had falsely reported attacks during the previous summer, at a rate of one per month. Subsequently, in late October and early November 1998 I received reports of another five such make-believe attacks.

We later discovered that this probably was related to activities by the mujahideen (freedom fighters). We knew that thousands of mujahideen, mostly indigenous to Indian-held Kashmir but also supported by freelance sympathizers from Pakistan, did operate against the Indian forces. They used to cross the Line of Control (LOC) in both directions at places which were thinly held and where the going was rough. I instructed the Military Operations and Military Intelligence Directorates at general headquarters and at the headquarters of the Rawalpindi Corps to carry out an assessment of the situation. During this time, the Indians continued to report "attacks."

The assessment was formally presented at the end of December. We realized that the number and frequency of reported attacks were unprecedented and could possibly be used by the Indians as a casus belli to launch an operation against us. We also had intelligence through various sources suggesting an Indian plan to conduct some operations in our Northern Areas. There was specific information of a possible Indian attack in the Shaqma sector; it was aimed at positions we had used to shell the road between Dras and Kargil in early summer 1998, in response to continuous artillery shelling by the Indians at the Neelum Valley Road on our side of the Line of Control (Map 1).

As a normal practice, the Indians used to move two reserve brigades from the Leh area each winter, to the Srinagar valley. In the winter of 1998 not only were these brigades retained north of Zojila, but India's Seventieth Brigade was deployed at Dras. It gave the Indians a window of opportunity because of the relatively early opening of the pass at Zojila, as compared with the Burzil Pass on our side. The availability of a paved road also gave India an advantage for supplying the area. There were large gaps between our defensive positions in the Kargil and Dras sectors, making it possible for Indian troops to cross the line too easily. India also brought in and tested special bunker-busting equipment in the autumn of 1998. We know that the Indian army had procured large quantities of high-altitude equipment, special weapons, and new snow scooters and snowmobiles. India appeared on the verge of an attack across the LOC.

Our sources of information were very reliable. India had been "creeping forward" across the LOC even after the Simla Agreement, which was reached between India and Pakistan after the war of 1971 and defined the Line of Control. India had tested us at Chorbat La, the

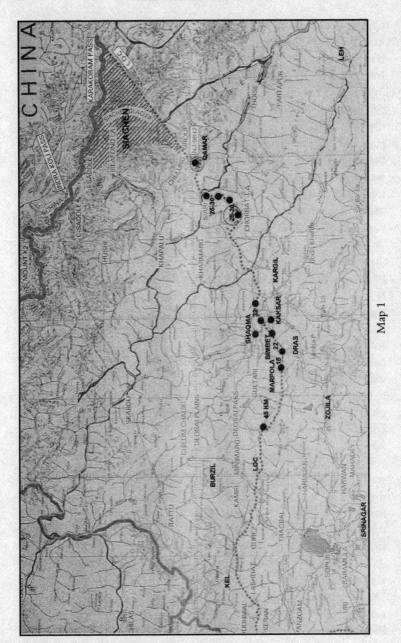

Map 1

Qamar sector and Siachen in the Northern Areas. Finally, frequent visits of the Indian defense minister, George Fernandes, to the Siachen and Kargil areas during the summer and autumn of 1998 suggested that India was considering more offensive operations.

The assessment of the GHQ staff and Rawalpindi Corps fit the logic of the situation. It was appropriate to allow the Rawalpindi Corps to prepare and present the FCNA plan of the defensive maneuver in the Northern Areas so as to deny any ingress across the LOC. A plan calling for plugging the gaps—ranging from nine to twenty-eight miles (fifteen to forty-five kilometers)—between our positions was formally presented and approved toward the middle of January 1999. Rawalpindi Corps and FCNA were to execute it.

The terrain and weather were forbidding. The operation had to be undertaken by limited forces, and security was crucial. Any leakage of information would have set off a race to the watershed, as had happened at Siachen. The terrain and resources were to India's advantage, for such a race. Our information therefore was shared on a "need to know" basis. Second line forces under the FCNA, called Northern Light Infantry, composed of locals of the area, were to occupy the forward positions. The troops were given special instructions not to cross the watershed along the LOC.

Our maneuver was conducted flawlessly, a tactical marvel of military professionalism. By the end of April the unoccupied gaps along seventy-five miles (120 kilometers) of the LOC had been secured by over 100 new posts of ten to twenty persons each.

With the forward movement of our troops to dominating positions, we began to understand exactly what Pakistani freedom fighters had undertaken. I was kept informed of all movements of the freedom fighters from March 1999 onward, when our troops started reaching the heights at the watershed. Finally, on May 7, I was given a comprehensive briefing of their positions.

The Indians were completely oblivious of our new strength along the LOC. The first confrontation between the two armies took place on May 2, when Indian troops bumped into our position in the Shyok sector. The second encounter took place with freedom fighters in the Battalik sector on May 7. The Indians suffered heavy casualties. Alarm bells started ringing at the Indian high command when another skirmish took place with the freedom fighters in the Dras sector on May 10, 1999. India overreacted by bringing its air force into action. Helicopter sorties were flown to ascertain the ingresses made by the freedom fighters. However, the actions of the Indian Air Force were not confined to the freedom fighters' locations; the Indians also started crossing over and bombarding positions of the Pakistan Army. This resulted in the shooting down of one of the Indian helicopters and two jet fighter planes over Pakistani territory. When the Zojila Pass opened to military traffic, an Indian buildup began. Our troops and the freedom fighters exacted a very heavy toll on Indian convoy traffic, forcing the convoys to travel in the dark of night. The Indians brought four regular divisions into the area, along with a heavy concentration of artillery. They even brought in the artillery of their strike formations (conventionally to be used in an offensive across the international border against Pakistan). Intense fighting erupted against the freedom fighters. The Indians also showed no hesitation in attacking our troops on the LOC on the ground and from the air.

On May 15, I ordered FCNA to improve our defensive positions in coordination with the freedom fighters to deny access to the watershed by India. By now the freedom fighters occupied over 500 square miles (800 square kilometers) of Indian-occupied territory: about 250 square miles (400 square kilometers) in the Mushko area, 40 square miles (100 square kilometers) in the Dras area, twenty square miles (fifty square kilometers) in the Kaksar area, eighty square miles (200 square kilometers) in the Battalik area, and twenty-three square miles (sixty square kilometers) in the Shyok area (Map 2). Our field commanders were fully engaged in supporting them in the face of the growing momentum of the Indian operations. We wanted to dominate the areas held by the freedom fighters. We established outposts to act as eyes and ears, and made raids and ambushes. The bravery, steadfastness, and ultimate sacrifice of our men in that inhospitable, high-altitude battlefield, against massive Indian forces, will be written in golden letters.

The Indian buildup continued during the entire month of May. India moved in artillery and infantry formations even at the cost of significantly depleting its offensive capability elsewhere along the international border. Evaluating this buildup at headquarters, we realized

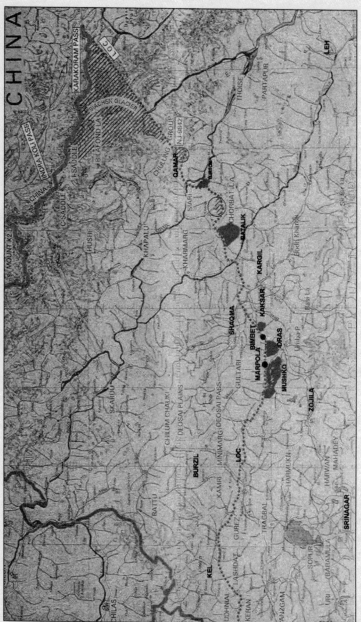

Map 2

that India had created a serious strategic imbalance in its system of forces. It had bottled up major formations inside Kashmir, leaving itself no capability to attack us elsewhere, and, most seriously, had left the field open for a counteroffensive with which we could choke the Kashmir valley. We had no offensive designs on the international border, and were reassured that India's offensive capability was restricted to Kashmir.

Having failed to dislodge the groups occupying the heights, the Indians resorted to mass attacks. Brigade-size attacks were launched to secure outposts held by as few as eight to ten of our men. These attacks gained little ground until the middle of June. Nonetheless, the Indian media hyped their success. On our side, our political leadership displayed a total lack of statesmanship and made no serious effort to rally the country.

Neither side's leadership had an appetite for war, but India worked hard to isolate us diplomatically. International pressure had a demoralizing effect on Prime Minster Nawaz Sharif. Meanwhile, the buildup on both sides continued. In mid-June, the Rawalpindi Corps headquarters was allowed to shift some of its regular troops from the Mangla garrison into FCNA's area of responsibility. These troops started reaching the mountains toward the end of June. Although they played only a limited role in the conflict in the few days that remained, they would be of great use during the consolidation of our positions on the watershed afterward. The positions held by our troops on July 4 are shown in Map 3. We had lost some ground in the Dras, Battalik, and Shyok positions, while the Kaksar and Mushko ingresses remained untouched.

Considered purely in military terms, the Kargil operations were a landmark in the history of the Pakistan Army. As few as five batallions, in support of the freedom fighter groups, were able to compel the Indians to employ more than four divisions, with the bulk of the Indian artillery coming from strike formations meant for operations in the southern plains. The Indians were also forced to mobilize their entire national resources, including their air force. By July 4 they did achieve some success, which I would call insignificant. Our troops were fully prepared to hold our dominating positions ahead of the watershed.

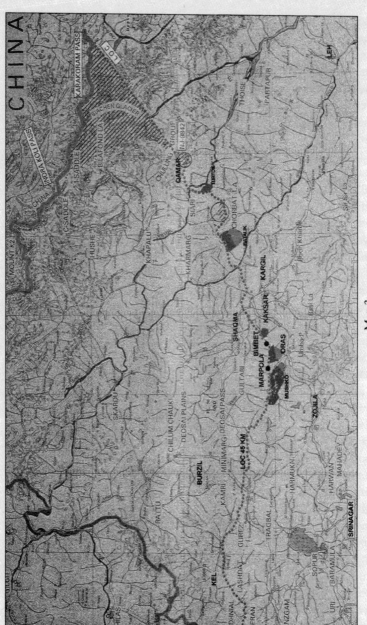

Map 3

Our nation remains proud of its commanders and troops, whose grit and determination I observed during my frequent visits to the forward areas. Many officers and men sacrificed their lives on the snow-clad peaks and in the boulder-ridden valleys of the Northern Areas. I would be remiss not to specially acknowledge the achievements, professionalism, and bravery of all ranks of the Northern Light Infantry. As a reward I later converted them into a regular group of the Pakistan Army. They now exist as a proud segment of the army's "queen of battle": the infantry.

July 4 marked a cease-fire, negotiated by President Bill Clinton with Prime Minister Nawaz Sharif. International pressure for a cease-fire was intense. President Clinton was the only statesman who had influence with both Pakistan and India. Yet in truth, it was no negotiation at all. Sharif agreed to an unconditional withdrawal. To make matters worse, misperceptions of the military situation were rampant. India raised the level of some of its achievements to mythical proportions. A hilarious example of this was the announcement of India's highest award for gallantry, given to a soldier posthumously, because he had died in the line of duty. Later, they found that the man was very much alive. On our side, I am ashamed to say, our political leadership insinuated that the achievements of our troops amounted to a "debacle." Some people even called the Pakistan Army a "rogue army."

As the chief of the army staff, I found myself in a very difficult position. I wanted to explain the military situation, to demonstrate how successful we had been, and point out the political mishandling that had caused so much despair. But that would have been disloyal, and very unsettling for the political leaders. In desperation they might do something to destabilize the state system, or to damage the fabric of the army. On the other hand, if they were allowed to continue to spin the events disingenuously, that would have been tantamount to disloyalty to my commanders and troops. The time has come for me to deal with some of the myths and faulty perceptions and present the truth, as I know it.

One myth is that the operation was launched without the army's taking the political leadership into its confidence.

This is a very unfortunate perception, because nothing could be farther from the truth. First, as noted above, there was no deliberate offensive operation planned, and moving to the unoccupied gaps along the line of control was not a violation of any agreement and was well within the purview of the local commander. The move to establish our defenses along the line was approved at both the corps and the army headquarters. The army briefed the prime minister in Skardu on January 29, 1999; and in Kel on February 5, 1999. During these briefings our defensive maneuver was explained as a response to all that was happening on the Indian side. Subsequently, the prime minister was also briefed on March 12 at the Directorate General Inter Services Intelligence (ISI), which included a detailed survey of the situation inside Occupied Jammu and Kashmir and also along the LOC. As the operation developed, he was briefed in detail by the director general of military operations on May 17. Later briefings were also arranged on June 2 and June 22.

A second myth is that the military situation on the ground was precarious, and the prime minister dashed to Washington to get the army out of it.

This disinformation is a much bigger lie. In their two months of operations the Indians came nowhere near the watershed and our main defenses. As a result of the ingresses ahead of the line, the Indians were able to clear only a few outposts in three (of five) areas. The briefing given by me personally to the Defense Committee of the cabinet on July 2, 1999, actually laid out the entire military picture. I covered all possible hypotheses of enemy actions in the air, at sea, and on land. The conclusions that I derived were:

- That the Indians were in no position to launch an all-out offensive on land, at sea, or in the air.
- That Pakistan was in a strategically advantageous position in case of an all-out war, in view of the massive Indian troop inductions inside Kashmir, resulting in a strategic imbalance in India's system of forces.
- That the Indian forces, despite their massive strength, would never be able to dislodge the freedom fighters and the NLI from the ingresses and positions held by them.

At that briefing the prime minister asked me several times whether we should accept a cease-fire and withdraw. My answer every time was restricted to the optimistic military situation; I left the political decisions to him. He wanted to fire his gun from my shoulder, but it was not my place to offer this. I also remember his minister, Raja Zafar ul-Haq, an ardent supporter of his, to have been the strongest proponent of no cease-fire and no withdrawal. Chaudhry Shujat Hussain, the interior minister at the time, who was to play a major political role after Nawaz Sharif's departure, said that whatever we did, we must stress that Kargil was "our joint effort and collective responsibility." Nawaz Sharif did not like this truth and stood up abruptly, saying that we would continue later—but this never happened. The meeting ended inconclusively. It was decided to meet again on July 5, 1999, to make the final decision. I went with all my family and some friends to the hill resort of Murree to relax over the weekend. At about nine PM on Saturday, July 3, I received an urgent call from the prime minister informing me, to my consternation, that he was flying to the United States and that I should meet him at Islamabad Airport immediately. I drove down from the hills and met him at about midnight. He put the same question to me again: Should we accept a cease-fire and a withdrawal? My answer was the same: the military situation is favorable; the political decision has to be his own. He went off, and decided on a cease-fire. It remains a mystery to me why he was in such a hurry.

A third myth is that the military hierarchy was not informed, and that even the senior army leaders were unaware of our maneuvers.

Any military professional would understand that our strengthening of defensive positions in a single formation's (FCNA's) area of responsibility was properly ordered. All formation commanders of the Rawalpindi Corps and all relevant officers at army headquarters were made aware of it as needed. The other commanders were informed immediately on the unreasonably escalated Indian response. All military information is shared on a "need to know" basis, and before this juncture they had little need to know it. The foregoing should also explain why the naval and air force chiefs were ignorant about it until the Indian response bordered on war hysteria.

A fourth myth is that we came to the brink of nuclear war.

The limits of our conventional forces were nowhere in sight, still less in danger of being crossed. I can also say with authority that in 1999 our nuclear capability was not yet operational. Merely exploding a bomb does not mean that you are operationally capable of deploying nuclear force in the field and delivering a bomb across the border over a selected target. Any talk of preparing for nuclear strikes is preposterous.

A fifth myth is that the Pakistan Army suffered a large number of casualties.

The Kargil conflict, as compared with earlier wars against India, was more intense and of longer duration. The Indians had mobilized troops far out of proportion to the situation, by massing a large number of infantry and artillery assets. The mountains favor defense. The Indians, by their own admission, suffered over 600 killed and over 1,500 wounded. Our information suggests that the real numbers are at least twice what India has publicly admitted. The Indians actually ran short of coffins, owing to an unexpectedly high number of casualties; and a scandal later came to light in this regard. Our army, outnumbered and outgunned, fought this conflict with great valor. The number of Indian casualties proves the fighting prowess and professionalism of the officers and men of the Pakistan Army.

The Kargil conflict emerged out of a tactical maneuver of limited dimensions but had significant strategic effects. As a result of the foresight and alertness of our senior commanders, India's planned offensive was preempted. The initiative was wrested from India, and an imbalance was created in the Indian system of forces. The military assets committed by the Indians in the Kargil conflict in particular and in Kashmir in general brought about a near parity of forces both in the air and on the ground along the international border. This nearly ruled out the possibility of India's deciding on an all-out war.

The Kargil conflict also brought about a significant change in the concept of operations at high altitudes. The myths about the inaccessibility of the terrain and the prohibitive effects of an inhospitable climatic environment on the conduct of operations were shaken by the resolve and resilience of the NLI troops.

I would like to state emphatically that whatever movement has taken place so far in the direction of finding a solution to Kashmir is due considerably to the Kargil conflict.

PART THREE

THE HIJACKING DRAMA

CHAPTER 12

PLANE TO PAKISTAN

"Sir, the pilot wants you in the cockpit," my military secretary Nadeem Taj said to me in a hushed tone. I had been lost in my thoughts, but the urgency in his voice jolted me back. "Now what?" I wondered. He could hardly have sounded so insistent if the pilot had simply wanted me to see our landing from the cockpit. The not-so-hidden finger of fate had intervened at regular intervals to write my destiny. I had the foreboding that the finger of fate was moving again.

Descending from 8,000 feet (2,400 meters), we were about to land in Karachi on a commercial flight from Colombo. The "fasten seatbelts" and "no smoking" signs had been switched on. I could see the lights of the city glittering below. In Colombo, a huge storm and a torrential downpour had flooded the runway and delayed our departure. Our flight had taken off forty minutes late. Then, passengers lingering in the duty-free shops had delayed us again at a stopover in Male. These delays were to prove providential.

Otherwise, our flight had been uneventful. Little did I know how eventful it was to become. I had no inkling about events that were unfolding on the ground, events that would change not only my destiny but also the destiny of my country.

It was October 12, 1999. The time was six forty-five PM. The flight was PK 805. The plane was an Airbus. There were 198 passengers on board, many of them schoolchildren. We were due to land in ten minutes.

After takeoff and dinner some of the children had come up to my seat, right at the front of the aircraft, and had asked for my autograph and taken photographs. I always enjoy meeting children, for their ideas are often new, and their way of looking at things is refreshingly different. They have few hang-ups and little of the cynicism that many adults have. Soon after, the cabin lights were dimmed and things settled down. The soothing hum of the big bird lulled people into contemplation or sleep. Sehba, seated alongside me by the window, pulled down her eyeshades and drifted off. As I've said, I was lost in my thoughts. All seemed well in the passenger cabin. It was peaceful.

"Sir, the pilot wants you in the cockpit," repeated my military secretary, his voice now even more insistent. There was definitely something strange going on. He motioned me to the front of the aircraft and told me the news: the pilot had informed him that our plane was not being allowed to land at any airfield in Pakistan and was being ordered to get out of Pakistan's airspace immediately. Only one hour and ten minutes of fuel remained.

I couldn't believe what I was hearing. It seemed preposterous.

I immediately told the stewardess to close the cockpit door, draw the curtains, and not let anyone in, lest the passengers discover what was happening and panic.

My aide-de-camp and military secretary told me that they had tried calling the Karachi corps commander and his staff on three different mobile phones to find out what was going on. They couldn't get through even though they kept changing their positions in the aircraft to try to catch the signal. They had also tried calling through the Pakistan International Airlines (PIA) ground relay-patch system but hadn't succeeded by this method either. Fifteen minutes' worth of precious fuel had been consumed before they summoned me.

When I entered the cockpit and asked the captain what the problem was, he told me that air traffic control was not giving any reason for denying him permission to land in Karachi but was insistently ordering him to get out of Pakistan's airspace immediately and land anywhere abroad. "Sir, I think that it has something to do with you," he said, stating what now seemed fairly obvious. The pilot had in mind the history of tension between Pakistan's civilian governments and the military. Nevertheless, the pilot's statement came as a rude shock to me. I knew that he was right, but why would they not let a commercial flight land in Karachi or anywhere else in the country? I could only guess that

Prime Minister Sharif was moving against me. Whoever it was, he was endangering a lot of innocent lives. I was not to know the full story until the drama in the air was over.

"We have hardly an hour's worth of fuel left," the pilot told me with a trace of desperation in his voice. I told him to ask air traffic control again why it was not permitting us to land, considering how little fuel we had. He did, and after about four or five minutes, during which time we kept flying to Karachi, the reply came: "Climb to 21,000 feet and just get out of Pakistan and go anywhere." Again, the air traffic controller refused to give any reason. They did not care where we went. They even suggested that our pilot should ask his company, PIA, for instructions. It was ridiculous. What could the management of PIA have told him? Air traffic control suggested that we head to Bombay, Oman in Muscat, Abu Dhabi, or Bandar Abbas in Iran—just about anywhere except (for some reason) Dubai. The controllers also informed our pilot that they had directed all airports not to let our plane land anywhere in Pakistan.

The whole thing seemed diabolical. Since India was the country closest to us, we would have no option but to go there, given our dangerously low fuel. This would put us in the hands of our most dangerous enemy, against whom we had fought three full-blown wars. It was unbelievable—an order of this kind coming from the Pakistani authorities to an aircraft of Pakistan's own national airline with Pakistan's army chief and chairman of the Joint Chiefs of Staff Committee on board. Air traffic control wouldn't dare do something so bizarre and treacherous without instructions from the highest level. I knew my army, and there was no question in my mind of a mutiny. Whatever else may have been going on, the army could never countenance sending its chief into Indian hands.

It could only be the civilian side of the government. No one below the prime minister could give such a drastic order. Sacking an army chief is one thing; but hijacking his plane and sending it to India is, as I have said, diabolical. Amazingly, it had not occurred to Nawaz Sharif that his coup against the army would also be a great victory for India. I am still flabbergasted that it didn't cross his mind how repulsive and embarrassing it would be to deliver the chief of the Pakistan Army, his army, into enemy hands. The people of Pakistan would have considered it high treason. I now understood that we were on a collision course not only with the ground below, but also with the government of Prime Minister Nawaz Sharif.

"Where can we go?" I asked the pilot. He said that he could go to either Ahmadabad, in India, or Oman, but we had to decide immediately because we were fast running out of fuel. "Over my dead body will you go to India," I declared angrily.

Tension in the cockpit was mounting, but I kept cool. After my tough training as a commando and years of military service, I have deliberately trained myself never to panic in a crisis. My attitude about death is that if it has to happen, it will happen. Not that I am a fatalist, but I can control my emotions. If you can't think rationally in an emergency, any slim chance of getting out of it is lost.

"I want to know the reason why they are not letting us land," I said. "This is a commercial flight. How can it be diverted?" The pilot passed my question on to air traffic control. Another agonizing wait of four or five minutes followed. It took so long because of a ludicrous chain, as I was told later. Our pilot's query to air traffic control was communicated to the chief of staff of the director general of the Civil Aviation Authority. He then took the message to his boss, who in turn phoned the prime minister's military secretary in Islamabad. The military secretary then took the message to the prime minister and sought his reply. There were six people from our pilot to the prime minister— seven, if you started with me. Given Nawaz Sharif's slow reaction time, he must have mulled over each answer and discussed it with those around him. It was a charade, but a most dangerous charade that carried the unmistakable stamp of the prime minister. Such an excruciatingly slow process of communication wasted precious time and fuel. It was a first in history; an aircraft hijacked in the air by someone on the ground, and not just someone but a prime minister sworn to protect the lives of his country's citizens.

While waiting for the reply we climbed to 21,000 feet (6,400 meters). It came just as we got there: "You cannot land anywhere in Pakistan. You have to leave Pakistan airspace at once." We couldn't believe it. Were they really trying to kill us all just to be rid of me? Now the pilot had more news for me—climbing to 21,000 feet had consumed so much fuel that we didn't have enough left to take us anywhere out of Pakistan. "Physically, this is not possible now," he announced. The tension ratcheted still higher.

Soon the only course left for us would be to try to ditch the plane somewhere. "Tell air traffic control that we are running out of fuel and don't have enough to leave Pakistan," I said to the pilot as a last resort. "No, forget the damn chap," I said as an immediate afterthought. "You just land in Karachi. There are over 200 people on board, and we are going to land in Karachi whether they like it or not."

Incredibly, air traffic control refused to budge. Without so much as a tremor in his voice the controller told our pilot that no airfield in Pakistan had lights on and there were three fire trucks blocking the runway in Karachi. "Landing in Karachi is out of the question because we will crash," the captain said to me plaintively. Now the tension in the cockpit was becoming extremely high—but quietly. I was angry, but I knew that I had to show calm determination and absolute self-control in my voice and actions. We could not afford to have the pilot or the rest of the cockpit crew lose focus. To their credit, they all remained composed and professional throughout the ordeal.

I told the pilot to tell the controllers again that we could not leave Pakistan's airspace, because we didn't have enough fuel. "We cannot get to any other country. You must allow us to land in Karachi," I told him to say.

Then, just minutes before our fate was sealed, we were told we could divert to Nawabshah, a semiurban town some 100 miles (160 kilometers) north of Karachi in the desert province of Sindh. "Do you have the fuel to take us there?" I asked the pilot.

"I can just make it, sir," he replied.

"OK, then, let's go to Nawabshah."

It was seven-thirty in the evening, forty-five minutes since I had been summoned, and we were about halfway to Nawabshah when the aircraft's radio crackled and a voice suddenly told our pilot to return to Karachi and land there. Our pilot was not sure if he could make it back to Karachi with the fuel remaining. He started calculating his fuel, and worrying about whether he was doing the sums correctly. None of us was totally comfortable about this sudden change of mind.

Who had given the order to allow us to land in Karachi so unexpectedly? What had caused this last-minute change of heart? Danger was on the ground—but where?

While we were still guessing what the motives might be and the pilot was feverishly doing his calculations, Major General Malik Iftikhar Ali Khan, the commander of an army division in Karachi, made radio contact with the aircraft. "Tell the chief to come back and land in Karachi," he told the pilot. "Everything is all right now."

I was still suspicious, so I spoke to Iftikhar myself. I had to make certain that it really was he, and not someone impersonating him. I also wanted to make certain that he was not being forced to call us back. This was the first time that I spoke on the aircraft's radio to anyone.

"Where is the corps commander?" I asked.

"Sir, the corps commander is in the VIP lounge. He is waiting for you at the gate. I am here at air traffic control."

"What is the problem?"

"Sir, I am sure you don't know, but about two hours back your retirement was announced and Lieutenant General Ziauddin Butt was made chief of the army staff. They were trying to divert your plane so that it does not land here. But the army has taken over now, and we have control of the airport. You turn back now. We will give you the details later."

I still wanted to make doubly certain.

"Can you tell me the names of my dogs?" I asked, because I knew that he knew them. If it was someone impersonating him or if he was under duress, he could or would not have given the correct names.

"Dot and Buddy, sir," he replied without hesitation. Even amid the tension, I could hear a smile in his voice.

"Thank you, Iftikhar," I said. "Tell Mahmood and Aziz that no one is to leave the country." Mahmood Ahmed was the commander of the Tenth Corps in Rawalpindi and Mohammad Aziz Khan was the chief of general staff; both were lieutenant generals.

I turned to the pilot and asked him about the fuel situation. "Can you take us back to Karachi?"

"We are midway and can just make it. But, sir, you have to make the decision fast. If there is turbulence along the way we might crash."

"Let's go back to Karachi, then," I said.

The next few minutes were agonizing, as you can imagine. A slight diversion, a wind sheer, or any turbulence would have meant the end of our fuel and a crash. Everything depended on a smooth landing. I returned to my seat and found Sehba in a state of quiet anxiety. She had seen an ashen-faced stewardess pass her by— ". . . as if she had seen a ghost," she told me. When my aide-de-camp offered me a cigarette and I took it, Sehba knew that something was definitely amiss, because I don't normally smoke cigarettes—contrary to the impression conveyed by a film clip that was later aired by television stations all over the world showing me with a cigarette dangling from my lips and a pistol in my hand. I knew that we were not supposed to smoke, so I asked the lady sitting across the aisle whether she minded. She turned out to be the principal of the Karachi Grammar School, and she was kind and tolerant. I was handed a cup of tea, which I literally gulped down, again something I don't normally do. Now Sehba was convinced that whatever it was must be very, very serious. She turned to me and asked what had happened. I told her that we were not being allowed to land and were running out of fuel, all because I had been dismissed and Ziauddin had been made the chief. Obviously, Nawaz Sharif did not want me around to counter his illegal action. "More than that I do not yet know," I told her. "But now we are landing." Sehba was horrified. I heard her utter a sound somewhere between a gasp and a scream. She later told me that when she saw that I was not in my seat and the aircraft was behaving in such a peculiar manner—first descending, then climbing, and then turning around twice—she thought we were going to crash.

We just made it, with only seven minutes of fuel to spare. The corps commander, Lieutenant General Usmani; the division commander, Iftikhar; and others must still have harbored suspicions, because after landing our plane was directed to the old airport terminal. The commandos traveling with me who were responsible for my security wouldn't let me near the door, for fear of a sniper. They went to the front themselves, forming a protective wall. But when I saw the corps commander on the stairs, I relaxed. He was the first person to enter the aircraft. He congratulated me on my safe landing. Then the soldiers came and surrounded me. I felt very proud of them.

When my feet touched the tarmac I still had no idea of any of the

details of what had happened. I was just relieved to be alive and more
than relieved that Sehba and all the other passengers, particularly the
children, were safe. Throughout this harrowing drama a memory had
kept nagging at the back of my mind. Now it came to the fore, Omar
Khayyam's famous quatrain:

> *The Moving Finger writes; and, having writ,*
> *Moves on: nor all your Piety nor Wit*
> *Shall lure it back to cancel half a Line,*
> *Nor all your Tears wash out a Word of it.*

As I walked to the car waiting for me on the tarmac, I wondered,
"God, what have I landed into?"

CHAPTER 13

THE CONSPIRACY

I have no compunction about admitting that the army was caught unawares by the prime minister's sudden action of dismissing me and following it up virtually simultaneously with sudden and abrupt changes in the military high command. His was the coup. It was a gross misuse and misapplication of the law: you cannot summarily dismiss the army chief, a constitutional appointee, without giving him just cause and affording him due process. Sharif intended it to be the final act before he assumed all power in the office of the prime minister.

The army's response was the countercoup.

With hindsight I can say that there had been scattered signs of what was coming, which failed to register. Mrs. Ziauddin, the wife of the officer who was supposed to replace me, asked another officer's wife about the deportment expected of a chief's spouse. In the presence of the wife of a major general, one of Ziauddin's relatives asked about the difference in the ranks worn by a full general as compared with a lieutenant general. But no one took such signs seriously.

I had felt comfortable going to Colombo because after months of tension with Prime Minister Nawaz Sharif over the Kargil issue, the two of us had finally arrived at a truce—or so I imagined. I had convinced him that we should display unity in public instead of making a spectacle of ourselves, with the prime minister blaming the army and its chief while shirking his own responsibility by denying his role in the affair. It was not credible for a prime minister to claim that something like Kargil could happen without his knowledge. Nawaz Sharif had not only strained credulity, he weakened his own position, for his opponents began saying openly that in this case he was not worthy of being prime minister. I thought we had agreed to move on.

Another reason why the army and I were relaxed was that the prime minister had recently elevated me to the additional position of chairman of the Joint Chiefs of Staff Committee concurrent with my existing position as chief of the army staff. Frankly, after that it didn't cross my mind that the prime minister would exploit my absence abroad to launch a coup against the army and myself.

Why Nawaz Sharif attempted the coup remains a matter of speculation. It cannot be said with certainty why he did so until all the actors involved from his side have spoken, and spoken truthfully. But how the army reacted to defend its honor is a study in presence of mind. Everyone worked together toward the common goal of stopping the prime minister's coup. The army was still smarting from the forced resignation of my immediate predecessor, General Jahangir Karamat, and was determined not to let another humiliation befall it. I had already conveyed an indirect warning to the prime minister through several intermediaries: "I am not Jahangir Karamat." My predecessor had retired quietly, and I did not want the prime minister to think he could violate the constitution so easily again. As it is, the Supreme Court later found that my dismissal was indeed illegal and unconstitutional.

The prime minister wasn't deterred. He was waiting for the right time to strike. I am inclined to believe, from the evidence I have gathered, that even though the prime minister had decided to remove me and my senior commanders, he and his cohort were at pains to make it look as if a sudden action had been forced on them. To their minds the right time was when I would be completely inaccessible to the army and thus unable to lead it, flying at 35,000 feet (10,000 meters) in foreign airspace.

Slowly but surely Nawaz Sharif was being fed disinformation to make him paranoid about me by people who stood to gain from my exit. He was constantly being told that I planned to remove him.

It is all very well to imagine that by cutting me off from all manner of communication they could successfully complete their coup before my plane landed, but the question still remains why they did it in such a clumsy and reckless manner: not allowing my plane to land, nearly letting it crash, and even suggesting that it go to India. I believe this had to do with the two fortuitous delays of my flight, first in Colombo and then in Male. Had my plane arrived on schedule, the army would not have had enough time to react and take Karachi Airport to prevent my arrest. Nawaz Sharif became nervous, indeed hysterical, when he realized that the army might in fact have time to strike back while my plane was still in the air.

To understand the prime minister's thinking, it is necessary to backtrack a few weeks. In the third week of September 1999, Nawaz Sharif's father-in-law died, and he went to Lahore for the funeral. As he was about to get into his car at the airport, his attorney general took him aside. Standing in the hot sun, the attorney general said that the army was going to remove Nawaz Sharif that very night. He would not tell the prime minister his source; he said only that he had foolproof inside information. Obviously, Nawaz Sharif had to take his attorney general seriously. In fact, the attorney general caused him so much worry that on reaching his in-laws' house Nawaz Sharif confided in his principal secretary, Saeed Mehdi, telling Mehdi to reassure the attorney general that while the prime minister had not divulged the substance of their conversation at Lahore Airport to him, he wished to know the source of the information. The attorney general responded by asking Mehdi to reassure the prime minister that his information was from a very important and credible insider and was absolutely reliable. This added to Nawaz Sharif's paranoia.

As is our custom, I too went to Lahore later that evening to offer my condolences to the prime minister. He could have taken this opportunity to discuss his attorney general's assertion with me, but he did not. Of course there was no army takeover that night, as none was intended, then or later.

A few days later, back in Rawalpindi, the prime minister's younger brother, Shahbaz Sharif, who was also chief minister of Punjab province, came to meet me regarding the tension with his brother, played up in the media in the wake of Kargil. I told him to tell his brother two things. One, I would not agree to give up my present position of chief of the army staff and be kicked upstairs as chairman of the Joint Chiefs of Staff Committee (JSJC) before my term was up. As far as I was concerned, he could make anyone from the navy or air force chairman of the JCSC; I didn't care. Two, I was recommending the retirement of the corps commander in Quetta, Lieutenant General Tariq Pervez. He was ill-disciplined, and I suspected him of plotting against me. The problem was that TP, as he was known in the army, was the brother-in-law of one of Nawaz Sharif's ministers and was using his relative's influence to bring about a premature change in the army's high command so as to position himself for promotion in the future.

"Give me one day," replied Shahbaz. The next day I was with the prime minister at his lunch for Admiral Bukhari, the navy chief. Sure enough, the prime minister took me aside and said, "I am also making you chairman of the Joint Chiefs of Staff Committee. Are you happy?" I said I was, now that I was staying on as army chief as well. But I told him that TP had to go and that I was going to recommend his retirement, as he was undermining military discipline. Nawaz Sharif feigned ignorance of who TP was, though I knew he was pretending. Yet he agreed to retire TP. Later I sent TP's dismissal papers to the prime minister, who promptly approved them.

Soon after that, the prime minister invited my wife and me to accompany him and his wife to Mecca for a pilgrimage in August 1999. He said that we would be leaving from Lahore early in the morning. I thanked him and said that we would arrive in Lahore the evening before, since it was an early-morning takeoff. He replied that in that case we should have dinner with his family at their new estate at Raiwind in Lahore.

In retrospect I am inclined to believe that all this was planned. He was certain that I would not refuse an opportunity to go to Mecca, and an early-morning takeoff meant that I would have to reach Lahore the evening before. And when he invited me to dinner, I could hardly refuse. He was lulling me into a false sense of security. I must say that it worked, because what the prime minister did on October 12 felt like an ambush.

Dinner was presided over by the patriarch of the family, the prime minister's father, known as Abbaji, which means Daddy. We were joined by Shahbaz. Throughout the meal, Abbaji kept up an uninterrupted monologue about his life and experiences. Neither son dared to interrupt him or offer an opinion of his own. Respecting elders is a most commendable Asian tradition, but these were no ordinary sons: one was prime minister and the other a chief minister. But so domineering was Abbaji's personality that both Nawaz and Shahbaz sat demurely at the table, like little children trying their best to remain in their father's good graces, speaking up only to help him remember things that he might have overlooked. Their sole aim was to try to please him. They behaved more like courtiers than sons. There was no question that Abbaji was the real decision maker in the family.

After dinner Abbaji turned to me and proclaimed grandly: "You are also my son, and these two sons of mine dare not speak against you. If they do they will be answerable to me." I was most embarrassed, but that was the way of the old man. Nawaz Sharif wore his usual expressionless face.

As it turned out, the dinner with Abbaji was quite a charade. The old man had already made up his mind that his son should dispense with me. He said to some people that he did not like the look in my eyes!

On October 9, 1999, while I was in Colombo, a news item appeared in an English-language newspaper stating that the corps commander in Quetta—TP—had been retired, for the absurd reason that he had met the prime minister without first seeking my permission. Obviously, the story had been planted by people who wanted to drive the prime minister crazy with apprehension that I might be plotting against him.

To this day I remain suspicious of TP. It could be that he wanted me out in order to reverse the decision to retire him. He was scheduled to retire just a few days before my fateful flight, but he had come to me and asked for an extension till October 13, to enable him to complete all his farewell dinners, which we in the army call "dining out." He also said that he bore me no ill will for retiring him: I was the chief and it was my decision, which he accepted as a soldier. Did he do this to buy enough time to hatch his own conspiracy against me? His brother-in-law, the cabinet minister, was an ally of the prime minister. Also, TP rated himself highly, and was convinced that he could fit into my shoes. He nearly gave the game away when a small news item appeared on the back page of the Rawalpindi edition of a mass-circulation Urdu-language newspaper, quoting TP as saying that after he took his uniform off in a couple of days he would reveal all about Pervez Musharraf and Musharraf's role in the Kargil affair. It was the kind of comment that could lead to a court-martial.

Nawaz Sharif was extremely upset by the newspaper story about TP's early retirement that ran on October 9, and he asked my spokesman to issue a denial on my behalf. The spokesman replied that he could not do so without clearance from me, and I was in Colombo. This infuriated the prime minister, because he felt that his request should have been honored whether or not I was in the country. He felt insulted and humiliated and said that he would talk to me on my return home. But my spokesman was only following the usual procedure. In my absence, the prime minister asked the Ministry of Defense to issue a clarification, which, quite properly, it did.

Later that afternoon the prime minister was to go to Lahore. Just before his departure, TP's cabinet minister brother-in-law, who had rushed back from a foreign tour, came to see him and gave him a file. As they came out of the room, the minister, walking behind the prime minister, gave the thumbs-up signal to the prime minister's principal secretary, Saeed Mehdi, who was waiting in the lobby. As Nawaz Sharif was about to board his helicopter, he asked Saeed Mehdi, without turning toward him, when Lieutenant General Ziauddin was due for retirement. Mehdi said that he would have to ascertain the exact date, but thought that it was sometime in April of next year. The prime minister then handed over the file and asked Mehdi to deliver it to the defense secretary. Mehdi asked whether he could read it, and the prime minister replied that he knew Mehdi would read it anyway, as he was only human. Saeed Mehdi later told me that the file contained a request from TP for an interview with the prime minister. This was odd, for even if they are corps commanders, lieutenant generals don't make farewell calls on the prime minister when they retire.

In return, Saeed Mehdi also handed over a file to the prime minister.

When the prime minister asked what was in it, Mehdi said that he had spent the whole night writing a note to him and requested that he read it during the flight. Mehdi claims that in the note, he said he could sense what was on the prime minister's mind but warned the prime minister to be very cautious and not be led astray by bad advice. He also suggested that before making any extreme decisions, the prime minister should get to know me better by meeting me more often, and that we should meet each other's families. But Nawaz Sharif's paranoia had reached a level where sensible advice bounced off his head.

Paranoia had made Nawaz Sharif so secretive that a day after his arrival in Lahore he flew off to Abu Dhabi with one of his sons and some of his closest cronies, presumably in search of a safe place to talk. It was October 10. Accompanying him, in civilian clothes, was Lieutenant General Ziauddin Butt. Zia is an engineer by profession and at the time was not only a lieutenant general but also director general of the Inter Services Intelligence agency. He was close to the prime minister, and Sharif was ready to hand over the reins of the army to him. Also on the flight to Abu Dhabi were Nawaz Sharif's speechwriter and the chairman of Pakistan Television (PTV), who was a member of the National Assembly. Although the decision to remove me had already been made, it seems that during the flight to Abu Dhabi, some of the finer details of the conspiracy were worked out.

They returned to Islamabad the same day, after calling on the president of the United Arab Emirates and ruler of Abu Dhabi, Sheikh Zayed bin Sultan Al Nahyan, and lunching with the crown prince.

On the morning of October 12, Nawaz Sharif flew to Multan and drove to a nearby town, Shujabad. Multan is a large city in southern Punjab, famous for its mosques, mystics, and mangoes. By going there Nawaz Sharif was perhaps trying to suggest that it was a normal day—business as usual—to create the impression that my sudden removal could have been triggered only by information suggesting that I was about to attempt my own coup. Of course, the trip to Shujabad was a feint. He took one of his sons and his speechwriter with him. His son gave the speechwriter some points for a speech and asked him to start drafting it in the plane as it waited in Multan, while the others drove off to Shujabad. When the speechwriter looked at the points, he remarked that it seemed that General Musharraf was going to be removed. The prime minister's son told him to just get on with it and not speak to anyone.

They had hoped to remove me while I was out of reach of the army. Because of the two delays of my flight, however, everything changed. They had to improvise. Apparently the only thing they managed to decide was that my plane should not be allowed to land in Pakistan. Somehow, they thought that the leaderless army would sit still in the face of treachery.

While Nawaz Sharif was attending a rally in Shujabad, he received a telephone call. I don't know to this day who made the call or what the caller told the prime minister, but immediately after the call Nawaz Sharif quickly wound up his business in Shujabad and rushed to Multan airport to fly back to Islamabad. I cannot help thinking that all this was staged, and he would have claimed later that that call had alerted him to my supposed plans for a coup. He asked that the defense secretary and his principal secretary, Saeed Mehdi, meet him at the airport at three PM, when he was due to land at Chaklala Air Force Base in Rawalpindi. He was trying to consolidate his power, but he failed to understand that he was actually about to lose power. This happens to people who don't understand the dynamics of power or its extent and limits. When he took off from Multan for Islamabad, he set himself on a course of political suicide.

The defense secretary was groggy that day. He had undergone an endoscopic procedure that morning and had still not recovered from the effects of the general anesthetic, when his phone rang. His wife said that he was sleeping and could not be wakened. According to the defense secretary, that first call was made to him as early as eleven thirty AM, before what now increasingly seems Sharif's staged phone call in Shujabad.

After warding off the caller many times, the defense secretary's wife was told that the prime minister urgently required her husband's presence at the airport. It was then that she reluctantly called him to the phone. He wondered what was so important that he was being forced out of bed in his groggy condition, but he went.

When Nawaz Sharif landed in Islamabad at three PM, he asked the defense secretary to accompany him in his car to the prime minister's house, about twenty minutes' drive away even with the traffic stopped. On the way he told the defense secretary what was on his mind—he wanted the secretary to issue a notification that General Pervez Musharraf had been dismissed and Lieutenant General Ziauddin Butt appointed in his place. The defense secretary kept asking him why he was doing this. As a recently retired lieutenant general and a former chief of general staff, he knew the army well. He advised the prime minister that another removal of the chief in this unconstitutional manner would grievously damage the morale of the army. But the prime minister remained adamant and insisted that his orders be carried out immediately.

When they reached the prime minister's house, the defense secretary told Nawaz Sharif that, as this was a very serious matter, he could not issue the notification unless he was ordered to do so in writing. Nawaz Sharif slapped him on the thigh and said angrily, "You are a coward!" The prime minister was met by Mehdi. Nawaz Sharif mockingly told him that the defense secretary was under the weather. He then asked the defense secretary to wait in another room.

When they had taken off from Multan, Nawaz Sharif's son had forbidden the speechwriter to draft the rest of the speech on the flight back to Islamabad, lest anyone in the entourage notice what he was doing. But once they got to the prime minister's house, the son took the speechwriter to the back lawn and told him to get on with it. Soon, the chairman of PTV came to assist him. Before they could get started, however, the chairman was told to get to his station in Islamabad immediately. Left alone, the speechwriter told the prime minister's son that he could not write like this and was at his best when he could dictate. The son told him to dictate and he himself would take down the dictation.

The prime minister proceeded to his office with his military secretary and Saeed Mehdi. As soon as they got there, the military secretary pulled all the telephone wires out of their sockets to ensure that no one was listening in case the phones were bugged. The prime minister then told the military secretary to pull out the order of my predecessor's removal, change the date, substitute my name for his and Lieutenant General Ziauddin's name for mine, and bring it to him for signature. It is as if they had a ready-made template to force an army chief out of office whenever they wished.

The prime minister asked whether he should make a speech. His military secretary said that he must explain his action to the nation, but Mehdi advised against it. Nawaz Sharif irritably told Mehdi to go and get on with preparing the removal order so that it could be given to the defense secretary. As soon as the order was ready, the prime minister signed it and took it personally to the president, whose house is a couple of minutes' drive away. All that the president noted on the order was the word "Seen." Through a constitutional amendment, Nawaz Sharif had made the president's office largely ceremonial, except that certain orders needed his authentication before they could be issued.

Back in the prime minister's house, the television cameras were waiting for Nawaz Sharif. He took two pips (rank insignia) off the shoulder straps of his military secretary, a one-star brigadier general (though in the Pakistan Army we call him only "brigadier"), and placed them on Lieutenant General Ziauddin, bestowing on him the rank of a full general and the title of chief of the army staff. So desperate was he to give a sense of finality to his deed that he placed the pips with his own hand, in order to have it shown on television. In a lighter vein, the military secretary remarked to Zia: "Sir, you have become a general but I have been demoted to a colonel."

Left alone to himself and his thoughts, the defense secretary was greatly agitated. He knew that the prime minister was set on a highly dangerous course. His agitation was compounded by the fact that he is a smoker but could not smoke in that particular room; also, he was still suffering from the lingering effects of the anesthesia. Despite being ordered to stay put, he went looking for a place to smoke. First he went to the deputy military secretary's room. Finding it empty, he proceeded to the military secretary's office. On the way there he saw walking toward him a group that included Ziauddin, the military secretary, and Mehdi. He noticed that Ziauddin was wearing on his uniform the insignia of a full general and an army chief.

They all gathered in the military secretary's room, and at five PM heard on television the Urdu-language news, announcing that General Pervez Musharraf had been removed and "General" Ziauddin had been appointed chief of the army staff. Zia moved forward and started shaking hands with all those in the room, including the defense secretary, and accepting their congratulations. But the defense secretary also knew that he had issued no notification and that the announcement did not carry the force of law.

The news traveled like wildfire. Phone lines were jammed. Nawaz Sharif's supporters gloated that they had scalped yet another army chief. The more pragmatic counseled caution. They were not sure that the army could stomach yet another insult. They had no idea how much worse was to come.

Soon after the broadcast, Saeed Mehdi gave the order for my removal to the defense secretary and told him to go to his office in the Ministry of Defense in Rawalpindi and issue the notification, so as to make my removal and Ziauddin's appointment legal. The defense secretary recalls that as he went toward his car, his brother, a member of Nawaz Sharif's cabinet, came running with the prime minister's brother Shahbaz, in a state of high agitation. "What has happened? What have you done? This is disastrous," they said. The defense secretary told them that he had nothing to do with it. If this is correct, then either they really were not privy to Nawaz Sharif's plot or they were faking it. Or, possibly, the defense secretary was simply protecting his brother. Not surprisingly, I can find hardly anyone today who admits knowing of Nawaz Sharif's plan or of having had anything to do with it!

The drive to the defense ministry took about thirty minutes. As his car reached Flashman's Hotel in Rawalpindi, the defense secretary received a call from Shahbaz Sharif on his cell phone saying that some soldiers had blocked the gate of the prime minister's house. "Which army is this?" asked Shahbaz. The defense secretary realized immediately that, as he had feared, the army had reacted. He also replied that there is only one army: the Pakistan Army.

CHAPTER 14

THE COUNTERCOUP

The countercoup—for there can be no other word for it—began at five PM, when the news of my removal was announced on television, and it took only three and a half hours. It would be over by eight thirty PM, when Lieutenant General Mahmood Ahmed, commander of the Rawalpindi Corps, entered the prime minister's house and took Nawaz Sharif into custody.

Just after five PM the army swung into action in the cities of Rawalpindi (where GHQ is located), Islamabad (some nine miles, or fifteen kilometers, away), Karachi, and Lahore, and later in Nawabshah when my aircraft was diverted there.

The action in Islamabad was the most tense and dramatic, though Karachi also witnessed high drama. More than once, officers and soldiers of the countercoup came eyeball-to-eyeball with the armed personnel of the coup. It was only by their presence of mind and the grace of God that a bloodbath was averted.

At five PM offices were closed and the high command of the army was either back home or involved in evening recreational activity. The chief of general staff, Lieutenant General Mohammad Aziz Khan, and Lieutenant General Mahmood Ahmed were playing tennis in an army club in Chaklala, about three miles (five kilometers) from army headquarters. Two commanding officers, lieutenant colonels Shahid Ali and Javed Sultan, belonging to the crack Triple One Brigade of the Rawalpindi Corps, were playing squash at the same club.

On hearing the news, they abandoned their game and rushed to the tennis courts to give the news to Generals Aziz and Mahmood. But those two had also already heard, and had hurried back to headquarters.

The director general of military operations (DGMO), Major General Shahid Aziz, had just gotten home and was sitting on his bed untying his shoelaces. When the news reached him, he retied his laces and rushed back to headquarters, telling his wife on the way out that he did not know when or if he would be back. He already sensed what he had to do. He also knew that the next few hours would be spent on the razor's edge. As his car drove out, he was disgusted to see his neighbor's wife distributing sweets at the gate of her house. The neighbor was none other than Lieutenant General Ziauddin; his wife was celebrating her husband's illegal elevation to the top army post.

Aziz Khan, Mahmood, and Shahid Aziz had not the slightest doubt that Nawaz Sharif's coup had to be thwarted. Enough was enough. They would lead the countercoup.

Consider the cast of actors and their relationship to me. Apart from being their chief, I played squash with the two commanding officers, Shahid Ali and Javed Sultan. Mohammad Aziz Khan was my appointee. The commander of the Rawalpindi Corps, Mahmood Ahmed, had been my regimental commanding officer when I was in charge of an artillery brigade in 1986–1987. The DGMO, Shahid Aziz, is my relative. The commander of the Triple One Brigade, Brigadier Sallahuddin Satti, was my brigade major when I was a brigadier. The officers critical to the countercoup in the other cities, Lahore and Karachi, were also my appointees. Only the head of our premier security service, the ISI, Lieutenant General Ziauddin, was close to Nawaz Sharif—but Ziauddin did not command any soldiers. The deck was stacked against the prime minister.

The DGMO—in this case Shahid Aziz—is the officer on whose orders the army moves, for his advice is regarded as orders from the chief. Thus the countercoup would be controlled by his office, which soon took on the appearance of a war room. The first decision was to issue orders to the Triple One Brigade, stationed in Rawalpindi, to take action. Part of the duties of the two commanding officers who were playing squash was to ensure security at the prime minister's and president's houses—Lieutenant Colonel Shahid Ali was responsible for the former and Lieutenant Colonel Javed Sultan for the latter. Lieutenant General Mahmood Ahmed ordered them via the commander of the Triple One Brigade to seal both houses and not allow anyone to enter or leave. He also told them to secure the television and radio stations. Orders were also issued that Ziauddin was to be denied entry to headquarters and to Army House (my official residence). My aged parents lived at Army House with us, and there was no denying that Ziauddin or someone from his staff might go there and cause them unnecessary worry.

Next, Shahid Aziz started calling corps headquarters in three of our four provincial capitals—Karachi, Lahore, and Peshawar—to assess the situation. There was no point in calling TP, the commander of the Quetta Corps—his loyalty lay elsewhere. But Shahid Aziz did call his second in command, and was told that all was well.

Lahore, about 270 miles (430 kilometers) from the capital, is home to the Fourth Corps. It is an important and sensitive city, as it is the capital of Punjab and a cannon's shot away from the Indian border. The Lahore Corps commander, Lieutenant General Khalid Maqbool, was in Gujranwala, about forty miles (sixty-four kilometers) from Lahore.

In his absence, the senior officer in Lahore was Major General Tariq Majeed. He was at home in his study when his wife shouted for him to come to the television room and hear the news about my dismissal. Livid, he telephoned headquarters and asked Shahid Aziz for orders. Shahid told him to detain the governor of Punjab and take over the two family estates of the prime minister, the television and radio stations, and the airport. He also told Tariq Majeed to secure every entry and exit point to the city.

Tariq Majeed called his brigadier, who commanded the Internal Security Brigade, and gave him his orders.

By five thirty PM lieutenant colonels Shahid Ali and Javed Sultan were making their way to Islamabad. They were under instructions to detain the prime minister and certain of his ministers and associates. When they arrived on Constitution Avenue, a wide double-lane boulevard leading to the prime minister's house and the television station, they found it teeming with well-armed police, looking as if they were expecting a mob. There were armored personnel carriers and three turret cars—the sort that have an opening in the roof—with the heads of crew members sticking out. Cement blocks and steel barriers had been placed on the road to slow down unfriendly or unidentified vehicles and prevent their entry into any sensitive building. It was a fairly awesome show of force that would normally deter anyone, or at least make anyone think twice. It was the best that Nawaz Sharif could muster, since he could not command any army units to do his bidding. But to the surprise of Shahid Ali and Javed Sultan, the police just stood aside and did not try to prevent them from proceeding. The police were being eminently sensible, for they knew that even if they overpowered the commanding officers and their soldiers, they would be no match for the stronger force that would inevitably arrive later. Perhaps they were also fed up with Nawaz Sharif's misrule.

When Ali and Sultan had left Rawalpindi, Shahid had called the major who headed the guard at the prime minister's house to tell him to seal it. But the major's wife said that he was out for a jog. Luckily, he was jogging on the grounds of the prime minister's house and was quickly contacted. He sealed the house immediately, informing the army guard there about what had happened and what was expected of them. He also told them that their chief had been treated unjustly and apprised them of the conduct of the impending operation, which he pretended was taking place under their chief's orders.

Similarly, the major in charge of presidential security was ordered by Javed Sultan to first seal the president's house and then go to the television station a short distance away and take it under his control. The president's house was sealed without resistance.

It was five forty PM in Karachi when the Karachi Corps commander, Lieutenant General Muzaffar Usmani, was called by Lieutenant General Aziz Khan and told to secure the airport and receive the chief when he landed there. Things started moving very fast after that, as Usmani issued rapid-fire instructions.

He ordered Brigadier Tariq Fateh, the director of Karachi Airport, to take over air traffic control and coordinate his actions with Brigadier Naveed Nasar, the commander of airport security. It will remain my abiding regret that all Tariq Fateh did was to go to the airport and sit inert in the office of the director general of the Civil Aviation Authority. This was a man whom I had helped considerably to get ahead in his career, but when the time came for him to stand up and be counted, he remained seated, waiting to see which side of the fence I would fall on—the winning side or the losing side.

By five forty-five PM troops were on the move in Lahore. They were split into four units: one went to the governor's house to detain Governor Sardar Zulfiqar Ali Khosa; the second went to the television station; the third went to the prime minister's family compound; and the fourth went to the prime minister's new family estate at Raiwind.

The governor was in his office, preparing to address a gathering of some 200 people. When two soldiers approached his room, the governor's private guards tried to stop them, but they were brushed aside. The commander entered the governor's office and asked the governor to accompany him to brigade headquarters. The governor accused the commander of insubordination and warned him of grave consequences.

By now all the initial action to thwart Nawaz Sharif's coup had commenced in Rawalpindi, Karachi, and Lahore. Shahid Ali and Javed Sultan had reached Islamabad. In Lahore Major General Tariq Majeed had issued orders to arrest the governor of Punjab, take the two estates of the prime minister as well as the television and radio stations, and seal all entry and exit points to and from the city. In Karachi, where distances are larger, troops were on the move.

After sealing the president's house, Javed Sultan's troops proceeded to the television headquarters, less than a mile (1.6 kilometers) away, and took it under their control. At six PM the English-language news began—without the announcement of my dismissal, which should have been the lead story. Alarm bells rang in the prime minister's house, where Nawaz Sharif and his associates were huddled together, glued to a television set.

•   •   •

The prime minister's military secretary, a brigadier, pulled rank and managed to get out of the prime minister's house. He rushed to the television station, where he pulled rank again on the major in charge, and asked him to stand down. For a few seconds there was a standoff, but the sensible young major realized that there was no point in resisting, because a stronger force would soon arrive to retake the station. The military secretary disarmed the major and his guard and locked them in a room. Just before the newscast finished, the anchorwoman was handed a piece of paper. She nervously read out an announcement that General Pervez Musharraf had been dismissed as chief of the army staff and had been replaced by Lieutenant General Ziauddin, who had been promoted to the rank of four-star general. But the nation, watching at home, sensed that something was amiss. The military secretary returned triumphantly to the prime minister's house.

At the beginning of the newscast the prime minister had panicked. My plane would land in Karachi in less than an hour, and the army would have its leader back. Any chance of defeating the countercoup would evaporate. I think it was at this point that Nawaz Sharif came to the conclusion that I must be prevented from landing in Pakistan.

He telephoned his adviser for Sindh, Ghous Ali Shah, who was stationed in Karachi. Sindh is our southernmost province, and its capital is Karachi, a cosmopolitan city of over 12 million—our largest commercial and financial center and main port city.

The prime minister instructed Shah to go to the airport immediately with a heavy police contingent to ensure that my plane did not land there. And in case its landing could not be prevented, the aircraft was to be parked in an isolated place—a "dumble," as it is called—and refueled immediately and sent out of the country.

Ghous Ali Shah was the de facto chief minister of the province. He had replaced the elected chief minister; this replacement was one in a long list of Nawaz Sharif's many undemocratic actions. He left for the airport accompanied by a strong police party and some of his provincial ministers and officials.

Next, the prime minister telephoned the director general of the Civil Aviation Authority in Karachi with the same instructions: don't let

Pervez Musharraf's plane land anywhere in Pakistan at any cost. Force it to go somewhere, anywhere, as long as it goes out of the country.

Five minutes later the prime minister repeated the same instructions to the chairman of Pakistan International Airlines (PIA), telling him to order his pilot to leave Pakistan. The chairman of PIA heard the instructions but remained neutral. As they were talking, my flight established initial contact with air traffic control at Karachi and informed the controllers that our estimated arrival time was six fifty-five PM.

At six ten the Karachi corps commander, Lieutenant General Usmani, ordered Major General Malik Iftikhar Ali Khan, the person who spoke with me in the plane from the air traffic control tower, to send the Immediate Reaction Group to Karachi Airport to ensure that my flight would be able to land there.

Restless and tense, the prime minister called the director general of the Civil Aviation Authority again, and instructed him that my flight should be diverted to Muscat or Abu Dhabi, but not to Dubai. The director general called air traffic control to ask about the progress of my flight, discuss the procedure for closing the airfield, and deny our aircraft landing permission unless he gave the clearance personally.

Just minutes later, Major General Iftikhar contacted air traffic control and gave contrary orders. The controllers were not to divert my flight. They were to allow it to land in Karachi. He was told, in response, that he should contact the office of the director general of the Civil Aviation Authority. Iftikhar smelled a rat and immediately issued orders to his brigadier, Jabbar Bhatti, to go to Karachi Airport and take over the air traffic control tower. Tariq Fateh was also told to get to Karachi Airport immediately and use force if necessary to ensure the safe landing of PK 805. But as I said, Tariq Fateh did nothing.

As the major at the television station had predicted, it was not long before a stronger detachment of troops headed by a young captain of the Four Punjab Regiment arrived at the television station, scaled its walls, and retook it without resistance. The television broadcast was switched off altogether. Screens across the country went blank. Soon a pink rose appeared, accompanied by martial music. By now people had guessed that a countercoup was in progress and that it would not be long before the second reign of Nawaz Sharif passed into history. The defense secretary, watching television in his ministry, realized it too. I wonder what Nawaz Sharif and his cohorts thought when they saw their television screens go blank, and then when the pink rose appeared. Knowing him, I think he would have been just a little upset.

Celebrations began. An expectant crowd gathered outside the television station. There were people from every walk of life—rich and poor, executives and laborers, men and women. Everyone was fed up with the regime and impatient to be rid of it. Many ambassadors and diplomats drove to the television station and got out of their cars to join the excited throng. No one was worried about violence. Soon, the crowd grew to such proportions that traffic came to a standstill. People started shouting slogans against Nawaz Sharif, and distributing sweets and sherbet. None of us in the hijacked aircraft knew any of this, of course. We were fast running out of fuel and trying desperately to land somewhere before we crashed.

Soon after the defense secretary saw the pink rose, a young major from Military Intelligence arrived at the Ministry of Defense and invited him to the Military Operations Directorate. When the defense secretary arrived there, the three leaders of the countercoup were waiting for him. He understood at once. They told him that they had no problem with him or his brother, who was one of Nawaz Sharif's ministers, but requested that he remain with them. They also told him that they knew he had not had lunch and that they had arranged a "very nice" dinner for him. Now there was no way the defense secretary could issue the notification of my replacement.

Until and unless the defense secretary signs the notification of the removal of an army chief, the chief still remains in his job. Officially and legally, even after the announcement on television, I was still the chief of the army staff. The Supreme Court later said as much in its judgment in a case brought against me: "General Pervez Musharraf, Chief of the Army Staff and Chairman Joint Chiefs of Staff Committee, is a holder of [a] Constitutional post. His purported arbitrary removal in violation of the principle of *audi alteram partem* was ab initio void and of no legal effect."

When Nawaz Sharif was sending my aircraft to India, was he not committing treason?

After retaking the television station, Lieutenant Colonel Javed Sultan proceeded to the president's house. Lieutenant Colonel Shahid Ali and his troops headed toward the prime minister's house. I am still glad that Shahid Ali did not know what Nawaz Sharif was trying to do to my plane, because had he known, he would have seen red. Anything might have happened. But all that he had been told was to apprehend the prime minister along with certain of his accomplices.

On the way, Shahid Ali received a call from Lieutenant General Saleem Haider, whom Nawaz Sharif had just nominated as commander of the Rawalpindi Corps in place of Lieutenant General Mahmood. He was in a rage because even though he was in uniform, the guards had stopped him at the outer gate of the prime minister's house and were not allowing him to enter. He had warned them of dire consequences, but to no avail. Shahid Ali politely but firmly told him that he should not insist on entering because as far as the guards were concerned Lieutenant General Mahmood Ahmed was still the Rawalpindi Corps commander. If he persisted, they were under orders to confine him.

The major had already sealed the prime minister's house, but Shahid Ali left some of his soldiers to guard the main gate at the outer perimeter before proceeding to the main building with about five other soldiers. There was another gate at the inner perimeter, with ten policemen guarding it. Shahid Ali shouted to them to lay down their arms. They complied promptly, every one of them. They knew that they were no match for the army's firepower, but any one of them could have been hotheaded or gotten skittish and started firing, causing casualties or even a bloodbath. They were placed under an armed guard, which took them to the main entrance, where they were made to sit aside with the other policemen who had already been disarmed.

It was just after this, when the Triple One Brigade had entered the prime minister's house and disarmed the policemen stationed at the gates, that our pilot radioed that he had only forty-five minutes of fuel left and could go only to Nawabshah if he could not land at Karachi. The charade of reaching the prime minister and getting his reply began. Instead of realizing that all was lost—Triple One was already on the grounds of his official residence and it would only be a matter of minutes before he himself was arrested and his government fell—Nawaz Sharif remained adamant and issued categorical orders that my flight had to be diverted out of Pakistan. He cannot be faulted for a lack of optimism.

By six thirty PM the Karachi runway was closed, its lights were switched off, and three firetrucks were parked across it. All domestic flights were diverted to other airports in the country, and international flights were held outside Pakistan.

Now the real action began. It was the closest that the two sides came to violence. Shahid Ali and his two or three soldiers reached the main porch of the prime minister's house. They were surprised to find it crowded with perhaps seventeen people. Nearby was a black car with four stars affixed to its plate, indicating that it belonged to a full general. Obviously, before arriving at the prime minister's house Ziauddin had arranged the paraphernalia of an army chief for himself. "General" Ziauddin, in uniform, stood on the porch with a major and two army commandos belonging to the elite Special Services Group. There were also troops from the police's elite force and the protection escort of the director general of Inter Services Intelligence. Also present was Lieutenant General Akram, who was my quartermaster general but whom Nawaz Sharif had just made chief of general staff in place of Lieutenant General Aziz Khan. Akram too was in uniform. Next to him was Brigadier Javed, the prime minister's military secretary. There were also the director general of the prime minister's security, a retired major general; and Sharif's principal secretary, Saeed Mehdi.

Shahid Ali deployed his few men around the porch. He approached Ziauddin. The military secretary warned him that if he did not keep his troops away, the prime minister's guards would open fire. If a firefight had started, God alone knows where it would have ended, or who would have been killed. It could have led to a rift in the army if soldiers had killed generals; and even the prime minister may not have survived it. As I have said, it was pure luck that neither Shahid Ali nor any of his soldiers knew that the prime minister had hijacked my plane.

A struggle to disarm each other's guards ensued. Shahid Ali asked Ziauddin to order his guards to lay down their arms. Ziauddin asked him to withdraw his troops instead and let Ziauddin proceed to army headquarters to take charge of his new office. When Shahid Ali refused, Ziauddin demanded to know whose orders he was following. Showing great presence of mind, Shahid Ali replied that he was operating under my direct instructions, that we had spoken only a few minutes earlier, and that I would soon be in Pakistan. Ziauddin retorted that orders from me were not valid, as I was no longer chief of the army staff and was, in any case, not present in the country because my plane had been diverted outside Pakistan. But Shahid Ali refused to listen.

Meanwhile, Lieutenant General Akram introduced himself in a commanding voice as the new chief of general staff. He ordered Shahid Ali to withdraw his troops immediately, at the same time threatening him with dire consequences if he did not comply. Akram desperately wanted Ziauddin to be allowed to go to headquarters and take charge of his new office. Ziauddin was simultaneously trying to seduce Shahid Ali to his side by making him all kinds of fantastic offers. In a movie it might have been hilarious; in real life it was deadly serious. At this critical juncture, Ziauddin and Akram also attempted to persuade Brigadier Sallahuddin Satti (both by coercion and bribery) to withdraw his troops from the TV station and the prime minister's house.

Bluffs and counterbluffs began. Akram pompously announced that troops from Mangla (about seventy miles, or 112 kilometers, away) and from Peshawar (about 105 miles, or 170 kilometers) had reached the outskirts of Rawalpindi and would soon reach Islamabad. Shahid Ali replied that as he spoke, and while these troops were still trudging toward Islamabad, tanks and armored personnel carriers were being deployed outside the prime minister's house. (What neither Akram nor Ziauddin knew was that Shahid Aziz had taken the precaution to block troop movement from Peshawar and Mangla and was in constant touch with the two commanding officers.) Just then, a reinforcement of twenty-five soldiers of the Triple One Brigade arrived. Shahid Ali ordered their immediate deployment and told them to get ready for action.

Two of the prime minister's guards who were commandos knew me as one of their own. Suddenly, they surrendered their weapons and changed sides. It was a turning point. Seeing them, the other guards of the prime minister and of Ziauddin started laying down their arms too.

Oblivious that his world was crumbling around him, Ziauddin was still clinging to his cell phone, giving instructions and also taking congratulatory calls. Shahid Ali on orders of his Brigade Commander stepped forward and snatched the phone from him. He ordered Ziauddin, Akram, and the others to go inside the house to be placed in protective custody. Ziauddin's last question was to ask Shahid Ali how many troops were involved in the operation. Shahid Ali bluffed: a battalion-size force had surrounded the main building of the prime minister's house, and three more battalions were deployed outside, he said. The police were completely disarmed. On hearing this, Ziauddin, Akram, and the military secretary looked very nervous and moved into the building immediately.

The worst was over in Islamabad. But my plane was still up in the air, running out of fuel, and going to what I thought was an uncertain finale in Nawabshah. It was well past seven PM by now.

While all this had been going on at the prime minister's house, many things started happening together in Karachi. Lieutenant General Usmani, along with his personal escort and the military police, reached Karachi Airport. Five minutes later, troops from Karachi's Malir Garrison also arrived. It was precisely at this time that air traffic control informed our pilot that Nawabshah Airport—like all the airports in Pakistan—was closed to our aircraft. And it was after this that the pilot called my military secretary, Nadeem Taj, into the cockpit to tell him about the unbelievable situation.

Back in Lahore, at about six forty-five PM, a company of some seventy soldiers reached the prime minister's family compound in a suburb called Model Town. They found a very heavy contingent of police deployed outside the boundary wall, on the roofs of the houses, and all over the lawns. When the police were told to surrender, they replied that they would await orders from Islamabad. The army deployed its recoilless rifles in a straight line, as if intending to blast the building in front of them. On seeing this, the police surrendered. No member of the immediate family was present in any of the houses.

At the same time, about 150 troops from the Lahore Corps reached the airport. Despite the fact that the police's elite force was already there, by seven thirty PM the airport was surrounded and secured without resistance.

There was no resistance at the Lahore television station either. The people on duty complied with instructions, and the Lahore station was the first to go off the air.

By this time, all entry and exit points to and from Lahore had been secured.

One of our cell phone companies with the largest number of subscribers at the time was Mobilink. A unit of troops was sent to the Mobilink tower to switch it off. I have to hand it to the engineer on duty there. He resisted, and with considerable spirit, for which I admire him, because he was not a fighting man. He had to be controlled with some effort.

The takeover of Lahore was complete by seven thirty PM.

When our pilot informed air traffic control at about six forty-eight PM that he could not go to Muscat, owing to his critically low fuel, the director general of the Civil Aviation Authority asked his air traffic controller an amazing question: could my plane go to Bombay? I have seen idiots and more idiots, but this question was beyond belief. The controller replied in the negative. So the director general instructed air traffic control to make it clear to our pilot that Karachi and Nawabshah airports were closed for "operational reasons" and that he should seek orders from his own authorities—that is, from the airline—to proceed further. The pilot said that his company had cleared him to land at Nawabshah, but the controller reiterated that Nawabshah was not available. It was ridiculous, but absolutely true. Our pilot replied that he had no option but to hold over Karachi and then declare an emergency and land or take a direct route to the nearest airfield.

What happened next remains one of the mysteries of that day. An air traffic controller elsewhere in Karachi, at Faisal Air Base, run by the Pakistani air force, asked the controllers at Karachi Airport about the estimated arrival time of an Air Force Boeing 737 VIP flight inbound from Islamabad. The controllers at Karachi Airport could not confirm the flight's arrival. I wonder what that was all about. Who was to come in on that flight? Or was it sent to take me somewhere in case I landed in Karachi despite the best efforts to keep me away?

•   •   •

It was at seven ten PM that controllers finally allowed our pilot to land at Nawabshah. It took five more minutes for us to be cleared for landing.

Nawaz Sharif didn't realize that with the army on the move in such force, it would all be over very soon—unless my plane crashed. I suppose he wanted to send me to Nawabshah on the assumption that the police could arrest me there without interference from the army. However, some army elements were in Nawabshah, helping Pakistan's largest electric utility collect bills and perform other tasks. Of course headquarters and the Karachi Corps remembered this and ordered the soldiers in Nawabshah to go to the airport and disarm the police and take me to safety in case my plane landed there. As it happened, things started moving so fast in Karachi that it was not necessary for my plane to land in Nawabshah. But the soldiers did get to Nawabshah airport and did disarm the police.

At seven eleven PM, a minute after our plane was allowed to land in Nawabshah, Brigadier Jabbar Bhatti of the Karachi garrison arrived at the wrong air traffic control tower at the old airport terminal building in Karachi. When he discovered his mistake, he made some controllers take him to the correct tower at the new terminal.

When he got to the correct tower, the director general of the Civil Aviation Authority was informed that Brigadier Jabbar Bhatti and his troops had arrived in the tower and were ordering the controllers to bring the aircraft to Karachi. On hearing this, the director general asked if "the person," meaning me, was to be off-loaded. Air traffic control replied that it knew only that my flight was to be brought back to Karachi. At that point the director general of the Civil Aviation Authority gave permission to allow my plane to land in Karachi. The runway was cleared and its lights were switched on.

A few minutes later Major General Iftikhar arrived in the air traffic control tower. The rest is history.

After the scuffle on the prime minister's porch, Lieutenant Colonel Shahid Ali and some of his soldiers entered the house and went to the private area, which is called the family wing. In the living room there, he saw Nawaz Sharif sitting with Ziauddin, Akram, Nawaz Sharif's son Hussain (who had gone with him to Abu Dhabi and Multan), Saeed Mehdi, and Saifur Rahman—the dreaded chairman of the Accountability Bureau, who had hounded many opponents of Nawaz Sharif. In the gallery, Shahid Ali saw someone rushing forward with a message from the director general of the Civil Aviation Authority that the aircraft was short of fuel, could not be diverted out of Pakistan, and might crash if not permitted to land. Later, it was discovered that this was the third such message that went unheeded.

Shahid Ali entered the room and placed everyone under arrest. "Has martial law been declared?" asked Nawaz Sharif plaintively. Shahid Ali said that he did not know. Saifur Rahman started crying. Nawaz Sharif looked dazed.

The prime minister's brother Shahbaz Sharif was nowhere to be found. Shahid Ali was told that he was in the bathroom. He asked Shahbaz to come out. Shahbaz shouted his acquiescence but did not come out for an inordinate amount of time. So Shahid Ali forced the door open to find Shahbaz Sharif standing in front of the toilet, flushing down the speech that Nawaz Sharif was to deliver after his coup had succeeded. Shahbaz was, in turn, flushed out of the bathroom. He insists to this day that he knew nothing of the coup plan. The prime minister's speechwriter, on the other hand, insists that Nawaz Sharif took no important action without first consulting his brother. God alone knows the truth.

By seven forty-five PM the countercoup had defeated Nawaz Sharif's coup throughout the country. My plane landed in Karachi at seven forty-eight PM. At eight thirty PM Lieutenant General Mahmood Ahmed, commander of the Rawalpindi Corps, arrived at the prime minister's house and held discussions with the captives for about an hour. Then they were taken to different army messes and confined there.

Back in corps headquarters in Karachi, we were somewhat dazed. We decided not to do anything precipitate. What was needed first and foremost was to reassure a bewildered nation, but without making any rash promises until we understood what we had gotten into. I started writing my speech by hand. When it was complete and met the approval of those present, I borrowed a flak jacket from an SSG commando, for I was in civilian clothes. The table hid my trousers as I spoke to my people at the unearthly hour of two thirty AM. As I reached the end of my speech, the thought again came to me: "What have I landed in?"

CHAPTER 15

ANATOMY OF SUICIDE

W hy did Nawaz Sharif do what he did? Why did he commit political suicide? This answer to this question may always remain a mystery.

I did my best to be cooperative as army chief. I regularly asked Nawaz Sharif how the army could help to improve his sagging government. He asked me to help shore up a failing megacorporation, the Water and Power Development Authority (WAPDA). I accepted this most difficult assignment. The army took over WAPDA's functioning, deploying 36,000 troops. We saved it from collapse. Nawaz Sharif also asked me to stiffen the back of a frightened judiciary in dealing with sectarian terrorists. I readily obliged. We opened several antiterrorist military courts and placed some restraints on these terrorist groups.

Such cooperation notwithstanding, there were areas of difference from day one. I thought they were minor, but perhaps Nawaz Sharif took them seriously. Only a few days after I took command of the army, he spoke very strongly against two major generals whose loyalty he doubted and asked me to retire them summarily. It was a very strange request. I replied that I could not do so without being given a formal charge sheet against them and without inquiring into details, giving the officers a chance to explain their supposed misconduct. He persisted in his demand directly and indirectly through intermediaries for more than a month. Finally, I flatly refused to oblige him. I told him that major generals couldn't be treated so arbitrarily on mere hearsay or suspicion.

The other disagreement arose a few months later, when the editor of the *Friday Times,* a weekly tabloid, was apprehended on the orders of the prime minister. I was first told to take over the case and keep the editor in the custody of the Lahore branch of Inter Services Intelligence (ISI). I did so with some reluctance, mainly to protect him from torture or mishandling by the police. I specifically instructed the ISI to keep him in a safe house, out of harm's way.

The story did not end there. I was shocked the next day when the prime minister placed an abominable demand on me—to court-martial the editor. At first I almost laughed and thought he must be joking. But the prime minister had done his homework. He said a court-martial is quite legal in cases of treason. It was a shocking suggestion that gave me my first glimpse into the deviousness of the prime minister's mind. Again, I flatly refused, explaining the adverse domestic and international consequences of such a rash action. My refusal ended in the release of the editor.

It could be that such affronts on my part made the prime minister realize his folly in selecting me for my position. He had probably thought that being the son of immigrant parents, I would acquiesce in his demands—that I would feel insecure and vulnerable and do his bidding. He couldn't have been more wrong. For one thing, such parochialism does not exist in the army, where we are all Pakistanis. Neither did Sharif understand that the patriotism of those who voluntarily left everything behind and came to Pakistan is beyond question. Pakistan was built as a refuge and a homeland for the Muslims of India to escape Hindu economic and political domination and social discrimination. My family was one of those that sought refuge in their new country. We have a great stake in its survival and prosperity. For us to acquiesce in anything that we believe will damage Pakistan would be unthinkable.

The Kargil episode created the biggest divide between the prime minister and myself. We had both wanted to put Kashmir firmly on the world's radar screen, politically as well as militarily. The Kargil initiative succeeded in doing so. Yet when external political pressure forced Nawaz Sharif to vacate the liberated area, he broke down. Rather than deriving strength through national solidarity, he blamed the army and tried to make himself look clean. He thought he would be more secure if he denied any knowledge of the Kargil operation. All kinds of carefully placed articles appeared, including a one-page advertisement in a newspaper in the United States, maligning the army and creating a divide between it and the government. It was in dealing with Kargil that the prime minister exposed his mediocrity and set himself on a collision course with the army and me.

Other than these visible disagreements between Nawaz Sharif and myself, I had ventured to advise him several times on how to improve his governance. This I did in response to a growing and widespread public outcry against the nation's rapid slide, and to the intelligentsia's specific pressure on me to react. Some people were even bold enough to ask me to take over, or to ask why I was not taking over to save the nation. While I agreed with their assessment, that the government was in bad shape, there was no institutional means or forum for me to raise issues and contribute toward rectification of the situation, especially after Nawaz Sharif had usurped all powers for himself, including the constitutional power of the president to dissolve the National Assembly. The president could thus no longer remove a prime minister and his government, so there was no check on the prime minister's power, and I certainly had no intention of mounting a coup. Better to let the political process, such as it was, take its course.

It is not unusual in Pakistan for the general public and the intelligentsia to approach the army chief and ask him to save the nation. In all crises, everyone sees Pakistan's army as the country's savior. Whenever governments have malfunctioned (as has frequently occurred), whenever there has been a tussle between the president and the prime minister (especially during the 1990s), all roads led to the general headquarters of the army. The army chief was regularly expected to put pressure on the prime minister to perform—to avoid corruption, nepotism, and sometimes, downright criminality. The army chief was also dragged in to mediate all disputes between the president and the prime minister.

In October 1999, the nation was fast headed toward economic and political collapse. Under these trying circumstances, I was working to shore up the prime minister and help him perform better. It was unfortunate that he distrusted my good intentions. Though he was a city boy, his mental makeup was largely feudal—he mistook dissent for disloyalty. His misplaced perception of my loyalty, coupled with the suspicion that I was planning a coup, must have led to Nawaz Sharif's paranoia.

There are three basic theories about why Nawaz Sharif did what he did.

Possibility 1: It could be that Nawaz Sharif planned to have me as army chief for only a year, though the normal term is three years. After a year I could be shunted aside to the chairmanship of the Joint Chiefs of Staff Committee. A pliable general (like Lieutenant General Ziauddin) could be promoted to ensure that he played a "positive" role in the national elections in 2002.

Possibility 2: As I said, perhaps Nawaz Sharif expected me to be more pliable, since my family had migrated from India at the time of Partition. But when he realized his error, he decided to get rid of me. Action against me, he may have thought, would establish his ascendancy over the army as well as please the Americans and the Indians.

Possibility 3: He feared a coup by me. His associates, including Lieutenant General Ziauddin, may also have fanned and fortified his paranoia. By this theory, he was trying to preempt me.

Whatever the reason, Nawaz Sharif committed political suicide. I have thought about it a lot and have come to the conclusion that whereas there was more than one reason propelling Nawaz Sharif toward the precipice, the most outstanding must have been that he wanted a pliant army chief for the next elections.

Our lower house of parliament, the National Assembly, had already passed the fifteenth amendment to the constitution, which was called the Shariat Bill. It would have made him as all-powerful as a medieval monarch. Through three constitutions, Pakistan has always styled itself an Islamic republic, but we have tried to maintain some distinction between governmental and religious authority. This amendment would also have consolidated all authority for enforcement of religious law in the hands of the prime minister. All that remained was passage by the upper house, the Senate. Nawaz Sharif was waiting for the Senate elections in early 2000, which would have guaranteed him a two-thirds majority in the Senate as well because of the nature of our system. All four of our provinces are represented equally in the Senate, and members are elected by their relevant provincial assemblies on the basis of the proportion of seats various parties have in that assembly. Since Nawaz Sharif's party had the largest number of seats in the four provincial assemblies combined, the result was a foregone conclusion. Once he had that, the Senate would have ratified the amendment.

Nawaz Sharif had already emasculated dissent in his parliamentary party through amendments to the constitution and had also taken away the power of the president to dissolve the National Assembly under certain circumstances. All he needed now to effectively make him a civilian dictator was to become "commander of the faithful."

Lieutenant General Ziauddin probably sensed what was on Nawaz Sharif's mind and cleverly urged him along, at the same time suggesting that he, himself, Zia, a loyal Kashmiri, was my best replacement. Ziauddin used the Kargil affair to frighten the prime minister into believing that I would remove him from office. His word as the director general of Inter Services Intelligence carried great weight.

The army's reaction to Nawaz Sharif's attempted coup has to be seen not only as a response to another humiliation by a prime minister, but also as a response to the abysmal political, social, and economic condition that Pakistan had reached. We stood at the brink of being declared a failed state, a defaulted state, or even a terrorist state. Economic growth had come to a standstill. The central bank was bankrupt, with only ten days' worth of imports in foreign exchange remaining. Nawaz Sharif had to freeze private foreign currency accounts after $11 billion of deposits went unaccounted for. Over one trillion rupees, around $20 billion, had been invested in development over eleven years, but there was almost nothing to show for it except a solitary 230-mile (370-kilometer) highway. Sectarian terrorism was on the rise, with Shias and Sunnis being killed regularly. The police were totally demoralized, lawlessness was rampant, and the law courts were overwhelmed. The public was also demoralized and beginning to display signs of hopelessness in the future of the country. The people had lost their honor and their pride in being Pakistanis. They were yearning for change. With the fifteenth constitutional amendment Nawaz Sharif wanted to usurp all power and become Ameer ul Momineen, "commander of the faithful," with dictatorial temporal and religious powers.

The spirit of loyalty is instilled deeply in all ranks of the army. At the lower ranks loyalty is toward the commander, and his word is to be obeyed without question. At the senior command level there is a larger sense of loyalty to a common cause or toward protection of the nation. The senior commanders had to decide whether their loyalty to a blundering prime minster was stronger than their loyalty to their own chief and their patriotism and love for the nation and its people. I am glad that at the moment of truth they took action in favor of their higher sense of loyalty to Pakistan and in accordance with what the nation would have desired them to do. I am proud of my army and the spontaneous support displayed by the Pakistani masses, who placed their trust in me to steer the nation to safety and prosperity.

PART FOUR

REBUILDING THE NATION

CHAPTER 16

PAKISTAN FIRST

Have you ever been thrown into the deep end of a swimming pool? People say that this is the best way to learn to swim, because if you don't, you sink. This is exactly how I felt when I reached Army House in Rawalpindi on the morning of October 13, 1999. I had been thrown into the deep end. I certainly had no intention of sinking. I was determined to give my best.

I set a number of things in motion immediately. One of my first thoughts was that the country must avoid another period of martial law. Overnight that thought had become a conviction. Our past experience had amply demonstrated that martial law damages not only military but also civilian institutions, because as the army gets superimposed on civil institutions the bureaucracy becomes dependent on army officers to make the crucial decisions that they themselves should be making. I therefore decided that there would be no martial law. If necessary, the army would be placed, not on top of civilian institutions, but alongside them, in sort of twinning capacity, in order to monitor their performance.

I called in my close army colleagues, General Mohammad Aziz and Lieutenant General Mahmood Ahmed, and told them what I had in mind. They had assumed that I would impose martial law and were therefore quite surprised by my decision. I reasoned with them, and soon they came around to my point of view.

We would remain a constitutional state, but we needed to restore our damaged constitution and create a transition government. We already had a president, but the presidency was a reduced post; what we needed was a head of government. Under our constitution the prime minister is the chief executive of the country and head of government. One of our most distinguished constitutional lawyers, Sharifuddin Pirzada, came up with an eminently sensible solution: keep the constitution operational, except for a few clauses, which could be temporarily suspended. I would become chief executive and head of government.

I took this idea to a meeting of the corps commanders. They too had assumed that martial law was coming, and here too I had quite a job convincing them that such a step would be disastrous. First, I let each one of them have his say, as is my normal practice (though it was new to the army). They were all of the view that given the circumstances that had been forced upon the army, there had been no option but to remove the government of Nawaz Sharif.

After each of them had spoken, I explained why I felt that martial law should not be imposed. They liked the idea of monitoring, rather than superimposition. My ascendance to power may be the only instance in history of a military takeover without the cover of martial law, but then we have had many firsts in Pakistan, including the reverse situation: a civilian president as chief martial law administrator (Zulfikar Ali Bhutto).

Once I had carried the army high command with me on this crucial question, we decided that I should speak to the nation again as soon as possible, explain the situation the country faced, and tell the people what I planned to do. The speech was scheduled for October 17.

We all wanted to ensure that this would be the last time the army was forced to assume leadership of the country. We had to set in place a system under which future army takeovers would be all but impossible.

At the same time, we started selecting my cabinet and other crucial members of my team. The only criteria we had were an impeccable reputation and a successful track record. To select my team I set up a committee of top army officers to identify and interview people, and then create a short list of three for each portfolio. I interviewed each of the finalists myself and made the decision.

The most crucial position was that of the finance minister, for the economy was causing us the most immediate concern. Out of a short list of three, I selected Shaukat Aziz, a capable international banker with a strong reputation. One factor that swayed my decision in his favor was that Shaukat Aziz is a self-made man from humble middle-class beginnings, like me. I had not met or seen Shaukat before this. I telephoned him myself and spoke to him. I said, "Pakistan needs you. Are you prepared to leave your job and do something for the nation?" He replied, "It would be my honor." I told him quite bluntly: "We will not pay you anything near what you are earning." He said that he did not care. So I summoned Shaukat Aziz to Islamabad and interviewed him.

We all thought that he was very good, definitely the man for the job. This is one decision I haven't regretted for a moment. He sacrificed his lucrative salary as an international banker and his high-profile, jet-set lifestyle to serve the nation. Along with the rest of my economic team, he was to do a tremendous job in salvaging the economy. Because he did such a good a job as finance minister, Shaukat Aziz would later become our prime minister.

I found a most capable governor of the State Bank in Dr. Ishrat Husain. He came from the World Bank and turned out to be the best governor we have ever had. The country was also lucky to get the services of the entrepreneur Razzak Dawood as commerce minister. He rationalized our trade regime to a large extent. I appointed Tariq Ikram, the regional director of Reckit and Coleman, as head of the Export Promotion Bureau. Together with the commerce minister, these men made an excellent team. Under them our exports, which had never exceeded $9 billion, passed $10 billion and kept increasing.

My cabinet had balance. It comprised men and women from all four provinces, with proven capabilities and successful track records in their respective areas of expertise. During the "dreadful decade of democracy," cabinets had been chosen by favoritism. Merit counted for little. In addition, my cabinet was small, starting with just ten people, a far cry from the scores of ministers, junior ministers, and minister equivalents we had had under previous administrations.

I shall never forget our first cabinet meeting. Having met most of them only once at the interview stage, I did not know my new ministers, except for two retired lieutenant generals who had both been senior to me in the army. I began by suggesting that we should all introduce ourselves, starting with myself. After I had spoken and given them a brief personal résumé, it was Shaukat Aziz's turn, because he happened to be seated to my right. He introduced himself in his impeccable internationalized English and thus set the tone. He was followed by Razzaq Dawood, who spoke fluently in his Americanized accent. The two or three people who followed also spoke in fluent English. When I looked down the line, my eyes fell on Zobeida Jalal, from Balochistan, the new education minister. She comes from one of our least developed provinces. The education of women there has not received the attention it deserves. It suddenly struck me that she might not feel entirely comfortable speaking in English and might be embarrassed. So to make it easy for her, I interrupted and said that we were all Pakistanis and could speak in either English or Urdu, our national language. To my surprise, when it came to her turn, Zobeida Jalal introduced herself briefly and to the point in perfect English.

I have no hesitation in admitting that initially I was quite overawed by what I had gotten into. My special worry was my utter lack of knowledge of economics and finance. I decided to learn on the job through anyone and everyone by asking questions unabashedly. In any case, what I soon realized was that none of this was rocket science. Every educated, sensitive Pakistani was well aware of the country's problems. It did not take me long to identify the maladies and work out remedies.

Our economy was shattered, and we were on the verge of bankruptcy. For years, our leaders had avoided any institutional checks and had misgoverned the nation with impunity. Corruption and nepotism were all too common. All government institutions and organizations and public-sector corporations had fallen prey to the most blatant corruption, facilitated at the highest levels of government, through the appointment of inept managers and directors. Corruption permeated effectively down from the top. From experience I have learned that in any organization in Pakistan, 10 percent of the people are incorruptible, 10 percent are incorrigibly corrupt (they will remain so, come what may), and the remaining 80 percent wait and watch to see which way the wind from the top is blowing and shift position accordingly. In the 1990s, the wind was blowing in the wrong direction.

One could write volumes on the rampant corruption, but for want of space, a few examples must suffice. One of the earliest briefings I received at the governor's house in Sindh was on the construction of the Right Bank Outfall Drain (RBOD), a pipeline for taking effluent to the sea. One point made in this presentation was that those involved had very conscientiously reduced the construction cost from 116 billion to 75 billion rupees. My gut feeling was that it was still too high. I detailed army engineers to survey the whole length of the RBOD and give me an accurate assessment of the cost. They worked through six months of sweltering heat, from March to August 2000, and concluded that the project could be done for only 16 billion rupees. Even after a few adjustments, the cost came to just 18 billion rupees, and the project is now under construction for that amount. The difference in the budget would have been pocketed as graft.

The biggest financial debacle that beset the nation was the frittering away of $11 billion of foreign-exchange deposits of private individuals and institutions that were held in trust by the State Bank of Pakistan. This money was misspent largely on meeting balance-of-payments deficits and debt servicing. I call it the biggest bank robbery in history. This led to a disastrous government decision: freezing all the foreign currency accounts to forestall a run on the banks. All Pakistanis, not to mention foreign investors, lost faith in Pakistan's government, and the result was a massive flight of capital.

In the middle of 2000 I was also told of an approved expenditure of 14 billion rupees for the refurbishment of the Marala Ravi Link Canal. The director general of army engineers told me that there was absolutely no need for this work—the project would have provided yet another avenue for looting the exchequer. I stopped the project. Six years later, the canal is running as smoothly as ever.

Another mind-boggling expenditure was the 1.1 trillion rupees spent on public-sector development projects from 1988 to 1999, roughly 100 billion rupees every year. There was hardly any visible major project undertaken during this period, other than the M2 motorway between Lahore and Rawalpindi, about which there were also many stories of underhand deals.

I came to believe that this enormous corruption took place at the top echelons of government, at the nexus of politicians, bureaucrats, and bankers, the last being handpicked by the politicians because all the major banks were nationalized.

Financial corruption aside, the government was rife with nepotism and incompetence. There was no strategic direction coming from the top. Nowhere, in any ministry, institution, organization, or department, did I see any clear vision or strategy. Pakistan was like a rudderless ship floundering in high seas, with no destination, led by inept captains whose only talent lay in plunder. The greatest victims were the poor people of Pakistan, who were fed false promises at each election, only to be disappointed. All the social indicators—health, education, income—were shamefully low and were continually deteriorating. Between 1988 and 1999 absolute poverty—people who earn $1 per day or less!—had risen alarmingly, from 18 percent to 34 percent. Public-sector corporations were headed, without exception, by sycophants; were overstaffed with political appointees; were losing money; and were dependent on government subsidies to keep them afloat. The hemorrhaging of public-sector corporations amounted to a colossal 100 billion rupees annually—taxpayers' money down the drain.

The critical issue that rendered democracy dysfunctional was the absence of checks and balances on the political leadership. The only check on the prime minister was the president's power to dissolve the National Assembly and dismiss the government. This was a safety valve, which, as we have seen, Nawaz Sharif got rid of by using his brute two-thirds majority, with disastrous consequences for him. Yet even this check invariably led to suspicion and acrimony between the president and prime minister.

Such a state of affairs left people disillusioned. Pakistanis started losing faith in their country. The young, in particular, were despondent. I had my work cut out for me. The ship of state had to be put on an even keel, its course and direction had to be charted, and a new, capable crew had to be installed to steer it. I was determined to take Pakistan ahead at full sail.

•   •   •

On October 17, 1999, I spoke to the nation again. I began:

> I took over in extremely unusual circumstances, not of my making. It is unbelievable and indeed unfortunate that the few at the helm of affairs in the last government were intriguing to destroy the last institution of stability left in Pakistan by creating dissension in the ranks of the armed forces of Pakistan. And who would believe that the chief of the army staff, having represented Pakistan in Sri Lanka, upon his return was denied landing in his own country and instead circumstances were created which would have forced our plane to either land in India or crash.

I did not mince words about the dire straits our country was in:

> Fifty-two years ago, we started with a beacon of hope and today that beacon is no more and we stand in darkness. There is despondency and hopelessness surrounding us with no light visible anywhere around. The slide down has been gradual but has rapidly accelerated in the last many years.
>
> Today, we have reached a state where our economy has crumbled, our credibility is lost, state institutions lie demolished, provincial disharmony has caused cracks in the federation.
>
> In sum, we have lost our honor, our dignity, our respect in the comity of nations. Is this the democracy our Quaid-e-Azam had envisaged? Is this the way to enter the new millennium?

I set myself a seven-point agenda. Some of these points, by their very nature, required so much time to implement that I knew that the best I could do was to start the process and take it to a stage where it could not be reversed easily. Those seven points were:

1. Rebuild national confidence and morale.
2. Strengthen the federation, remove interprovincial disharmony, and restore national cohesion.
3. Revive the economy and restore investors' confidence.
4. Ensure law and order and dispense speedy justice.
5. Depoliticize state institutions.

6. Devolve power down to the grassroots.
7. Ensure swift accountability across the board.

I promised that the recovery of national wealth was a task that would be ruthlessly pursued. From the seven points I identified four areas of special focus:

1. Revival of the economy.
2. Introduction of good governance. This included all elements of social development: health, education, and the emancipation of women.
3. Alleviation of poverty.
4. Political restructuring to introduce sustainable democracy.

These were the points on which I kept a relentless focus while I was running the government as chief executive.

I established the National Accountability Bureau (NAB) to put the fear of God into the rich and powerful who had been looting the state. A special NAB ordinance was issued to give power and full autonomy to the organization. I wanted an army general as chairman, a general who was scrupulously honest, clearheaded, and bold enough to move against the rich and powerful without being swayed by their influence. In Lieutenant General Muhammad Amjad I saw all these qualities. He exceeded my expectations. In a short time he established his own and his organization's credibility. Later, lieutenant generals Khalid Mabqool, Muneer Hafiez, and Shahid Aziz led the NAB equally effectively. The effects of the NAB were felt far and wide. Billions of rupees of plundered national wealth were recovered. Kleptocrats were prosecuted.

I know that people everywhere thirst to punish rulers for their sins, but bringing corrupt and criminal rulers and politicians to account is never easy. Unlike businesspeople who leave a paper trail of the loans they have taken from banks, people in powerful government positions know better than to leave a convenient trail of evidence behind them for future prosecutors. Yet we managed many prosecutions, plea bargains, and recovery of unpaid bank loans, though not to the extent that I had hoped for, particularly among politicians and public officeholders.

I needed an organization—a think tank—to research and recommend reforms in various areas. I called it the National Reconstruction Bureau (NRB). Here I needed a person with a fertile analytical mind, very well read, focused, and painstakingly industrious. I felt that Lieutenant General Tanvir Hussain Naqvi (retired) filled the bill eminently. I must say he delivered far beyond what I had hoped. The first task that I entrusted to him was to produce a local government system to decentralize our entire political system. He wrote a full Local Government Ordinance, setting detailed rules for the district-level governance that we evolved and introduced. It has been recognized by the World Bank as a silent revolution in Pakistan. It is to General Naqvi's credit that he accomplished the very big task of producing a new Police Ordinance 2002, replacing the one of 1861. This brought police rules in harmony with the prevailing environment. The nation owes him gratitude.

What I did not know at the time was that the judgment of the Supreme Court in a case challenging my takeover was to severely restrict me in implementing my agenda. On May 12, 2000, the Supreme Court, while justifying the removal of Nawaz Sharif's government and the takeover by the army because the Supreme Court deemed my dismissal as army chief illegal, placed two restrictions on me that were to have far-reaching consequences. First, it required me to hold elections in three years. With hindsight, I realize that I needed more time to fulfill my agenda, though at that point I thought three years were adequate. I did not realize then that what Pakistan needed was not mere reform but restructuring. I also did not know how quickly time passes. I sometimes regret that I did not appeal to the Supreme Court for more time—at least five years. Our system of sharing funds between the federal government (which we call the center) and the provinces, and our sharing of powers and responsibilities between the center and the provinces, could not be finalized by me. I did initiate a study on the restructuring of the government and the civil service, but could not bring this to fruition. Nevertheless, all these studies were initiated at the National Reconstruction Bureau, and a number of ideas were generated.

The events of 9/11 and its aftermath came to distract us from these issues. I was forced to pursue security ahead of restructuring.

The second restriction imposed by the Supreme Court was that I could not introduce structural changes in the constitution: "That no amendment shall be made in the salient features of the Constitution i.e. independence of the Judiciary, federalism, parliamentary form of Government blended with Islamic provisions." This meant that correcting a dysfunctional democracy would have limitations.

On closer analysis, however, I realized that my basic idea of introducing sustainable democracy in Pakistan could be achieved within these constraints. Our new system of local government, the bedrock of any democratic system, was provided for in our constitution but had never been implemented by politicians, who, selfishly, did not wish to devolve power to the grassroots.

In retrospect, I believe that my decisions not to abrogate the constitution and not to impose martial law were both correct. I am inspired by a letter written by Abraham Lincoln in 1864:

> My oath to preserve the Constitution imposed on me the duty of preserving by every indispensable means that government, that nation, of which the Constitution was the organic law. Was it possible to lose the nation and yet preserve the Constitution? By general law life and limb must be protected, yet often a limb must be amputated to save a life, but a life is never wisely given to save a limb. I felt that measures, otherwise unconstitutional, might become lawful by becoming indispensable to the preservation of the Constitution through the preservation of the nation. Right or wrong, I assumed this ground and now avow it.

I have always agreed with these views of Abraham Lincoln. In fact, I found this passage so inspirational and so beautifully worded that I have kept it in my briefcase ever since I first read it in 1990. Little did I know then that I might have to fall back on it one day. In the predicament in which I was placed, I thought I could preserve the nation in such a way that the constitution would also remain functional. In my own way I sorted out the conundrum: I preserved both the limb and the body. But if there ever had to be a choice, the body would outweigh the limb.

If the nation goes, so does the constitution. But if the constitution, especially a flawed one, goes, the nation still remains and can always give itself another constitution or correct the flaws in the first one. Thus our ultimate duty is to preserve the nation. The choice may be stark, but it is obvious: Pakistan comes first—always. We achieved the ideal: preserve both the body and the limb, the nation as well as the constitution.

CHAPTER 17

THE QUEST FOR DEMOCRACY

I ardently believe that no country can progress without democracy, but democracy has to be tailored in accordance with each nation's peculiar environment. Only then can it be a functioning democracy that truly empowers the people and produces governments to address their needs. If it does not function, then it merely creates a facade without spirit or substance. There are many, many systems that deserve to be called democratic. Transplanting one system to another country just won't do, as has been amply proved in Pakistan and elsewhere, if that system is too alien. It can be rejected by the body politic, like a foreign substance in a human body.

Sadly, a functioning democracy is exactly what has eluded Pakistan ever since its birth on August 14, 1947. This lack lies at the root of most of our ills. The problem is that while most of us know that the Greek word *demos* means "the people," hardly anyone takes notice of the other vital Greek word, *kratein,* "to rule." Thus "people's rule" or "rule by the people," which is the spirit of democracy, is entirely forgotten. What we in Pakistan have consciously constructed instead is rule by a small elite—never democratic, often autocratic, usually plutocratic, and lately kleptocratic—all working with a tribal-feudal mind-set, "in the name of the people" with democratic camouflage. This small elite comprises feudal barons, tribal warlords, and politicians of all hues. In Pakistan we inherited a feudal, patriarchal society. The population is divided into vertical compartments of provinces, tribes, clans, castes, and subcastes. People generally do not vote across these compartments or across their tribe, caste, or clan boundaries. Elections therefore involve shifting coalitions of different clans or tribes, negotiated by tribal or clan leaders, rather than appeals to independent voters. The system lends itself to incompetence and corruption, leading to poor governance. It creates the illusion of democracy because we do have elections; but we forget that elections are but a tool of democracy, not an end in themselves.

Our history of dysfunctional democracy has caused us great grief, most hauntingly in the separation of East Pakistan in 1971.

Our suffering over the last six decades has been a learning experience, however, and happily, more and more thoughtful people believe that there is no other option but genuine democracy. Our contentions are not about whether we should have democracy. Our contentions are about how best to make democracy work for the country and our nation and about setting up a system that will produce the genuine democracy for which the people yearn.

This brings me to the many yardsticks used to measure democracy. People must have the option of throwing a government out at regular intervals, through elections. The media have to be free, within the norms of civilized behavior. Socialists, who invariably describe their countries as "people's democracies," believe that democracy demands the equitable distribution of wealth, access to social welfare and education, and equal opportunities. I am no socialist, yet I share these ideals. I believe that the most honest yardstick, and one that is often forgotten by the well-heeled, is the human condition. I believe that a system is useless if it does not improve the human condition significantly and continuously. Then it matters little, especially to the vast hungry multitude, what the system is, or whether or not the system passes under the label of democracy.

A system of elections must put into office a government that is sensitive to the frustrations and aspirations of the people and does its utmost to address them. Anything else cannot be called democratic by any stretch of the imagination. In Pakistan, we have had too many elections that only empowered an elite class whose primary objective is to preserve, protect, and fortify its privileges even at the cost of the country and neglect of the people. Similarly, I know that economic growth is vital to continuing progress, but in itself it is meaningless unless the quality of life of the ordinary citizen, starting from the poorest, improves with it. This cannot happen in the absence of good governance. What is the use of macroeconomic success if its benefits do not filter down to the people? After all, why do we make all these political and administrative arrangements, including the creation of nation-states, if not for the benefit of our citizens? When those benefits fail to reach them, they lose faith in the state, and the state can even collapse.

A brief political history of Pakistan shows how we have failed to create a true democracy. The death of the father of the nation, Quaid-e-Azam Muhammad Ali Jinnah, thirteen months after independence, was a serious setback. With his departure the infant state of Pakistan lost its lead politically, physically, and metaphorically—and even ideologically. We took nine years to finally produce a constitution in 1956, and even this constitution violated the basic tenet of one person, one vote. The population of East Pakistan, although larger than that of west Pakistan, we equalized through a device called the "parity principle." This device gave the same number of seats in parliament to a minority in west Pakistan as it did to the majority in East Pakistan. To justify the parity principle, the four provinces of the western wing, comprising the Punjab, Sindh, North-West Frontier Province (NWFP), and Balochistan, were cobbled together into a single unit to be called the province of "West Pakistan." Naturally, the people of the three smaller provinces of west Pakistan felt highly aggrieved by this unpopular decision, for they believed that it would not only emasculate their culture but also deprive them of their fair share of resources. Though the politicians of East Pakistan with their own vested interests and agendas had agreed to this unholy arrangement, the Bengali people there, overall, felt that they had been duped because their votes were watered down.

National elections under the new constitution were to be held in early 1959. But on October 8, 1958, the president at the time—a retired civil and military official, Major General Iskander Mirza—in collaboration with the army chief, Ayub Khan—dissolved parliament, threw out the government (which was itself unelected and lacking legitimacy), abrogated the constitution and declared martial law, of which General Ayub Khan became the chief administrator. However, the two found it difficult to share power, and only twenty-one days later, on October 28,

1958, President Mirza was sent packing to London, never to return. General Ayub Khan then became president of the country.

President Ayub Khan lifted martial law in 1962, when he introduced our second constitution. Sadly, this constitution retained all the antidemocratic elements of the first, namely the parity principle and the "One Unit of West Pakistan."

Despite the fact that under President Ayub Khan Pakistan witnessed more economic development than ever before, its benefits did not sufficiently reach the masses. Instead, wealth became concentrated in a few hands, mostly a new class of industrialists known as the "twenty families"—later, twenty-two families. While this perception was not fully correct, the wily Bhutto exploited it to undermine the good performance of Ayub.

In 1968–1969 general discontent among the masses led to a popular upheaval. The main themes of the discontent were economic disparities between eastern and western Pakistan, the concentration of wealth in twenty-two families, an acute sense of deprivation and alienation in East Pakistan, and a general political suffocation of the public. All these complaints were used effectively by opposition political leaders. Ayub Khan could not sustain this pressure and decided to resign in March 1969.

But as he was leaving, instead of following the constitution and handing power over to the speaker of the National Assembly, Ayub handed it over to the army chief, General Yahya Khan, who abrogated the constitution and declared martial law. Pakistan had come full circle, back to 1958. However, General Yahya was under pressure to implement two of the most popular demands of the anti-Ayub agitation: to end the parity principle and break the "One Unit." This he did, thereby taking western Pakistan back to its four provinces. In that sense, we were back to the days before the constitution of 1956.

General Yahya Khan held fair elections in December 1970, but by then so much had happened to polarize the eastern and western wings of Pakistan that each wing voted parochially. The East Pakistanis voted for their own party, the Awami League, virtually unanimously. As I have said earlier, it won outright, with a majority of seats in the National Assembly, and earned the right to form the government without entering into a coalition with anyone.

Ayub's protégé, the former foreign minister Zulfikar Ali Bhutto, whom he often called "my son," had fallen afoul of his mentor and formed his own Pakistan People's Party (PPP). It won two of the four most populous provinces of the western wing and had the second highest number of seats in the National Assembly, but fell well short of a majority. This new assembly too was charged with making a new constitution, but this time in ninety days. The Awami League's majority meant that East Pakistan could frame a constitution that gave it the provincial autonomy it desired—but this was completely unacceptable to the power elite of western Pakistan. Bhutto threatened the newly elected members of the National Assembly from western Pakistan that if they went to Dhaka, the capital of East Pakistan, where the assembly was to meet, they should buy one-way tickets—because if they returned he would break their legs. During all this time, the leader of the Awami League, Sheikh Mujibur Rahman, made no attempt to reach out to the people of western Pakistan, nor did he do anything to neutralize the maneuvers of Zulfikar Ali Bhutto.

In frustration, Yahya Khan postponed the inaugural meeting of the National Assembly, which was to be held in March 1971, and arrested Sheikh Mujib and his party's leadership, declaring them to be traitors. The already alienated and deprived population of East Pakistan rose up in arms, abetted and supported by India. What began as a political standoff quickly became an armed conflict, as we have seen earlier.

Needless to say, India took full advantage of the brewing crisis. India helped the Bengalis raise an army of guerrilla fighters, called the Mukti Bahini. It also gave refuge to many leaders of the Awami League and a large refugee population escaping the civil war.

As a major commanding a company of the Special Services Group of commandos in western Pakistan, I witnessed these events with great sadness and trepidation. During this crisis, India signed a Treaty of Peace and Friendship with the Soviet Union. It used the pretext of the economic burden of a large refugee population to attack Pakistan in the eastern and western wings. With the link between eastern and western Pakistan severed, and with a hostile population, the military there did not stand a chance. Our ally, the United States, stood by and did nothing substantive to help us, unlike India's ally the Soviet Union. Yahya appointed Bhutto deputy prime minister and foreign minister and sent him to the UN Security Council to negotiate a cease-fire. But Bhutto rejected a resolution proposed by Poland that might have prevented the loss of East Pakistan. It seems he had concluded that he could never come to power as long as East Pakistan was there. Our army in East Pakistan surrendered, 90,000 military and civilian personnel were taken prisoners of war, and East Pakistan seceded to become Bangladesh. That was the day I cried.

We had a "new Pakistan" now, as Bhutto called it, comprising only the western wing. From being the largest Muslim country and the fifth largest country in the world, we stood woefully diminished. Bhutto assumed total power as president, without a constitution. Worse, he used the lack of a constitution as a pretext to become chief martial law administrator. An autocrat at heart, Bhutto got a kick out of being head of a martial law regime.

What was left of the National Assembly, a minority, was convened to form a new constitution for Pakistan. Not only were we back to the situation of 1947, we were now in a diminished country.

In 1973, the remaining rump assembly agreed to a new constitution. The good thing about this was that it was passed by consensus. Ironically, even though Bhutto had acquired great popularity on a platform of Islamic socialism and providing basic needs like food, shelter, and clothing to the poor, he soon had to get into partnership with tribal chieftains and feudal landlords, the very men whose political power he had ostensibly come to break. Instead, he opted for the soft target, the business community, and went in for large-scale nationalization of industries, banks, and financial houses. This broke the back of a nascent industrial base, an economic engine that could have provided an urban, modern countervailing force to tribal-feudal power. The nationalized industries were handed over to bureaucrats and party cronies and soon became hotbeds of corruption.

Zulfikar Ali Bhutto masqueraded as a democrat but ruled like an autocrat. During his time the press was suppressed more than ever before or since. Many editors and journalists were arrested for dissent, and newspapers and journals were closed down. Political opponents were arrested on spurious charges; some were incarcerated in a notorious gulag-like prison called the Dalai Camp and some were even murdered mysteriously.

When the time came for the next general elections in 1977, nine powerful opposition parties formed an alliance and presented a united front to oppose Bhutto's People's Party. Bhutto rigged the ballot extensively. He even had himself elected unopposed, by arresting his opponent and preventing him from filing his nomination papers in time. The people had had enough and rose up, often violently. Many people were killed on the streets, and thousands were arrested. Bhutto went into negotiations with the opposition alliance to come to an agreement and end the agitation. They failed, and on the night of July 5, 1977, the army took over, declared martial law, put the constitution into abeyance, and placed Bhutto and some of his henchmen under arrest. Inevitably, the army chief, who was then General Zia ul-Haq, became chief martial law administrator and later also assumed the office of president. Two years later he had Bhutto hanged after a conviction for murder in a highly controversial trial.

Zia ruled for eleven years. Since the anti-Bhutto agitation had been fueled by the slogan of introducing Sharia (Islamic law), General Zia found it a convenient platform to adopt, and one that came naturally to him. He was helped immensely by the Soviet Union's invasion and occupation of Afghanistan. The mujahideen resistance to the Soviets, as is now well known, was one of the turning points in modern history. The United States helped find and fund and arm the mujahideen, as did many European and Muslim countries, most notably Saudi Arabia. It was in Pakistan's interest to help the Afghans as well, for now the borders of the Soviet Union had effectively reached Pakistan, and there was a very real danger that if the Soviets settled down in Afghanistan, they could soon invade Pakistan for access to its warm waters for their navy.

Pakistan became a frontline state. We fought the war with the Afghans, the Americans, the Europeans, and the Saudis, and we won. But we paid a very heavy price. Kalashnikovs, mortars, rockets, Stinger missiles, and other sophisticated armaments found their way into Pakistan's arms market. Soon Pakistan was awash in weapons of the most lethal kind, weapons that remain in private hands to this day. Worse, a drug culture soon took root, and it involved heroin, no ordinary drug.

Hard-line mullahs and their seminaries were given official patronage by Pakistan, the United States, Saudi Arabia, and other allies during this period, and they were charged with producing indoctrinated fighters against the Soviet Union. No one complained, therefore, when President General Zia ul-Haq introduced a regressive Islamization in the country. He introduced Islamic laws and established Islamic courts to run parallel with the normal judicial system.

In 1985, President Zia revived the constitution and held elections in which people could run as individuals but not as members of any party. The deal Zia offered to the politicians was that the new National Assembly had to pass the eighth amendment to the constitution, giving the president the power to dissolve the National Assembly. This clause actually proved useful, for it acted as a safety valve that prevented military takeovers, until Nawaz Sharif revoked it.

In late May 1988 Zia used the eighth amendment to dissolve the National Assembly and dismiss the government. Yet he did not form a caretaker government to hold elections within ninety days, as the constitution required. By this time Zia had become very alienated and isolated. It was on his return from Bahawalpur after attending an Abrams tank demonstration that his aircraft mysteriously crashed on August 17, 1988. The Zia era was over.

The chairman of the Senate, Ghulam Ishaq Khan, a retired bureaucrat who had also been President Zia's finance minister, became acting president and held elections in November of the same year. Benazir Bhutto's People's Party won the highest number of seats in the National Assembly but fell short of a majority. However, Benazir Bhutto was able to form a coalition government, and there followed eleven years of sham democracy rotating between her and Nawaz Sharif, with caretaker governments in between. It was a decade of political musical chairs. Benazir Bhutto's government was removed in 1990. Nawaz Sharif became prime minister after the elections that followed. His first term, though not so bad as the second, was characterized by cronyism, plundering, and poor governance. President Ghulam Ishaq Khan removed him in 1993. The Supreme Court restored his government, but he and the president still could not get along. Both asked the army chief, General Waheed Kakar, to mediate. The result was the resignation of both the president and the prime minister. New elections made Benazir Bhutto prime minister for a second time, again in a coalition. She picked up where she had left off. In 1997, the president, a nominee of Benazir Bhutto's party, dismissed her government. The fourth election in nine years brought Nawaz Sharif back to power, but with a difference. This time he had a brute two-thirds majority in the National Assembly and could bludgeon through any amendment to the constitution he wanted. He used his majority to silence dissent. He forced the army chief out of office. He attacked the press and arrested many journalists. And he had his party's goons physically attack the Supreme Court.

In the midst of all this, India exploded five nuclear devices on May 11 and 13, 1998. India had first exploded a nuclear bomb in 1974, setting off an expensive nuclear arms race in the subcontinent. Pakistan responded with tests of its own on May 28, 1998. Economic and military sanctions were slapped on Pakistan, setting back our already woefully weakened economy. Fearing that people would withdraw their foreign exchange deposits, Nawaz Sharif froze all foreign currency accounts. This had an even more disastrous effect on our fragile economy, as disastrous perhaps as Zulfikar Ali Bhutto's rampant nationalization of the 1970s. Taking advantage of the public's elation over the nuclear tests, Nawaz Sharif got the National Assembly to pass the fifteenth constitutional amendment, giving him dictatorial powers under the pretext of bringing in what he called an Islamic government. All that remained was for the Senate also to pass the amendment, as it would have done in early 2000. We were well on our way to Talibanization. Sharif got rid of the power of the president to dissolve the National Assembly and dismiss the government. After emasculating the president, he tried to make the judiciary subservient to the executive, taking on the chief justice of Pakistan, Sajjad Ali Shah, and even going so far as to get his party's shoddy political storm troopers, many of them parliamentarians, to physically attack the Supreme Court building. The honorable judges had to hide in their chambers to escape a thrashing. The entire sordid episode was recorded by the security cameras in the

Supreme Court building. In the battle that ensued between the prime minister on one side and president and chief justice on the other, the army chief—now General Jahangir Karamat—was again asked to intervene as mediator. When the crunch came, he decided to side with the prime minister; that decision led to the president's resignation and the election of a new president handpicked by Nawaz Sharif. This was the same army chief whom he would later force to resign for saying the right thing, which amounted to advising the prime minister about honest and good governance and the formation of a National Security Council to formally consult with and advise him and also help institutionalize the perennial dragging in of the army chief as an arbitrator by the president and the prime minister. After General Karamat's resignation I became chief of the army staff. Then came Kargil; Nawaz Sharif's capitulation in Washington on July 4, 1999; his effort to make the army and me the scapegoats; and his reckless attempt to hijack my plane and deliver his army chief into enemy hands.

CHAPTER 18

PUTTING THE SYSTEM RIGHT

Given Pakistan's checkered political history, alternating between martial law and sham democracy, the way to true democracy has been difficult, requiring travel on several different paths at once. Our main political parties have in reality been no more than family cults, a dynastic icon at their head. Remove the icon, and the party evaporates. Hardly any of our political parties have been democratic on the inside, and therefore these parties never bother to hold genuine internal elections. The head of the party is the party. A party head appoints whom he (or she) wishes, almost always sycophants, to party positions. These sycophants always look upward to the boss who appointed them rather than downward at the party workers who ought to elect them.

I noted the absence of democracy at the grassroots level and the absence of effective checks and balances over the three power brokers of Pakistan: the president, the prime minister, and the army chief. These were the main impediments to sustainable democracy. Each of these problems needed to be solved.

More broadly, when I took power, I knew that freedom needed to be spread to everyone, and guaranteed. I will discuss the emancipation of women and other issues of rights in Part Six. But without a system that could produce true democracy—the sort that I have described earlier, one that gives rise to governments that improve the human condition continuously and significantly—none of the other changes would have made any difference. Former prime ministers Nawaz Sharif and Benazir Bhutto, who had twice been tried, been tested, and failed, had to be denied a third chance. They had misgoverned the nation. Furthermore, they would never allow their parties to develop a democratic tradition, as was clear from the fact that neither Benazir Bhutto's party nor Nawaz Sharif's had held internal elections. In fact, Benazir became her party's "chairperson for life," in the tradition of the old African dictators! For both individuals, legal cases were pushing against them. All I had to do was make clear that the charges would not be dropped. Benazir Bhutto had already run away from the country and absconded from the law during Nawaz Sharif's time. Later, Nawaz Sharif and his family were happy to sign a deal with my government to go into voluntary exile in Saudi Arabia, a deal he now brazenly denies. Both have chosen to avoid the rule of law by staying away, though they keep insisting now and again that they will return, even together, in order to keep alive the morale of their party members and remain politically relevant.

They were the heads of two significant political parties—the Pakistan People's Party (PPP) and the Pakistan Muslim League (PML-N). And because these parties were run like dynasties, candidates who could provide alternative leadership were nonexistent or mere pygmies. It did not appear practicable to maintain those parties alone. Something more had to be done.

I was very conscious that in doing something more, with whatever political restructuring I did, I had to satisfy two international concerns. One, the process must remain democratic; and two, elections, whenever they were held, had to be fair and transparent.

Thus, before we could proceed with elections, we needed another political party. Without a fresh option, Bhutto and Sharif could still run the show from abroad.

Nawaz Sharif had been convicted of hijacking my plane. He faced life imprisonment. He could not withstand the rigors of isolation and confinement. He used his previous contact with Crown Prince (now King) Abdullah of Saudi Arabia, who asked me to allow Nawaz Sharif to go into exile there. I could not turn this request down, since it came from a great friend of Pakistan who also genuinely called me a brother—and I in return called him an elder brother. I also thought that sending the entire family of Nawaz Sharif out of the country might be politically advantageous. It would avoid the prolonged destabilizing effect of a high-profile trial. I obliged. We struck a deal. I would give Nawaz Sharif a conditional pardon, and he and certain members of his family would go to Saudi Arabia for ten years and remain out of politics. They would also give up some of their properties as reparation for their misdeeds. This deal was signed by all the elders of the Sharif family, including Nawaz Sharif, his brother Shahbaz Sharif, and their father. It must be said that Shahbaz Sharif initially refused to sign and did not want to leave Pakistan. But we could not have this partial acceptance. So anxious were Nawaz Sharif and his father for Nawaz to avoid serving the sentence that they persuaded the younger brother to sign. The entire family thus left for Jeddah. In retrospect, I now feel that the decision was absolutely correct and beneficial for Pakistan. It facilitated the creation of a new political party.

In early 2006 Nawaz Sharif approached me through a very dear friend of mine for permission to go to London to be with his seriously ill son. Wishing the boy well, I readily agreed. Having reached London, however, Nawaz Sharif reneged on his promise not to indulge in politics. He showed a lack of character, launching a tirade of lies and distortions against me. Exile and isolation are an opportunity for introspection and critical self-analysis. Nawaz Sharif apparently learned nothing from his exile and failed to grow intellectually or politically.

I needed a national political party to support my agenda. I had the option of forming a new party, but I decided—and the emotion of a soldier had a lot to do with this—to revive the Pakistan Muslim League (PML), the party of Quaid-e-Azam Muhammad Ali Jinnah that had led us to freedom and to our own country.

My principal secretary, Tariq Aziz, an old and trusted friend, had the idea in advance of the elections of 2002 of converting the PML(N) back to a true PML(Q), the Q standing for Quaid. Chaudhry Shujat Hussain and his cousin Chaudhry Pervez Ilahi, seasoned politicians from Gujrat in the Punjab, were prominent within the PML(N). Tariq Aziz's idea was to encourage them to reconstitute the PML(N) into the PML(Q). The Chaudhry cousins had been victims of some mudslinging, but they were good men. I agreed to the proposal. Tariq Aziz then introduced them to me, and I asked them to spearhead the effort to galvanize and reinvent the Muslim League. I must say, to their credit, that they demonstrated complete commitment to my cause and tremendous grassroots political skills. They reinvigorated the PML and identified it with Quaid-e-Azam by adding the Q. Most of the members of PML joined the fold of the new PML(Q) with Chaudhry Shujat as the president. What was left of the party called itself PML-N to identify itself with Nawaz Sharif. I realize, however, that many joined the new party because of their support of and commitment to me. I must also acknowledge the active role played by my friend Tariq Aziz in drawing people to me. He showed complete loyalty to me personally and to my agenda.

Thus PML(Q) was formally launched on August 20, 2002, with the hope that it would dominate the elections of that year.

We were cobbling together and launching the new Pakistan Muslim League in the wake of 9/11, when I had taken a firm stand against terrorists (as I will discuss in Part Five). My popularity was at a peak after the dust of my decision about 9/11 started settling and the masses realized that Pakistan was firmly on a progressive path. The ranks of the PML swelled accordingly. The politicians of PML saw me as their leader, but—ironically—I was not trying to play politics. My idea was to remain above the fray, and avoid joining any party. Still, I had to transfer my popularity to the new party before the elections scheduled for October 2002. How to do it? I decided that we should hold a national referendum on my office. I knew it would result in a sizable vote in my favor, and I could then transfer that demonstrated popularity to the embryonic PML(Q) by voicing my support for the party. Many of my close associates disagreed with this approach, but I overruled them and decided to hold a referendum. It was held on April 30, 2002. The question asked of the people was:

> For the survival of the local government system, establishment of democracy, continuity of reforms, end to sectarianism and extremism, and to fulfill the vision of Quaid-e-Azam, would you like to elect President General Pervez Musharraf as President of Pakistan for five years?

The referendum went smoothly. There was a very high turnout, and the overall count was very strongly in my favor. There were some irregularities, though. I found that in some places overenthusiastic administrative officials and bureaucrats had allowed people to vote more than once, and had even filled out ballot papers themselves. I also later found that this absolutely unwarranted "support" was helped along by the opposition in certain areas where they have a hold and where they stuffed ballot boxes in my favor so as to provide supposed evidence for claims of foul play. The whole exercise ended in a near catastrophe.

In retrospect I realize that in Pakistan, unless there is an opposition candidate or an alternative party that can monitor the process, any opinion poll will end in a fiasco. Detractors will cry foul, and you will not be able to prove otherwise. That was the case with this referendum; it placed inordinate demands on the dedication, honesty, and integrity of individual polling staff and the administration.

Finally, in a national broadcast, I had to come clean. I thanked the people for their support but also admitted that some excesses had indeed taken place without my knowledge or consent. I took full responsibility for them and for the wrong decision of the referendum in the first place, and offered my deep regrets. Telling the truth, however unpleasant, gives the public the chance to forgive and forget. But tell lies, as our politicians habitually do, and the people will punish you.

As the election of October 2002 approached, I involved myself more and more in political issues. I soon realized that political reforms in some areas were a sheer necessity. The first amendment I proposed was to reduce the voting age from twenty-one to eighteen years. After all, if young people can be considered mature enough to get married at eighteen, or to get a driver's license, why can they not be responsible enough to vote? Thus we decided to empower youth.

Women, I have always believed, suffer special discrimination in the male chauvinist world, especially in developing countries. Redressing this problem at its core would require political empowerment. We created sixty reserved seats for women to mitigate the acute gender imbalance in the National Assembly, knowing that women would be their own best advocates to remove gender bias and societal inequities. This arrangement does not exclude them from contesting the other seats in the Assembly. When elections were held in October 2002, a total of seventy-two women were elected to the National Assembly, twelve from general seats. This has set the stage for the irreversible process of the empowerment of women, as I will discuss in Chapter 30.

The census of 1997 conducted under the auspices of the army had shown that Pakistan's population had risen to 140 million. The number in the National Assembly and the provincial assemblies was based on a census held decades earlier when the population was much smaller. Constituencies had become bloated. We therefore raised the number of seats in the National Assembly from 217 to 342. Of these, 272 are directly elected general seats, sixty are reserved for women on the basis of proportional representation, and ten are reserved for non-Muslims in accordance with their population ratio. We did the same proportionally in the four provincial assemblies.

The separate electoral system that had been followed for the minorities, in which non-Muslims could vote only for non-Muslim candidates on reserved seats, predictably led to a feeling of isolation from mainstream politics. No Muslim needed their vote, and this fact reduced their significance. We gave them a joint electoral system in which minorities vote for any candidate, and also allowed them to retain the reserved seats. With this change, all candidates have to solicit minority votes and therefore have to address the concerns of minorities. They are now mainstreamed into national political life.

We also made it incumbent on all candidates for the Senate, the National Assembly, and the provincial assemblies to be university graduates or the equivalent (ten years of school and four years of college or university). This was done not only to have better-educated parliamentarians but also to sift out many undesirable politicians, thus giving our parliaments a new, younger, more enlightened outlook.

We established a rule that no one could be president or prime minister more than twice, whether the terms were consecutive or not and whether either term had been fully served or not. Many people thought this law has been brought in to prevent Nawaz Sharif or Benazir Bhutto from ever becoming prime minister again. This is partially true, but above all, the new rule was enacted to encourage new blood to compete for high offices. It will be a check on the dynastic rule of a few individuals.

Imposing checks and balances on the three power brokers of the country was always high on my agenda. I was convinced that unless this was done, democracy could not be sustained or good governance guaranteed. There had to be an institutional way of motivating the prime minister to perform well, aside from presidential censure and later denouncements or the ad hoc, unconventional, but popular norm of the army chief's "advising" the prime minister to govern better. It almost invariably happened that the prime minister would refuse to listen, and this refusal would lead to intense acrimony between him and the president or even the army chief. This invariably resulted either in dissolution of the Assembly by the president or, once the power of the president to dissolve the Assembly was removed, the danger of the imposition of martial law by the army chief.

The president could also be impulsive and attack the prime minister because of very personal whims. When the president had the authority to dissolve the Assembly under Article 58(2)b of the constitution, this could—and very much did on one occasion—lead to an unwarranted interruption of democracy. An unreasonable president needed to be checked.

The last and perhaps most important check had to be imposed on the army chief. In Pakistan's political environment the opposition always tends to undermine the government, fairly or unfairly. The easiest way to do this, though unconstitutional and undemocratic in the extreme, has been to incite the army chief against the prime minister. This situation is compounded when the prime minister is grossly misperforming and people who are generally concerned about the well-being of the country reach out to the army chief to save it. I saw this happening with every army chief after 1992, when I became director general of military operations. Between October 1998 and October 1999, when I myself was the army chief in Nawaz Sharif's government, I know how many people—both men and women—taunted me for not acting against the prime minister. "Why don't you take over? Are you waiting for Pakistan to be destroyed?" they would ask. Such situations, far too frequent during the 1990s, put the army chiefs in a quandary. An impulsive army chief, having failed to change the prime minister's behavior by persuasion, could take over. This must never be allowed to happen in the future if democracy is to be sustained. Martial law is never an answer to political malaise.

A foolproof, institutional system of checks is essential. I proposed the National Security Council (NSC), a body that would be chaired by the president but would have no executive function. It should be only a consultative body, neither above nor below parliament. We ultimately defined the membership of this body to include the prime minister, the four provincial chief ministers, the leader of the opposition in the National Assembly, the Senate chairman, and the speaker of the National Assembly, plus four men in uniform—the chairman of the Joint Chiefs of Staff Committee and the chiefs of the army, air force, and navy. That makes thirteen: a chairman and twelve members. I know that the army chief only should be brought in to keep him out of politics, but interservice sensitivity demands the inclusion of all four four-star commanders.

With the NSC composed thus and meeting at least once a quarter, I am convinced that we have instituted a check on the three power brokers. The prime minister has to perform, or he will come under pressure from the NSC—or at least from the leader of the opposition and the uniformed members. The president had better not be impulsive when no member of NSC is with him. The army chief can never take over, because he has an institution available to voice his concerns (and the concerns of a worried public) to the prime minister and can then allow the constitution and the political process to take their course.

I am aware of the opposition of certain politicians to the NSC, and especially to the inclusion of the uniformed members. I am also conscious of western concerns of keeping the military out of political institutions. In spite of all this I am certain that the NSC, coupled with the safety valve of the presidential power to dissolve the National Assembly, is the best way possible to sustain democracy and avoid martial law. It is tailored to the Pakistani environment and will remain applicable until we mature enough to be able to create effective checks and balances within our parliaments and political institutions.

Unfortunately, the leader of the opposition in the National Assembly, Maulana Fazal ur Rehman, whose appointment was supported by the PML(Q) on the assurance that he would attend the NSC's meetings, backed out after pledging that he would attend. He belongs to the alliance of six religious parties and has been boycotting these meetings. They are either ignorant of the efficacy of the NSC or simply trying to sabotage my political reforms so that they can return to their bad old ways of the bad old days.

In any developing country, where political and governmental institutions are not entirely mature, there is always a large gap between formulation and implementation of policy. Traditionally, Pakistan has had a central (federal) government and large regional (provincial) governments, but local affairs have been either unregulated or managed by the provincial governments. It is said that "all politics is local." If the masses are to participate effectively in the political process, democracy has to permeate down to the grassroots. This was lacking in Pakistan.

In fact, genuine democracy has to evolve from the grassroots upward, not be thrust from the top down. The base of the pyramid has to be very strong, or else it will collapse. A local government system that is genuinely empowered politically, administratively, and financially lies at the heart of democracy because it is best equipped to understand and also to address the needs and problems of the common people. This is what touches the people most, not assemblies in far-flung provincial or national capitals.

As noted earlier, we achieved a silent revolution with our Local Government Ordinance of 2000. This ordinance did away with the vestiges of the colonial era, when a deputy commissioner and a superintendent of police ran districts like lords. With the stroke of a pen they were both subordinated to the elected mayor (*nazim*). I had to withstand tremendous pressure and intrigue from the bureaucracy trying to nip this system in the bud, but we held our ground and succeeded in putting the new system in place. If, over time, it succeeds—as, God willing, I am convinced it will—history will call it ingenious.

The first local government elections were held in five phases, from December 30, 2000, to July 5, 2001. Each local government has three tiers: the union council at the lowest level, the *tehsil* (or subdistrict) council, and the district council. The district is headed by the *nazim* (equivalent to a mayor). Each union council (the lowest body, representing a population of 15,000 to 20,000) has thirteen members, four of whom must be women. We also gave one reserved seat in each union council to a non-Muslim. Four seats are kept for workers and peasants, thus mainstreaming the poor. The districts are allocated development funds from the center (i.e., the federal government) and the provinces, but they can also raise their own revenues. This, I believe, is the true empowerment of the people.

The first district governments were formally installed on August 14, 2001. I addressed all the *nazims,* motivating them to work for the uplift of their areas and their people. Unfortunately, the members of the National Assembly and the provincial assemblies felt threatened by the new local governments. They did not realize that their actual job is to legislate, not manage every village and neighborhood. I am sure that as our democracy gradually matures, this realization will dawn. When the local government system really takes root and people start voting only for the genuinely honest and deserving, rejecting the corrupt and inefficient, we will have achieved a bloodless revolution.

The district governments of 2001 functioned reasonably well for their first term of four years. How well they functioned depended, however, on the mayors. Wherever the elected *nazims* were good, progress was very visible. The districts that elected the wrong candidates stagnated. The second local government elections were held in 2005. The campaigns were conducted with much greater fervor and resulted in the election of better candidates. Voters exhibited an increased maturity, at least at the local level. We will have to wait for Pakistan's next general elections in 2007 (the assemblies have a term of five years) to see whether that maturity extends to the national and provincial levels. I am very glad that in many places, corrupt and inept council members were rejected in the second local government elections. Another encouraging sign was the massive rejection of religious groups in the North-West Frontier Province and also in Balochistan, where they are part of the ruling coalition at the provincial level. Their support dropped from 76 percent of the total provincial assembly seats in the provincial elections of 2002 to 24 percent of the total seats in the local elections of 2005. This was partially because of their own poor governance. I also made an effort to make people aware of the dangers of supporting the mullahs.

In retrospect, notwithstanding all the allegations and counterallegations of vote rigging and inept performance, I see the local government experience as very positive. I always look at the glass as half full. Obviously, such a glass is also half empty, but it will gradually be filled with more experience and maturity.

The Supreme Court had given me three years to stabilize Pakistan, hold elections, and hand over power to an elected government. By 2002, we had the new local governments in place, a new political party, and the economy stabilized to a considerable extent. The shock of 9/11 was being absorbed. I can say with some pride that for three years I had the most efficient and compact cabinet in the history of Pakistan. My team performed exceptionally well, and we turned the tide in all areas of governance. I salute all my cabinet ministers and the heads of the main public corporations and departments who worked so selflessly, with such patriotic zeal, and gave the country and myself such complete loyalty.

Several people advised me not to hold elections, and to ask the Supreme Court for more time. They thought that the reforms we had introduced needed time to mature. But I was adamant—not only because I had given my word to the people to hold elections as desired by the Supreme Court, but also because I firmly believed that it was absolutely essential to set a democratic dispensation in motion, the earlier the better.

We went ahead with the elections under a Legal Framework Order (LFO) that gave legal cover to all the electoral and political reforms we had introduced. The elections were held in the fairest and most transparent manner, irrespective of all allegations to the contrary. The PML(Q) won the largest number of seats in the National Assembly, but not an outright majority. The only locality where it got an outright majority was in the Punjab provincial assembly; there, it comfortably formed the provincial government. In Sindh, Benazir Bhutto's new Pakistan People's Party Parliamentarians (PPPP) won the most seats but also fell well short of a majority. So the coalition in that province was up for grabs. In Balochistan, the PML(Q) won the most seats, but not enough to form a government. In the North-West Frontier Province the religious group of the Muttahida Majlis-e-Amal (MMA) won an outright majority and formed the government there.

At the national level, the PML(Q) had the choice of entering into a coalition with either the MMA or the People's Party. A coalition with the Muttehida Qaumi Movement (MQM), the fourth largest group in the National Assembly, would have fallen short of a strong majority. The People's Party has always claimed the progressive and liberal ground. If this claim was taken at face value, it was the logical first choice for the coalition. It was a good opportunity for them to demonstrate that they were truly liberal and not just a family cult that practiced fascism rather than liberal democracy, as when this party was in power in the 1970s. But all efforts by the PML(Q) to work with them failed, for the sole reason that Benazir Bhutto would not countenance anyone else from her party becoming prime minister. She treats the party and the office like a family property. A coalition with the MMA after 9/11 would have had a very negative international fallout, but still, it was attempted as a last resort. The MMA demanded the prime minister's office for a man who would have been quite unacceptable both internationally and domestically. He even came to me personally to ask for the coveted position, committing himself to a very reconciliatory approach toward the United States and the West and complete support against al Qaeda and other extremists. We faced a dilemma.

At that point, a group of stalwarts from the People's Party proved bold enough to disagree with the self-centered attitude of their chairperson, Benazir Bhutto. They formed a bloc called the Patriots. They have since taken the old name Pakistan People's Party (three P's) to differentiate themselves from Bhutto's Pakistan People's Party Parliamentarians (four P's.) This new PPP, together with MQM and the PML(Q), formed the government with a thin majority. That led to regional bargains. The PML-Q and MQM agreed to form a government in Sindh. This in turn led to a period of peace and harmony in Karachi, the commercial hub of Pakistan that the MQM dominates.

Some people at home and abroad questioned the credibility of the elections. Some even accused the "establishment"—i.e., the intelligence agencies and me—of supporting the MMA because it won so many additional seats unexpectedly. These charges are not only false but absurd. If I had wanted to rig the process, why would I have done so for the MMA? That would have made no sense, but conspiracy theories are popular in Pakistan.

While all the negotiations were going on, we needed to authenticate the Legal Framework Order by bringing it into the constitution of Pakistan as an amendment. In effect, we needed to save the constitution and our nascent democracy by ratifying the steps already taken. Such a constitutional amendment required a two-thirds majority in the National Assembly. The only way this could be achieved was to get the PPPP or the MMA on board. The MMA was more amenable because it wanted the assemblies to function so that it could exercise power. Extensive meetings were held by the leaders of PML(Q) and MMA. My chief of staff, Lieutenant General Hamid Javed, also participated. These were tough negotiations, and I realized that the MMA was anything but straight. Its members tended to be devious in the extreme, changing their stance regularly. The sensitive issues involved included my remaining president for another five years, my remaining in uniform or not, the creation of the National Security Council, and restoring to the president the power to dissolve the National Assembly. I give full credit to the PML(Q) team led by Chaudhry Shujat Hussain and my chief of staff, who after a laborious and often very frustrating series of parleys finally thrashed out a joint strategy with the MMA. We agreed to present the seventeenth constitutional amendment as a bill in the National Assembly after (as proposed by the MMA) taking the National Security Council out of the bill and proposing it separately in the National Assembly as an act, which the MMA would support. As a quid pro quo, and in good faith, I also gave my verbal commitment to retire from the army and remove my uniform by December 31, 2004. Thus the seventeenth amendment to the constitution of Pakistan was passed with more than a two-thirds majority. No sooner was it passed than, as agreed, the act to allow the NSC was proposed. The clerics showed their hypocritical face by turning against it. However, the act was passed because it needed only a simple majority, which we had. Our reforms were now constitutional and legal, and I could constitutionally hold the two offices of president and chief of the army staff until 2007.

• • •

I was quite serious when I announced that I would remove my army chief's hat by December 31, 2004. But events that soon began to unfold started putting doubts in my mind. On the domestic front, not only was the MMA continually reneging on its promises, the Maulanas also started to adopt a very confrontational approach. The war against terror was also heating up in South and North Waziristan, with the army entrenched and fully involved. Over and above all this, Pakistan in general and Dr. A. Q. Khan in particular came into the international limelight on the sensitive issue of nuclear proliferation, which needed the most careful handling. As all this was happening domestically, the conflict in Iraq had gathered momentum and Pakistan was being asked to contribute troops. This situation too needed deft handling. Finally, after the ten-month Indo-Pakistan border standoff in 2002, there was a thaw in our relations when Prime Minister Vajpayee agreed to visit Pakistan in January 2004. This process needed to be taken forward with great sensitivity.

With all this facing Pakistan, with so many pulls in different directions, there was a dire need for unity of command in governance. By this I imply a single authority over the three important organs of government—the bureaucracy, the political system, and the military. Whether anyone liked it or not, circumstances had vested this command in me. In the changed environment, I thought that removing my uniform would dilute my authority and command at a time when both were required most. Therefore, much against my habit and character, I decided to go against my word. I decided not to give up my uniform.

In the wake of the elections of 2002, the PML(Q) elected Mir Zafarullah Khan Jamali as leader of the parliamentary party, and with the additional votes of its coalition partners, he was elected prime minister. For the first time Pakistan had a prime minister from Balochistan, its smallest province. He was very personable, and I certainly liked him.

When I took over the reins of Pakistan I already held two offices—chairman of the Joint Chiefs of Staff Committee (JCSC) and chief of the army staff. Soon after the takeover I assumed the office of chief executive of Pakistan. I also took over as president of Pakistan on June

20, 2001. Thus I was wearing four hats. I became president for two reasons: one was protocol, because of my regular contacts and dealings with the leaders of other states; the second was that after the elections in October 2002, I would have to vacate the office of chief executive—it would disappear, in favor of the elected prime minister. I had already taken off the hat of chairman of JCSC in October 2001, appointing General Aziz in my place. I was then left with only two hats: president and army chief. The entire electoral college comprising the Senate, the National Assembly, and the four provincial assemblies confirmed me as president of Pakistan by giving me a vote of confidence on November 16, 2002.

Although I had followed democratic and constitutional norms to retain the two offices, my remaining in the post of army chief gave Pakistan's detractors an excuse to doubt my intentions, and to question the credibility of our democracy. But I listen to my conscience and to the needs of my country. I do what I do if I think it is best for my country, not to get certificates of approval from foreign organizations and media. I do what I think will make my people happy.

Normally, the leader of the largest or majority party in the National Assembly becomes prime minister, but it was decided to separate these two offices so that Chaudhry Shujat could get on with the crucial job of consolidating the PML(Q). Also, Shujat did not wish to be prime minister, not least because of his indifferent health.

Jamali soon formed his cabinet, and the government started functioning. The cabinet was large because all partners in the coalition had to be accommodated; this is one of the detrimental features of a coalition government in the parliamentary system. Jamali's government chugged along as best as it could till 2004.

During this period serious differences developed between Jamali and his party president, Chaudhry Shujat. The differences spread to the extent that the party started feeling that the prime minister and party chief were working at cross-purposes. I tried my best to resolve their differences, but failed. I also felt that Jamali could not cope with the demands of his office. People started jockeying for his position, realizing that he might not last. The nation was once again faced with uncertainty, which, given our recent economic upswing, we could ill afford. There were all sorts of rumors, including one that I would dissolve the

National Assembly. I had no such intention, of course; but facts have never stopped wild speculation from running rampant. Worse, the party could not agree on a replacement prime minister. When matters came to a head, I had to intervene. I had come to the conclusion that Shaukat Aziz, our successful finance minister, would make the best prime minister. But the difficulty was that Shaukat was in the Senate, and the prime minister has to be a member of the National Assembly. It was therefore decided that Jamali would resign as prime minister; that the party president, Chaudhry Shujat Hussain, would become prime minister for a couple of months; and that Shuakat Aziz would run in two by-elections (two for the sake of caution) for seats voluntarily vacated for him in the National Assembly.

I did not discuss any of this with Shaukat Aziz. He was simply presented with a fait accompli. On the day Jamali resigned, Shaukat was in Rawalpindi, setting a huge cache of narcotics on fire. Driving back to Islamabad, he received a call from my chief of staff, who, without telling him why, asked him to go immediately to Chaudhry Shujat Hussain—"And good luck to you," my chief of staff said at the end of the conversation. Shaukat was nonplussed. When he got there, Chaudhry Shujat remained mum, because I had told him not to reveal anything until Jamali formally announced his resignation. Shuakat Aziz was told only that the prime minister had resigned.

I had also requested that when Jamali announced his resignation, he should inform the nation that Shaukat Aziz would be prime minister and Chaudhry Shujat would hold the office for only an interim period. This Jamali failed to do, for whatever reason. I telephoned Shujat and told him to call a press conference immediately and give the whole plan to the nation. That is when Shaukat discovered that he had been earmarked for the second hottest seat in Pakistan, something that was brought home to him with a bang when the assassination attempt was made on him.

That evening I attended a small dinner at a friend's house, where Shaukat was also to be present. The dinner had been arranged days in advance, and not everyone present knew then that on this day Shaukat Aziz would be named as the future prime minister. When it came time for dinner, a woman asked, "But aren't we going to wait for Shaukat?" Obviously she hadn't heard the news. I could not help smiling, and I said, "Shaukat will be coming late." He actually arrived after dinner. When he did, I stood up, embraced him, and asked all the guests: "Let us give a good round of applause to the new prime minister."

To the credit of Jamali, I would like to say that he was extremely loyal to me and his cooperative role in the changeover was most praise worthy. In him I have a good friend. After the change I had a family get-together with him, at his house, where I expressed my gratitude to him for his services to Pakistan.

Our party system is still evolving. There were innumerable factions of the Pakistan Muslim League that had splintered away at different times and for various reasons. There were also a number of other small parties. It was always my desire to consolidate like-minded political parties, so as to have a smaller number of them. I started an effort in this direction, approaching several friendly factional leaders. I was very glad to see a positive response. The finale of this exercise was my calling all the concerned leaders and asking them to give up their small fiefs in favor of one Pakistan Muslim League. They were all gracious enough to agree.

Who was to be the president of the party? I felt very honored when all the leaders said that they would accept anyone I nominated. After due consideration of all the pros and cons I decided in favor of Chaudhry Shujat Hussain. The participants, without exception, agreed with my choice again.

As I said, our system still has a long way to go before achieving stability and true democracy. But we are making progress, slowly but surely, from election to election. True democracy will dawn when each political party introduces genuine democracy within itself, when a party's federal and provincial council members are elected by party workers and in turn elect the various party office holders.

The blown-up bridge, after the assassination attempt of December 14, 2003

The blown-up gas station, after the assassination attempt of December 25, 2003

The recovered face of one bomber provided a key break in the investigation

Childhood

With my father and my brothers,
Javed (*right*) and Naved (*center*)

With my parents and brothers

Just before entering the Pakistan
Military Academy

As a newly commissioned officer
of the Pakistan Army

As a young officer with my brothers,
Naved (*center*) and Javed (*right*)

Sehba Musharraf

With Sehba, as newlyweds

Ayla (*left*) and Bilal (*right*)

As a lieutenant colonel,
with Sehba, Ayla, and Bilal

With Sehba, as brigadier general,
during my stay at the National
Defense College

With Sehba, Ayla, and Bilal

As a major general

With my parents,
Sehba, and children

As a brigadier general, with Sehba,
at the Shangrila Hotel in Skardu,
in the Northern Areas

Receiving Prime Minister Nawaz Sharif in the Kel sector of Kashmir, south of the Kargil sector, before the Kargil conflict, February 5, 1999

The Corps Commander for the Northern Areas and Kashmir briefing Prime Minister Nawaz Sharif and his key cabinet members, February 5, 1999

Prime Minister Nawaz Sharif addressing the troops in the Kel sector of Kashmir, February, 5, 1999

As chief executive,
chairing a meeting
with my first cabinet

Casting my vote during
the referendum of 2000,
accompanied by my mother
and Sehba

Waving to the crowd during
the Centenary Convention
of the PML party

Arriving at the National Day Parade, March 2005

Inspecting an aircraft at the Pakistan Aeronautical Complex

Addressing a large gathering in the Northwest Frontier Province

Inspecting the rehabilitation of the Sukkur Barrage, on the Indus River in Sindh

At the groundbreaking of the Diamer Bhasha Dam, April 2006

Inspecting construction work at the Mirani Dam in Balochistan

At the home of polo: Shandur, the highest polo ground in the world

With the National Cricket Team's captain

Meeting with the National Junior Squash Team

Always a sportsman: Working to develop the army's first water-sports club, in Mangla, North Punjab

With H.R.H. Prince Karim
Aga Khan, a great friend
of Pakistan

Coming out of the
Holy Kaaba, Mecca

With the custodian of
the two holy mosques,
King Abdullah bin
Abdul Aziz

With U.N. Secretary General
Kofi Annan, September 2004

Reviewing the Guard of Honor
in the Great Hall of the People,
Beijing, with President Hu Jintao
of the People's Republic of china

With Sehba at Panda Park
in Chengdu, China, 2006

With Sehba, Tony Blair,
and Mrs. Cherie Blair

With President George W. Bush
at Camp David

With Sehba, President Bush,
and Mrs. Laura Bush at Camp David

Former U.S. President Bill Clinton visited Pakistan after the earthquake of 2005

With Sehba, Australian Prime Minister John Howard, and Mrs. Janet Howard

With Japanese Prime Minister Junichiro Koizumi

With French President Jacques Chirac

With Indian Prime Minister
Dr. Manmoham Singh

With India's former Prime Minister
Atal Bihari Vajpayee, 2002

With Indian President
Dr. Abdul Kalam and
Prime Minister Manmoham
Singh, 2005

At the Taj Mahal with Sehba

Visiting the collapsed Margalla Towers in Islamabad after the earthquake of 2005

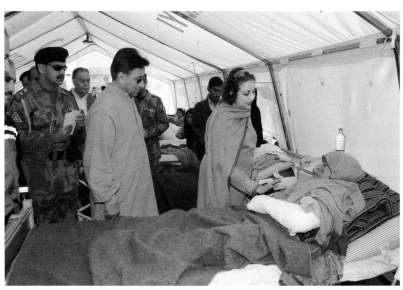
Visiting an earthquake victim in a field hospital in Muzaffarabad

CHAPTER 19

KICK-STARTING THE ECONOMY

The item at the top of my agenda in 1999 was the revival of Pakistan's sick economy. I have already described how our new team helped define our problems. Here, I will delve into some of the specifics, enough to convey a sense of what we faced, and what we have achieved.

Commercial banks and other financial institutions were riddled with cronyism. Public-sector enterprises were grossly mismanaged, and they formed a large part of our economy, including such companies as the Water and Power Development Authority, the Karachi Electric Supply Corporation, Pakistan Railway, Pakistan Steel Mills, Pakistan National Shipping Corporation, Pakistan International Airlines, the Cotton Export Corporation, and the Rice Export Corporation of Pakistan.

The persistence of large fiscal and current-account deficits, and the consequent public and external debt, were a major source of macroeconomic imbalance in the 1990s. Tax revenues and exports were stagnant. Foreign-exchange inflows were declining.

Many people began to talk of Pakistan as a failed state. Our growth was slowing; investment rates were decelerating; and the external debt burden was ballooning, having grown from $20 billion to $39 billion between 1988 and 1999. We were overwhelmed by the cost of debt servicing, and our physical and human infrastructure was in distress. Poverty had almost doubled, from 18 percent in 1988 to 34 percent in 1999.

As a novice in economic policy making and management, I devoted my initial few months to assembling a team of technocrats in the fields of finance, commerce, trade, banking, and privatization so as to understand what really happened during the 1990s that had led to such a disastrous outcome. Only then could we formulate a strategy for economic revival. I outlined the broad framework of this strategy to the nation on December 15, 1999, but kept adjusting and fine-tuning it over the next six years. I wanted to ensure that our economic direction was clearly defined and known to everyone, particularly those in the private sector who had to make investment decisions, produce goods and services, and engage in trade.

With the help of my advisers, I realized early on that we had to avoid quick fixes and make some very tough decisions. I paid no heed to those who advised me that these decisions would cost me politically and my popularity would suffer. It was high time that we did the right things for the sake of our national interest rather than for personal or parochial interests. The strategy that emerged consisted of four objectives:

1. Achieving macroeconomic stability.
2. Making structural reforms to remove microeconomic distortions.
3. Improving the quality of economic governance.
4. Alleviating poverty.

We focused on these four objectives as part of an integrated strategy, because macroeconomic stability in the absence of structural reforms would prove to be short-lived. Structural reforms cannot be successfully implemented if the quality of economic governance remains poor. The ultimate objective of all our efforts to revive the economy remained the alleviation of poverty. I was convinced that the interconnections between these four objectives were strong and that they had to be pursued together. This approach, of course, posed a dilemma. The results of such a strategy would not be visible for a few years. The majority of the people had been suffering hardship for almost a decade and wanted results now. They had run out of patience. Nonetheless, I decided that I owed it to my country to provide a sustainable solution to our economic ills, even if it incurred some short-term displeasure.

Luck was not on our side in the initial few years, and the economy suffered serious shocks and reversals. An unprecedented drought lasted three years, hurting our agriculture and the rural economy. A global recession slowed demand for our exports. On top of everything else, India mobilized its troops on our borders, and we were forced to retaliate, putting a further strain on our economy. Despite these shocks we remained steadfast on our chosen course and pursued our strategy.

We invited Pakistani experts from both outside and inside the country to advise us in critical areas. A former official of the World Bank headed a task force to recommend reforms in our tax system. This task force proposed ways to widen the tax base, document the economy, and bring eligible taxpayers into the tax net, partly by automating the tax collection process and reducing the discretionary authority of tax collectors.

Another economist formerly with the World Bank headed the Debt Management Committee, which formulated a strategy for external debt management. A retired top government official submitted a report on agricultural taxation. An Economic Advisory Board was formed comprising senior businessmen of the country, senior officials of the Finance Ministry, and the governor of the State Bank of Pakistan to make suggestions for removing the hurdles and obstacles facing the economy, through a policy of deregulation, liberalization, and privatization.

The governor of the State Bank spearheaded reforms in the financial and banking sector that not only have made our banking system healthy and efficient, but also for the first time have given middle- and lower-income groups access to banking credit. Interest rates, which were above 20 percent in the 1990s, were brought down dramatically to an average level of 5 percent, thus lowering the cost of doing business. This action, along with consumer, agricultural, and small- and medium-enterprise (SME) financing, was critical in stimulating the economy. Industrial capacity, which was lying idle in almost all sectors, was revived by making credit available on easy terms. Tariff rates on industrial machinery and raw materials were lowered. Exchange rates were tied to the market rather than administered directly; whereas in the past the rupee was continually devalued, we were now able to provide a stable exchange rate to our exporters and importers and to foreign investors.

One of the tough decisions we made in the year 2000 was to approach the International Monetary Fund (IMF) for assistance. I was quite aware that IMF programs were highly resented by the people of Pakistan, but we wanted to use the IMF to achieve our strategic objectives. Unfortunately, the problem in the past had been that the rulers entered into agreements with the IMF to draw down their financing, with no intention of implementing any of the agreed-on reforms. Pakistan was known as a one-tranche country: it drew down the first tranche, which is automatic upon approval by the IMF, and then abandoned its agreed-on program, including the remaining payments, because the rulers did not have the confidence or popularity to make some politically unpopular decisions.

Why did our government succeed in completing the IMF program ahead of time and then in saying good-bye to the fund? We had our own homegrown program of reforms that reflected our priorities and the realities of Pakistan. We developed our own strategy of implementation and then approached the IMF for assistance. Instead of taking the IMF's assistance by accepting its conditions, which are often divorced from Pakistan's reality, we sold the viability of our own strategy to the IMF and took assistance from it on that basis. The major advantage the country drew from having a credible program with the IMF was that our entire stock of external debt with bilateral creditors at the Paris Club (a consortium of developed European countries, North America, and Japan that extends loans to highly indebted countries under a collective arrangement) was restructured on highly favorable terms. The agreement granted a repayment period of thirty-eight years, with a fifteen-year grace period. In real terms this restructuring meant that our debt stock was reduced by at least 30 percent. Subsequent write-offs brought about a further reduction in the value of our external debt obligations. To my mind, it was simply absurd that we had to spend almost 66 percent of our revenues in servicing our debt. I told my economic managers that this situation was untenable and thus unacceptable and they had to take steps to reverse it: i.e., debt servicing should be reduced to the 22–25 percent range while public-sector investments should be tripled. The Pakistani people needed water reservoirs, lining of watercourses, roads and highways, ports and terminals, electricity and gas, schools, health clinics, and safe drinking water. Our growing urban centers such as Karachi and Lahore required major improvements. We could do none of this unless we diverted resources from debt servicing.

To the credit of my economic managers, we paid off all our most expensive loans; secured debt relief; obtained new, favorable loans; and paid off the remaining foreign currency deposits owed to foreign banks and financial institutions. All this gave us the fiscal space for public investment. Furthermore, our credit ratings have improved significantly in recent years. Pakistan is perhaps the only developing country that has graduated out of the IMF program and directly entered the international financial markets. The lesson that I draw for Pakistan and other countries from our relationship with the IMF is that we should not shift the blame for our own inadequacies onto the IMF and use it as a scapegoat. If you know what you are doing and have a coherent strategy of your own, the IMF and other international financial institutions can be deployed for the greater good of the country. When we are not ourselves sincere in our intentions and have no appetite to fulfill our obligations and responsibilities, it is no use blaming others.

In the area of economic governance our main endeavor was to level the playing field and close loopholes that favored a select, privileged few. The ad hoc system of regulations, which dominated our decision making in the 1990s, was replaced by a transparent, uniform, across-the-board system. Accountability mechanisms were strengthened, and people found guilty of corruption were taken to task irrespective of their status and connections. This deterrent effect has reduced corruption at the higher levels of policy makers. I cannot claim that we have been able to get rid of corruption at the middle and lower levels, but we have made a good beginning.

During the first two or three years, when we were working hard on macroeconomic stabilization, there was a lot of criticism of our policies. I was quite blunt in my public pronouncements and always maintained that growth would take place only when macroeconomic stability was firmly established. After stabilization, when growth picked up as predicted, the critics shifted their stance: now they bellyached that unemployment and poverty had not been reduced. Now that both the unemployment rate and poverty have begun to decrease, there is a hue and cry that income inequalities are sharpening. It is true that high growth brings some bad side effects, such as inflation and temporary income inequalities, but these problems can be taken care of by the right policy instruments.

In one of my very early briefings, I was told that all our major economic woes flowed from our high deficits. My immediate question was: "What is our main source of income, and where do we mainly spend?" The answer was that our spending was largely on ourselves—apart from debt servicing, this spending involved the costs of government and defense along with subsidies to virtually all public-sector corporations that were hemorrhaging in the amount of almost $2 billion per year. Our earnings came mainly from taxes.

The goal became clear. We had to reduce expenditures. I cut the budget, froze the defense budget, and appointed able people to lead all the government enterprises. Freezing the defense budget was the toughest decision. We did it in spite of India's increasing its budget manifold, and in spite of the near war hysteria created in 2002 when India amassed its forces on the border for ten months. I had only one question to ask of the new directors of public-sector enterprises, whom I had selected carefully: "Can you turn this setup around to profit instead of loss?" If the answer was a confident "yes," the man was selected. I must say most of them delivered. They turned their enterprises around. The steel mill, which had been running at a loss of billions of rupees virtually since its inception, became profitable in billions; the Pakistan National Shipping Corporation, which was losing billions, recovered and got into a position to buy two oil tankers with its own income. Also, the railways, the Water and Power Development Authority, Pakistan Television, and several smaller government concerns turned their red ink into black or at least checked their decline considerably.

Once I had taken action to cut expenses, my next worry was to increase earnings. Generating more revenue was easier said than done. The people of Pakistan were not at all accustomed to paying taxes. We had a very narrow base bearing the heavy load of perpetually increasing taxes. I decided against levying additional taxes and instead moved in favor of broadening the tax base. This involved documenting our economy. I called on teams of personnel from the army and the Central Board of Revenue. They started visiting all businesses and asking these businesses to fill out tax forms. That led to a serious confrontation with shopkeepers and traders, who came out on the streets and refused to comply. They even hid their goods in secret warehouses and stores, removing them from the shops to avoid evaluation by the visiting revenue teams. Law and order broke down in several places, leading to ugly scenes between traders and the law enforcement agencies.

I came under tremendous pressure to back off, but I refused. I was convinced that without broadening the tax net we could not reduce the fiscal deficit or generate funds for our vastly ignored development needs. I bore the brunt of all the traders' daily strikes for months. I toured several large cities, meeting with industrialists and traders and asking them to see reason. Ultimately we wore them down, partly by incorporating some of their suggestions for improving our new system. The drive was hugely successful, though I certainly cannot claim that we have caught all the defaulters in the tax net. We eased up when we realized that we could catch the rest of them in the tax net by using less visible or obvious methods through the Central Board of Revenue.

All in all, we brought the deficit down from around 8 percent (it had even crossed into double figures in the mid-1990s) to under 4 percent. Revenues increased from 302 billion rupees in 2000 to 700 billion rupees in 2006, an increase of over 130 percent in five years. This was no mean achievement compared with the eleven-year period from 1988 to 1999, when revenue increased by only 50 percent, from 200 billion rupees to 302 billion rupees. What made me really proud of this achievement was the fact that the upsurge in revenue collection did not require any increase in the rates or incidence of taxes. In fact, we reduced tax rates on several items as well as the number of taxes.

All these improvements gave us funds for projects in our Public Sector Development Program (PSDP). Between 1988 and 1999, PSDP remained stagnant between 90 billion and 110 billion rupees. In 2006 the allocation stands at 300 billion rupees—an increase of 300 percent.

In 1999 we had an alarming deficit of approximately $5 billion in our external balance of payments. This had forced us to borrow every year from international financial institutions. The point came when we had to take short-term commercial loans at unaffordable interest rates because we could not do without them, as no institution offering better terms was prepared to lend to us any longer.

I saw that earnings came from exports of approximately $8 billion (they never crossed $9 billion in our history); remittances from expatriate Pakistanis, which stood below a paltry $1 billion per annum; and foreign direct investment (FDI), which was negligibly low at $300 million. Our expenditure was mainly in approximately $10 billion of annual imports and debt servicing at a whopping $5 billion per annum. No wonder there was a persistent deficiency of $5 billion to $6 billion every year.

I launched a concerted drive to rectify this serious imbalance. Reducing the import bill was not in our interest, because the expenditure was mainly on industrial needs and other essential, irreducible items. Major foreign exchange spending was on the import of petroleum and petroleum products, the price of which is not in our hands and the demand for which is price-inelastic; and on tea and edible oil, both of which are staples for the poor and fairly inelastic too. The only expense to be reduced was debt servicing, and as mentioned earlier, we managed to achieve that reduction. Ironically, 9/11 came to our rescue. With Pakistan joining the coalition against terrorism, we earned the sympathy of the Paris Club. On the whole, the entire package resulted in the reduction of our annual debt servicing liability from $5 billion to $2 billion.

All these changes helped set the stage for growth, but I knew we needed to encourage specific revenue. We took each source of earning separately and strategized on how to increase it. Exports could be increased only if we became more aggressive in marketing our products. Our exports were mainly focused on agriculture and textiles. There was no value addition in the former, and the latter, I came to know, accounts for only 6 to 8 percent of total world trade. Sixty-one percent of total world trade is in heavy industry, engineering, and the high-technology sectors. It was patently obvious that we needed to emphasize an export-led industrial sector. We redid our entire tariff structure to shift the focus from merely facilitating trade to encouraging indigenous industry. This I knew was a long-term measure, but I am proud to see our changed focus paying off. Our industrial growth was 18.2 percent in

2004 and 14.6 percent in 2005. In the short term we needed to diversify our goods and markets. We reinvigorated the Export Promotion Bureau (EPB) under its dynamic chairman, Tariq Ikram. High-quality ministers in commerce and industries working in tandem with the EPB did the trick of boosting our exports. In 2006 we have achieved a target of over $18 billion—an increase of around 125 percent in five years. That, by any standards, is no mean achievement.

Foreign direct investment (FDI) had almost dried up. In 1999 it stood at a pitiable $300 million. In 2001, when I was discussing Pakistan's debt and investment problems with Premier Zhu Rongji of China, he offered a helpful perspective. Investors, he said, are like pigeons. When a government frightens them with poor decisions, they all fly off together. When the government improves its policies to attract them back, they return only one by one. He advised me to persevere and they would return. Then he observed that Pakistan seemed to be suffering from what he called a "debt and investment dilemma." On debt, he said, "Your dilemma is that you must *not* borrow, because it increases your debt servicing liability, but you *must* borrow if you wish to develop rapidly." As to investment, he said, "Your dilemma is that you want to draw in FDI to increase your sagging foreign exchange reserves, but the investor looks at the health of your foreign exchange reserves before he invests."

I personally spearheaded the campaign to increase our exports and FDI. First we adopted the course of deregulation, liberalization, and privatization. We created strong regulatory mechanisms to ensure transparency and checks and to provide a level playing field for all investors in all sectors of the economy. We also introduced rules and regulations to create a very investor-friendly environment. Armed with these positive environmental changes, I met with business communities wherever I went around the world to increase trade, joint ventures, and investment in Pakistan. We achieved phenomenal success. In 2005 FDI crossed $1.5 billion, up 500 percent from 1999. We appointed an able, dynamic young man as investment minister, and I personally started chairing joint meetings of investors and government stakeholders to remove bureaucratic obstacles across the table. Our few hotels had been nearly empty during the "dreadful decade of democracy." Now occupancy rates are 100 percent, and this situation has attracted many famous international hoteliers to build more four- and five-star hotels. There is also a simultaneous rush of investors in other booming (and blooming) sectors of our economy. I know our policies are bearing fruit, and investment in 2006 should touch $3 billion—ten times more than in 1999.

The third area that needed to be put right was remittances from expatriate Pakistanis. When we compared our performance with other countries that have large expatriate populations, we realized that our level of remittances, which was around $1 billion, was appallingly low. The main reason for this, I found, was the efficiency of the *hawala* or *hundi* system: the informal, underground system of transferring money from expatriates to their relatives in Pakistan. While the informal system took only one day to deliver money, even to remote villages, our banks would take no less than seven days and were not even easily accessible. This lazy, careless bureaucratic attitude was inevitable because our banks were nationalized. We pushed the banks to reform, to ensure access to Pakistanis abroad and to transfer their money faster. We got the post office, which had far greater access to the people, to integrate itself in the banking system to improve services. In addition to all these corrective actions, 9/11 resulted in a remittance boon. The international law enforcement community focused on the financial underworld and started tightening the screws. The informal *hawala* operators were hounded. As a result of fast, improved banking services and my personal interventions, motivating expatriate Pakistanis wherever I went to reinstill confidence in them, expatriates started using banks for their remittances. Perhaps the most important factor, at least psychologically, was the continuing stability of the rupee, minimizing the difference between the official exchange rate and the unofficial rate. It was no longer worthwhile to use the risky informal system, especially now that the hassles at banks had been reduced considerably. Our remittances soared to over $4 billion in 2005—up 400 percent from 1999.

Our efforts to address the external balance-of-payments deficit resulted in a surplus of $2 billion in 2004.

Because we were highly successful in reducing the fiscal deficit and converting the current account deficit into a surplus, our economy started showing a very healthy recovery and even went into overdrive. All macroeconomic indicators became positive.

History judges leaders by results. Let my results do the talking, through a look at what I inherited in 1999 and what we achieved by 2005.

In 1999, we were on the verge of default. The dreaded words "failed state" were on everyone's lips. That is a distant memory now. The economy is on an upsurge.

Our gross domestic product (GDP) has risen from $65 billion to $125 billion—almost double in five years—and we now are in a different league altogether. International financial institutions look on us very differently and with respect.

The growth in GDP rose from 3.1 percent to a healthy 8.4 percent in 2005. We will achieve 7 percent in 2006 in spite of the negative effect of rising oil prices and the reconstruction effort following the earthquake.

Our overall foreign debt has been reduced from $39 billion to $36 billion.

With such a reduction in debt and such a rise in GDP, the critical debt-to-GDP ratio fell from an unhealthy 101 percent to a much healthier 59 percent. A fiscal responsibility law has been passed, making it illegal for future governments to become indebted beyond 60 percent of GDP.

Per capita income has risen from $460 to $800. We are now in the middle-income category of countries—up from the low-income category.

Foreign exchange reserves have risen from a paltry $300 million (equal to two weeks of imports) to $12.5 billion (equal to ten months of imports).

Exports are hitting $17 billion for 2006, whereas they were only $7.8 billion in 1999.

Our imports have increased phenomenally. Our import bill is still more than our export earnings, but I am happy to say that the rise in imports has been healthy and positive, because apart from the near-doubling of our demand for oil, most of the rest of our import expenditure is on capital goods. We are bringing in machinery for building new factories and infrastructure and for expanding and modernizing existing facilities. This, I believe, is short-term deficit for long-term surplus, because most of the new factories will produce goods either for export or as substitutes for goods that we are importing. Such investment creates many job opportunities as well. I know that in some industries middle management and certain kinds of skilled workers are already hard to come by. We are prospecting for oil and gas on a very large scale, and increasing our hydroelectricity generation with the building of five big dams, so our bill for imported oil will come down. The fact that we are converting our power generation plants from imported furnace oil to indigenous natural gas is beginning to make a difference as well. And when gas and oil pipelines, possibly from Iran, Qatar, or Turkmenistan, go through Pakistan to China and—we hope—India, we will earn transit fees. Further, not only can we use some of the oil and gas being transported in these pipelines ourselves, we can use the pipelines to export our own oil and gas when we have a surplus.

Revenue collection has increased from $5.1 billion to $11.7 billion. This phenomenal increase of 130 percent is not from an increase in the number or rates of taxes. Rather, it is due to a reduction in the number and rates of taxes, broadening of the tax base, rationalization of the tax regime, documentation of the economy, and introduction of a self-assessment scheme that has reduced the interface between the taxpayer and tax collector, thus decreasing opportunities for corruption. All these factors have contributed to the huge increase in revenue.

Our external debt and liabilities were a disastrous 347 percent of our total foreign exchange earnings. This figure has now been brought down to 137 percent. We are a far cry from 1999, when Pakistan compared poorly even against the "highly indebted poor countries" (HIPCs), whose ratio of debt is over 250 percent of foreign exchange earnings. It would have been a sorry day for our ego had we, a nuclear and missile state, been put in the HIPC category.

Remittances jumped 400 percent, from $1 billion to over $4 billion.

The strong position of our foreign exchange reserves stabilized the eroding rupee. Under my watch, the exchange rate has hovered around sixty rupees to one U.S. dollar over the last four years.

The 100 Index of the Karachi stock exchange, which remained bearish at under 1,000 points, has become constantly bullish, rising to around 11,500 points in 2006. Some say this is the best-performing stock exchange in the world.

Pakistan has also joined the international capital markets for the first time. We first offered euro bonds in Europe and Asia, then launched Islamic bonds in the Gulf and the Middle East, and finally offered dollar bonds in the United States and Europe. All these were oversubscribed by renowned private investment houses. In fact, our dollar bonds drew loans of hundreds of million dollars for long-term durations: ten to thirty years. The very fact that private ventures are prepared to extend loans to Pakistan for such long terms at interests rates of merely 2 percent above U.S. government rates shows the confidence of the international financial community in Pakistan's rising economy.

Our credit rating in Moody's and Standard and Poor's (S&P) had hit rock bottom in 1999. It has now moved up to B+ with Moody's and BB with S&P.

The downside of the sudden upsurge in the economy was a rise in prices. The income of the salaried class and the earnings of others have improved, resulting in increased purchasing power and thus increasing the demand-supply gap. This has caused an upward trend in inflation, which had neared almost 10 percent but has now been brought down to around 7 percent. The sharp rise in international oil prices has played its part as well. This has been a cause of considerable worry for the government and for me personally because at the end of the day the masses form opinions about the government based more on price rises than on macroeconomic gains. I remain conscious of this and am sensitive to the dire need to check inflation.

No efforts to revive the economy will be complete unless the macroeconomic gains are transferred to the masses as improved living standards. The best way to improve people's living conditions is to enhance their earnings by providing them with gainful employment, opening up avenues for self-employment, scaling up investment in human capital, and maximizing the impact of existing public spending on education and health. Central to achieving this objective is the promotion of stronger economic growth.

Ending poverty is an imperative, not a choice. Alleviation of poverty demands understanding clearly where poverty actually resides and then deciding how each area is to be addressed. Pakistan is an agrarian society, with over 65 percent of the population living in rural areas. This majority depends on basic agriculture and animal husbandry for sustenance and bears the brunt of poverty. In the remaining 35 percent of the people—the urban population—poverty can be subdivided into the educated unemployed and the uneducated unemployed. Both categories needed help and rectification.

Logically, the main effort for rural uplift had to go to the agricultural sector. The major constraint in Pakistan's agriculture has been the availability, or unavailability, of irrigation. In this connection, my government launched over 300 billion rupees' worth of water-related projects, most of which are likely to be completed during the next two to three years. These projects include the construction of various canals and dams, the lining of watercourses with bricks to stop leakage and spillage, and the upgrading of the irrigation and drainage systems. After the completion of these projects, 2.88 million acres of new land will be available for cultivation, allowing a quantum leap in agricultural growth, increasing the incomes of farmers, providing more jobs for the rural workforce, and reducing poverty in rural areas.

We cannot be satisfied with just bringing additional areas under cultivation, however. We also have to conserve water and ensure its optimum utilization. This we are doing by launching an extensive laser leveling program for all agricultural land (to prevent waste of water by finely calibrating the level of land) and encouraging modern drip irrigation (to save water). The brick lining of our watercourses, costing $1 billion, will be a major contributor to water conservation. We have also concentrated on yield intensification to increase the per-acre output of crops and thus multiply farmers' earnings. I introduced a farmers' welfare package to encourage increased production. By ensuring that farmers would have easy access to banks, we have increased agricultural loans by 500 percent; we have also introduced an ingenious easy-to-return three-year revolving-credit system for them. This has saved farmers from the cruel clutches of the middleman to whom he once had to sell his crops very cheaply in order to repay his loan on time.

All these measures have greatly increased agricultural output. We have had bumper cotton and wheat crops, breaking all previous records. But this still did not give me the satisfaction of having done enough for the poorest segment of our society. We evolved a long-term plan as well. Pakistan happens to be the world's fifth largest producer of milk, but we produce hardly any other dairy goods. We also have some of the best fruit in the world, and high-quality vegetables, but we are not adding value to them for export. I have made a deliberate decision to launch agro-based industries in the rural areas. We have initiated a "white revolution" by launching a special milk collection and chiller storage system. This will encourage a modern dairy industry to spring up, producing cheese, yogurt, butter, and milk powder for local consumption and export. We are also encouraging food and fruit processing to add value to our exports and contribute toward job creation for the rural workforce.

I am quite satisfied with our efforts for rural uplift. But addressing the issue of educated unemployed youth in the country in general and the urban areas in particular has always remained high in my thoughts. Information technology and the telecommunication industries are two of our major drivers of economic growth because of their enormous potential for creating jobs in urban areas. This sector has witnessed unprecedented growth during the last four and a half years and has emerged as a major source of foreign investment, thanks to the development efforts and reforms that we have introduced.

In 1999, only thirty-nine cities in Pakistan were connected to the Internet. By 2006, 2,000 cities and towns were connected to it. In 1999, fiber-optic connectivity was limited to only about forty towns; today 1,000 towns have it. Bandwidth costs for the transmission of two megabytes per second have been reduced from $87,000 to $1,400. Pakistan's telecom industry has been a major success story. In only three years, from 2003 to 2006, teledensity, which is the number of telephones as a percentage of the population, has increased from a meager 2.9 percent to 16 percent; cell phones have increased from 600,000 to over 30 million; and wireless local loop is taking root in the rural areas.

Information technology (IT) and telecommunications are bridging the digital divide not only across the globe but within the country as well. They are playing an important role in Pakistan's socioeconomic development. The extraordinary growth in the IT and telecom sectors has created enormous employment opportunities, directly and indirectly, for educated youth at call centers, in telecom engineering, as telecom salespersons, in customer service, in finance, in accounting, and so forth. This is one of the fastest-growing sectors of the economy, and its pace is likely to accelerate even more in the years to come.

Last but not least come our efforts to create jobs and alleviate poverty among the urban uneducated unemployed. We thought that industry, together with building and construction, would generate the maximum number of jobs. Building and construction are particularly labor-intensive and therefore ideally suited to the uneducated unemployed. We took special measures to encourage this industry. Our actions and strategy paid dividends. Today there is a boom in both these sectors, and the demand for labor is so high that workers' incomes have automatically shot up. As far as labor and other construction-related personnel like draftsmen are concerned, it is a seller's market.

While working toward improving the country's macroeconomic indicators and initiating wide-ranging structural reforms, my government was never oblivious to the plight of the deserving segments of society. We continued to pursue targeted intervention to address the problems of poverty and to generate income and employment through our public works program and our food support program, by providing microcredit, by distributing *zakat* (charity) and so on. Strong macroeconomic gains allowed us to raise development spending annually from less than 100 billion rupees to 300 billion rupees in just six years. These resources are being utilized to create jobs, improve education and health services, and strengthen the country's physical infrastructure. As a result, for the first time in our history, poverty and unemployment are showing a downward turn.

PART FIVE

THE WAR ON TERROR

CHAPTER 20

ONE DAY THAT CHANGED THE WORLD

September 11, 2001, was an uneventful day in Pakistan, at least while the sun was high. That evening I was in Karachi, inspecting work at the beautiful gardens of the mausoleum of our founder Quaid-e-Azam Mohammad Ali Jinnah. I was happy to be in the city I love. Little did I know that on the other side of the globe, yet another event involving aircraft was about to alter the course of my life, and the course of Pakistan. Little did I know that we were about to be thrust into the front line of yet another war, a war against shadows.

Nearly two years earlier, at the start of my hijacking crisis, my military secretary had whispered in my ear that the pilot of my flight wanted me in the cockpit. Now he came up to me again and whispered: an aircraft had crashed into one of the towers of the World Trade Center in New York City. I had been familiar with the World Trade Center ever since terrorists had tried to blow it up in 1993. They had done considerable damage and six people were killed. One of the masterminds of that attack, Ramzi Yousef, had fled to Pakistan and had been arrested by our security service in 1995.

At first, I dismissed the news report as an accident involving what I thought must have been a light private aircraft. I continued with my inspection. But at the back of my mind there was the nagging thought that this had to be a most peculiar accident. Either the pilot had to be utterly inept to have hit such a tall building, or the plane had to be so totally out of control that it couldn't be prevented from hitting the tower.

When I returned home, I went directly into a meeting with Karachi's corps commander. We were deeply engrossed in discussion when my military secretary slipped into the room and started fiddling with the television set.

"What is the urgency?" I asked, a bit irritated.

"Please watch what's on television, sir," he said.

He had found CNN. I could not believe what I saw. Smoke was billowing out of both towers of the World Trade Center. People were jumping out of windows. There was sheer panic, utter chaos. It was not a light private aircraft that had been involved but two fuel-laden commercial Boeings full of passengers. The planes had been hijacked and deliberately crashed into the twin towers. This could hardly be an accident—it had to be a deliberate, brazen act of terrorism. I learned that two other aircraft had also been hijacked—one had hit the Pentagon; another had gone down in a field in Pennsylvania. Commentators at the time said that second one had been heading for the White House. This was war.

We were still glued to the television when we saw one tower go down, and a few minutes later the second. It was unbelievable. Smoke from burning aircraft fuel and the dust and debris from the largest buildings in the world made the scene look like a nuclear explosion.

The enormity of the event was palpable. The world's most powerful country had been attacked on its own soil, with its own aircraft used as missiles. This was a great tragedy, and a great blow to the ego of the superpower. America was sure to react violently, like a wounded bear. If the perpetrator turned out to be al Qaeda, then that wounded bear would come charging straight toward us. Al Qaeda was based in neighboring Afghanistan under the protection of those international pariahs, the Taliban. Not only that: we were the only country maintaining diplomatic relations with the Taliban and their leader, Mullah Omar. September 11 marked an irrevocable turn from the past into an unknown future. The world would never be the same.

I went to the Governor House. The foreign office advised me to give a statement. I wrote one quickly and said on national television that we condemned this vile act, that we were against all forms of terrorism and stood with America at this appalling time, and that we would assist it in any way we could.

•   •   •

The next morning I was chairing an important meeting at the Governor's House when my military secretary told me that the U.S. secretary of state, General Colin Powell, was on the phone. I said I would call back later, but he insisted that I come out of the meeting and take the call. Powell was quite candid: "You are either with us or against us." I took this as a blatant ultimatum. However, contrary to some published reports, that conversation did not get into specifics. I told him that we were with the United States against terrorism, having suffered from it for years, and would fight along with his country against it. We did not negotiate anything. I had time to think through exactly what might happen next.

When I was back in Islamabad the next day, our director general of Inter Services Intelligence, who happened to be in Washington, told me on the phone about his meeting with the U.S. deputy secretary of state, Richard Armitage. In what has to be the most undiplomatic statement ever made, Armitage added to what Colin Powell had said to me and told the director general not only that we had to decide whether we were with America or with the terrorists, but that if we chose the terrorists, then we should be prepared to be bombed back to the Stone Age. This was a shockingly barefaced threat, but it was obvious that the United States had decided to hit back, and hit back hard.

I made a dispassionate, military-style analysis of our options, weighing the pros and cons. Emotion is all very well in drawing rooms, newspaper editorials, and movies, but it cannot be relied on for decisions like this. Underlying any leader's analysis has to be a keen awareness that on his decision hangs the fate of millions of people and the future of his country. It is at times like these that the leader is confronted by his acute loneliness. He may listen to any amount of advice he chooses, but at the end of the day the decision has to be his alone. He realizes then that the buck really stops with him—this is no facile cliché.

My decision was based on the well-being of my people and the best interests of my country—Pakistan always comes first. I war-gamed the United States as an adversary. There would be a violent and angry reaction if we didn't support the United States. Thus the question was: if we do not join them, can we confront them and withstand the onslaught? The answer was no, we could not, on three counts.

First was our military weakness as compared with the strength of the United States. Our military forces would be destroyed.

Second was our economic weakness. We had no oil, and we did not have the capacity to sustain our economy in the face of an attack by the United States.

Third, and worst of all, was our social weakness. We lack the homogeneity to galvanize the entire nation into an active confrontation. We could not endure a military confrontation with the United States from any point of view.

I also analyzed our national interest. First, India had already tried to step in by offering its bases to the United States. If we did not join the United States, it would accept India's offer. What would happen then? India would gain a golden opportunity with regard to Kashmir. The Indians might be tempted to undertake a limited offensive there; or, more likely, they would work with the United States and the United Nations to turn the present situation into a permanent status quo. The United States would certainly have obliged.

Second, the security of our strategic assets would be jeopardized. We did not want to lose or damage the military parity that we had achieved with India by becoming a nuclear weapons state. It is no secret that the United States has never been comfortable with a Muslim country acquiring nuclear weapons, and the Americans undoubtedly would have taken the opportunity of an invasion to destroy such weapons. And India, needless to say, would have loved to assist the United States to the hilt.

Third, our economic infrastructure, built over half a century, would have been decimated.

The ultimate question that confronted me was whether it was in our national interest to destroy ourselves for the Taliban. Were they worth committing suicide over? The answer was a resounding no. It is true that we had assisted in the rise of the Taliban after the Soviet Union withdrew from Afghanistan, which was then callously abandoned by the United States. For a while, at the embryonic stage, even the United States had approved of the Taliban. We had hoped that the Taliban, driven by religious zeal based on the true principles of Islam, would bring unity and peace to a devastated country. But they were fired by a misplaced messianic zeal inculcated in them by half-baked, obscurantist clerics, a zeal that was contrary to the moderate, tolerant, progressive spirit of Islam of the majority of the Pakistani people.

After the Taliban came to power, we lost much of the leverage we had had with them. The peace that they brought to Afghanistan was the peace of the graveyard. Nevertheless, we still supported them, for geostrategic reasons. If we had broken with them, that would have created a new enemy on our western border, or a vacuum of power there into which might have stepped the Northern Alliance, comprising anti-Pakistan elements. The Northern Alliance was supported by Russia, India, and Iran. Now we were no longer constrained by these concerns. We had new, more deadly ones. Now we could detach from the Taliban. In any case, they did not stand a chance. Why should we put our national interest on the line for a primitive regime that would be defeated?

On the other hand, the benefits of supporting the United States were many. First, we would be able to eliminate extremism from our society and flush out the foreign terrorists in our midst. We could not do this alone; we needed the technical and financial support of the United States to be able to find and defeat these terrorists. We had been victims of terrorism by the Taliban and al Qaeda and their associated groups for years. Earlier Pakistani governments had been hesitant about taking on the militant religious groups that were spreading extremism and fanaticism in our country. General Zia had openly courted them for political support, and Nawaz Sharif was in the process of setting himself up as "commander of the faithful," sort of a national imam. For my part, I have always been a moderate Muslim, never comfortable with the rhetoric or the ways of the extremists. I moved against them when I banned a number of extremist religious organizations in February 2001 because they were involved in sectarian militancy. But now here was a chance to confront them more boldly and openly. Second, even though being a frontline state fighting terrorism would deter foreign investment, there were certain obvious economic advantages, like loosening the stranglehold of our debt and lifting economic sanctions. Third, after being an outcast nation following our nuclear tests, we would come to center stage.

What of the domestic reaction? The mullahs would certainly oppose joining the United States and would come out into the streets. There would be an adverse reaction, too, in the North-West Frontier Province bordering Afghanistan, for obvious reasons. Sindh, specially Karachi, and Balochistan would be neutral or lukewarm. But what of the Punjab, which is the heart of Pakistan? Would it react negatively? I thought that by and large it would not. If I could make the Punjabis understand why I went with the United States, they would understand me—why unnecessarily take on a superpower, and for what? The Punjabis are a very pragmatic people. As for Karachi, which has many seminaries, some of which are run by extremists from the Frontier Province, there certainly would be some street protests. But the bulk of Karachi's people would not support it. So my considered opinion, based on the ethos of the country and the inclinations of the people I knew so well, was that there would be no unbearable reaction or street protests.

This was a ruthless analysis, deliberately devoid of emotion, which I made for the sake of my country. Richard Armitage's undiplomatic language, regrettable as it was, had nothing to do with my decision. The United States would do what it had to do in its national interest, and we would do what we had to in ours. Self-interest and self-preservation were the basis of this decision. Needless to say, though, I felt very frustrated by Armitage's remarks. It goes against the grain of a soldier not to be able to tell anyone giving him an ultimatum to go forth and multiply, or words to that effect. I have to say, though, that later I found Armitage to be a wonderful person and a good friend of Pakistan.

On September 13, 2001, the U.S. ambassador to Pakistan, Wendy Chamberlain, brought me a set of seven demands. These demands had also been communicated to our foreign office by the U.S. State Department through what is called a non-paper.

1. Stop al Qaeda operatives at your borders, intercept arms shipments through Pakistan, and end all logistical support for Bin Laden.
2. Provide the United States with blanket overflight and landing rights to conduct all necessary military and intelligence operations.
3. Provide territorial access to the United States and allied military intelligence as needed, and other personnel to conduct all neces-

sary operations against the perpetrators of terrorism and those that harbor them, including the use of Pakistan's naval ports, air bases, and strategic locations on borders.

4. Provide the United States immediately with intelligence, immigration information and databases, and internal security information, to help prevent and respond to terrorist acts perpetrated against the United States, its friends, or its allies.

5. Continue to publicly condemn the terrorist acts of September 11 and any other terrorist acts against the United States or its friends and allies, and curb all domestic expressions of support [for terrorism] against the United States, its friends, or its allies.

6. Cut off all shipments of fuel to the Taliban and any other items and recruits, including volunteers en route to Afghanistan, who can be used in a military offensive capacity or to abet a terrorist threat.

7. Should the evidence strongly implicate Osama bin Laden and the al Qaeda network in Afghanistan and should Afghanistan and the Taliban continue to harbor him and his network, Pakistan will break diplomatic relations with the Taliban government, end support for the Taliban, and assist the United States in the aforementioned ways to destroy Osama bin Laden and his al Qaeda network.

Some of these demands were ludicrous, like "curb all domestic expressions of support [for terrorism] against the United States, its friends, and its allies." Such a demand depends on the interpretation of what constitutes verbal support for terrorism and on the limits of dissent and freedom of expression. I found the expression "Should the evidence strongly implicate Osama bin Laden and the al Qaeda network in Afghanistan . . ." self-contradictory, because if the United States was still searching for evidence, how could it be so sure that "Osama bin Laden and the al Qaeda network in Afghanistan" were the perpetrators of 9/11? I also thought that asking us to break off diplomatic relations with Afghanistan if it continued to harbor Osama bin Laden and al Qaeda was not realistic, because not only would the United States need us to have access to Afghanistan, at least until the Taliban fell, but such decisions are the internal affair of a country and cannot be dictated by anyone. But there was no point in arguing over what seemed to be a hurriedly drafted document. We had no problem with curbing terrorism in all its forms and manifestations. We had been itching to do so before the United States became its victim.

We just could not accept demands two and three. How could we allow the United States "blanket overflight and landing rights" without jeopardizing our strategic assets? I offered only a narrow flight corridor that was far from any sensitive areas. Neither could we give the United States "use of Pakistan's naval ports, air bases, and strategic locations on borders." We refused to give any naval ports or fighter aircraft bases. We allowed the United States only two bases—Shamsi in Balochistan and Jacobabad in Sindh—and only for logistics and aircraft recovery. No attack could be launched from there. We gave no "blanket permission" for anything.

The rest of the demands we could live with. I am happy that the U.S. government accepted our counterproposal without any fuss. I am shocked at the aspersion being cast on me: that I readily accepted all preconditions of the United States during the telephone call from Colin Powell. He did *not* give any conditions to me. These were brought by the U.S. ambassador on the third day.

Having made my decision, I took it to the cabinet. As expected, there was some concern from the ministers that they had not been consulted. Doubts were also expressed in the corps commanders' meeting that followed. In both meetings I went over my analysis in detail and explained how and why I had come to this decision. I answered every question until all doubts were removed and everyone was on board. I then went on national radio and television on September 19 to explain my decision to the people. As I had thought, the reaction was limited and controllable.

Then I began meeting with a cross section of society. Between September 18 and October 3, I met with intellectuals, top editors, leading columnists, academics, tribal chiefs, students, and the leaders of labor unions. On October 18, I also met a delegation from China and discussed the decision with them. Then I went to army garrisons all over the country and talked to the soldiers. Everyone was rightly concerned that if Afghanistan was bombed, many innocent Muslim lives would be lost. I allayed this fear by saying that first we would try to persuade Mullah Omar to make Osama bin Laden and his top lieutenants leave Afghanistan; that way, Afghanistan could avoid any military strike by the United States.

It all came down to two men: Mullah Omar and Osama bin Laden.

CHAPTER 21

OMAR AND OSAMA

Mullah Omar and Osama bin Laden are perhaps the most notorious names in the world today. To most of the world they are terrorists; to those who are generally referred to as radicals, they are cult heroes. To almost everyone, they are enigmas. The world knows almost nothing about the nature and biography of Mullah Omar, the man who led the Taliban regime and, in my opinion, continues to run the remnants of the Taliban today. Much more is known about Osama bin Laden's life history, at least until five years ago. After that point, for most of the world, Osama dropped out of sight. Thanks to direct contacts and intelligence, I can now fill in some of these gaps for both men. Along the way, I will clarify some parts of the known record.

It has famously been said that "short-term gain for long-term pain" is foolhardy, but this is exactly what happened to the allies in the jihad against the Soviet occupation of Afghanistan, not least the United States, Pakistan, and Saudi Arabia. We helped create the mujahideen, fired them with religious zeal in seminaries, armed them, paid them, fed them, and sent them to a jihad against the Soviet Union in Afghanistan. We did not stop to think how we would divert them to productive life after the jihad was won. This mistake cost Afghanistan and Pakistan more dearly than any other country. Neither did the United States realize what a rich, educated person like Osama bin Laden might later do with the organization that we all had enabled him to establish. Worse, the United States didn't even consider the rebuilding and development of Afghanistan after the Soviets departed. America simply abandoned Afghanistan to its fate, ignoring the fact that a wretchedly poor and unstable country, armed to the teeth with the most sophisticated weapons and torn apart by warlords, could become an ideal haven for terrorists. The United States also ignored what might happen to Pakistan, now that the deadly drug heroin had been introduced into our country and we were awash with weapons of the most lethal kind. Worse, America imposed sanctions against us under the totally biased Pressler Amendment, passed in 1985, which banned military and economic assistance to Pakistan unless the president of the United States certified, year by year, that we did not possess a bomb. I cannot think of a better way of losing friends.

But I believe our greatest oversight was to forget that when you help to organize and use people fired by extraordinary religious or ideological zeal to achieve your objectives, you must consider that they might be using you to achieve their objectives and are only temporarily on your side for tactical reasons of their own. In Mullah Omar's case the objective was to gain power in Afghanistan. In the case of Osama bin Laden it was perhaps to get help from America, Pakistan, and Saudi Arabia to create al Qaeda, obtain funding and arms, and finally secure a base from which to operate. In such situations, who is using whom becomes murky. We—the United States, Pakistan, Saudi Arabia, and all those who were allied with us in the Afghan jihad—created our own Frankenstein's monster.

The Taliban were not a new, post-Soviet phenomenon. They were taught by the same teachers in the same seminaries that had produced the mujahideen. But now the label had changed. When we sided with the Taliban, it was for good reasons: first, that they would bring peace to Afghanistan by bringing the warlords to heel; second, that the success of the Taliban would spell the defeat of the anti-Pakistan Northern Alliance. There was nothing wrong with our intentions, except that we did not realize that once the Taliban had used us to get to power, we would lose influence with them.

Mullah Muhammad Omar was born in the village of Nauda, Kandahar, purportedly in 1959. He has four wives and four children—two sons and two daughters. One daughter was killed in August 1999 in a bomb blast.

Mullah Omar visited Pakistan for two weeks during the early part of the Afghan jihad against the Soviets, as an ordinary mujahideen foot soldier. During the jihad he joined a couple of mujahideen organizations, one after the other. It is said that during a battle one of his eyes was badly injured, and that he removed it himself with a knife (without anesthesia) and sewed his eyelid up. But others say that he was treated in a hospital in Peshawar and the eye was surgically removed. Many people naturally tend to believe the first, heroic version, which has contributed to the legend of Mullah Omar.

After the Soviet withdrawal in 1989 and up to 1994, Mullah Omar became an imam of a mosque in a small village of the Maiwand district, west of Kandahar. He saw the chaos that Afghanistan fell into after the capture of Kabul by the mujahideen in April 1992, with numerous warlords controlling different parts of the country. The public had little security from murder, rape, theft, and extortion.

The Taliban movement began in Maiwand in June 1994. It took off quite abruptly, mainly owing to the lawlessness in that area. It was sparked by a single incident: two young boys were abducted, viciously raped, and killed by an Afghan gangster turned checkpoint commander and his associates outside Kandahar. The public, already desperate, naturally became agitated and started protesting violently. Mullah Omar and his small, unknown band of Taliban rushed to the checkpoint, disarmed the violators, and killed some of them. The Taliban were seen as protectors of the defenseless against rapacious warlords and gangster officials. They then started cleaning up various areas. Their fame spread rapidly. Followers joined up within Afghanistan, and from certain seminaries in Pakistan, mainly in the North-West Frontier Province, Balochistan, and Karachi.

Mullah Omar was appointed *amir*—leader—of the Taliban in October 1994. In 1996, a grand assembly, also called a *shoora,* of 1,500 religious scholars held in Kandahar appointed him *amir-ul-momineen* or "commander of the faithful." By that time, after a swift offensive, the Taliban were already occupying 90 percent of Afghanistan.

The arrival of the Taliban on the scene was a spontaneous reaction to the chaos and lawlessness in Afghanistan and to the atrocities committed by former mujahideen commanders, warlords, and gangster officials. Though this movement began at home, the Pakistani government under Benazir Bhutto tried to take the credit for having created, raised, and launched it, in the hope that the Taliban's rapid military success would be to Pakistan's political advantage. Benazir Bhutto's interior minister, Major General Naseerullah Babur (retired), naively started calling the Taliban "my children." It was only later, when "his children" became disobedient, that Benazir's government disowned them. The truth is that the Taliban did not ask for or receive any help from Pakistan in their earliest stages.

The United States, I suspect, did not disapprove of the Taliban phenomenon for the same reason that we did not—the Americans hoped that the Taliban could bring peace and stability to Afghanistan. The governments of Saudi Arabia and the United Arab Emirates (UAE) may even have helped the Taliban discreetly, while their citizens helped openly with donations. Because of the stalemate between the warring tribal factions, the western powers in general and the United States in particular welcomed the emergence of a "third force," hoping for a return to some normality. When they later became disillusioned, it was easy for them to dissociate themselves from the Taliban.

Not so for us. The Taliban were all Pukhtoons from an area bordering Pakistan's North-West Frontier and Balochistan provinces, which also have an ethnic Pukhtoon population. We have strong ethnic and family linkages with the Taliban. The opponent of the Taliban was the Northern Alliance, composed of Tajiks, Uzbeks, and Hazaras, backed by Russia, India, and Iran. How could any Pakistani government be favorably inclined toward the Northern Alliance? Any such inclination would have caused serious strife and internal security problems for Pakistan.

We invited Mullah Omar to Pakistan a number of times after he gained power, but he always refused, citing wartime conditions in his country. We also offered to send him for *umra,* the small pilgrimage to Mecca, but he parried this offer too. He always met delegations from our intelligence agency but never allowed any of his field commanders to interact with us; he said they were continuously involved in operations. Thus our relations with the Taliban were never smooth; in fact, they were quite uncomfortable.

•   •   •

We could only watch in horror as the Taliban unleashed the worst abuses of human rights in Afghanistan under the cloak of their own peculiar interpretation of Islam, an interpretation that the majority of Muslims reject and which gives a bad name to a great religion. Once, visiting players of a Pakistani football team were arrested by the Taliban government for wearing shorts during a game, and their heads were shaved as punishment. The Taliban refused to allow women to step out of their homes, even to go to the market, and refused to allow girls to attend school.

They were infamous for torturing adulterers and murdering their enemies. Once they locked up a number of Iranians in a shipping container, let them starve and suffocate, and finally shot them with Kalashnikovs through the walls of the container.

Pakistan's first official interaction with Mullah Omar took place in the last week of October 1994 at a place called Spin Boldak on the Pakistan-Afghan border. The purpose of this first meeting was to seek safe passage for a Pakistani humanitarian and relief convoy. The meeting took place in an operations room during a battle against some mujahideen commanders. Omar bluntly refused at first, because of the ongoing fighting along the route, but toward the end of the meeting he agreed reluctantly. The convoy was hijacked later, but not by the Taliban.

After Osama bin Laden arrived in Jalalabad in southern Afghanistan in May 1996, Arabs from various countries who had left after the Afghan jihad started returning there to join him. They already knew him from the jihad days. They supported the fast-growing Taliban movement too. Soon Uzbeks, Bangladeshis, Chechens, Chinese Uygurs, and Muslims from south India, Europe, America, and even Australia started to arrive in Afghanistan to help the Taliban cause. The Al Rasheed Trust, based in Pakistan, was one of the main supporters of the Taliban movement and provided logistical and media help from Karachi.

On September 19, 1998, our director general of Inter Services Intelligence and Prince Turki Al Faisal, who was then the head of Saudi intelligence and is now his country's ambassador to Washington, met with Mullah Omar in Kandahar. This meeting came in the wake of al Qaeda's bombing of the U.S. embassies in Kenya and Tanzania.

The prince informed Mullah Omar about Osama bin Laden's involvement in the bombing, and shared information about his plans, luckily unearthed and foiled, to blow up the U.S. consulate in Jeddah. He reminded Omar that three months earlier, in June 1998, the Taliban had given a firm commitment to Saudi Arabia, through the prince, that they would expel Osama bin Laden from Afghanistan and hand him over to the Saudis. Yet they had done nothing. The prince also reminded Mullah Omar about Osama bin Laden's promise to the Taliban that he would not involve himself in any terrorist activities while he was in Afghanistan. This promise was belied by a press conference in Khost in 1998, at which Osama boasted of inspiring people to commit terrorist acts. Osama had also masterminded unrest in the Kingdom of Saudi Arabia. Yet the Taliban still had not handed him over to Saudi Arabia, as promised.

Our director general of Inter Services Intelligence also stressed to Mullah Omar that both Pakistan and Saudi Arabia had sincerely supported the jihad in Afghanistan against the Soviets. He said that his earnest advice to Mullah Omar was either to expel Osama from Afghanistan or hand him over to the government of his native country. The director general also told Mullah Omar that Osama's links inside Pakistan were a source of great concern. Dissociating from Osama would facilitate recognition of the Taliban government by other countries.

Mullah Omar surprised both the prince and our director general by responding that he had made no promises to Saudi Arabia. He was effectively calling the prince a liar. He launched into a litany of his own woes, complaining that his government was under tremendous pressure; that no other country would offer Osama asylum; and that he faced a threat from Iran, which was supporting the Northern Alliance against the Taliban. He complained that the Saudi government should have helped him at this critical juncture; instead, it was adding to the pressure on him over Osama.

The prince had remained calm till this point. Now he lost his composure. He pointed an accusatory finger at Omar. This did not go down well with Mullah Omar and the twenty or so raw Taliban guards in the room. Suddenly, Mullah Omar stood up and stalked out in fury. One of the guards followed him. Omar returned a few minutes later, his hair dripping with water, his shirt and sleeves drenched. "I went into the other room and poured cold water on my head to cool off," he told the prince. "If you had not been my guest I would have done something dire to you."

Omar proposed the formation of a council of Islamic scholars from Afghanistan and Saudi Arabia to decide Osama's fate. He bitterly objected to the presence of American troops on Saudi soil, which was also one of Osama's complaints, and said that the Muslims of the world would unite to liberate the kingdom. He said that the older generation of Saudis had a great deal of self-respect and would never have allowed America's entry into the sacred land. He accused Saudi Arabia and Pakistan of giving him only one percent support in what he called the "Osama crisis." He said that he had obtained a written promise from bin Laden not to violate the Taliban's trust by involving himself in any militant activity from Afghan soil.

The prince became even more annoyed, and accused Omar of insulting the Saudi people, Saudi religious scholars, and the royal family. He would not tolerate further disgrace, he said. If the Taliban ever entered Saudi Arabia with nefarious intent, he would be the first to fight them. Then he got up, gave the salutation *wa salaam,* and left.

Now it was Mullah Omar's turn to be shocked. He had been playing to the gallery—his guards and the other Taliban around him. He asked what had happened. Our director general of Inter Services Intelligence replied that it seemed that the prince did not wish to continue the discussion and had left for the airport. But Mullah Omar still did not comprehend that he had made an enemy out of one of the few people who could have truly helped extricate the Taliban from the mess created by Osama bin Laden's presence in Afghanistan.

How do you negotiate with such a man? He was (and is still) caught in a time warp, detached from reality. But we could not simply abandon Afghanistan to the Taliban by withdrawing recognition and closing down our embassy in Kabul. God knows that the Taliban gave us enough cause: once, they burned our embassy and beat up our ambassador, who had to be flown back to Pakistan on a stretcher.

One of the worst things the Taliban did was to blow up two gigantic historic statues of the Buddha that had stood for centuries in a place called Bamiyan. When Omar first threatened to do this, the world could only turn to Pakistan to try to persuade him to change his mind.

Virtually the entire world had made the mistake of not recognizing the Taliban regime and establishing embassies in Kabul. I had propounded a different approach, asking several important world leaders to recognize the Taliban so that we could put collective pressure on them to change. If seventy or eighty countries had established embassies in Kabul, we might have been able to exert some influence on them. I said so to President Bill Clinton, and to then Crown Prince (now King) Abdullah bin Abdul Aziz al Saud of Saudi Arabia, and to Sheikh Zayed bin Sultan Al Nahyan of the UAE. Crown Prince Abdullah was most critical of Mullah Omar and called him a liar. "I can never join a liar," he said to me. "I hate liars."

So it was left to us to try to persuade Mullah Omar not to destroy the statues. When we went alone to negotiate with him on behalf of the world, we found him to be on another wavelength. He said that God wanted him to blow up the statues of Buddha because over the years God had caused rain to create huge holes at their bases where dynamite could be planted. This was a sign from the Almighty that the statues were to be destroyed. Mullah Omar paid no heed to us, and—tragically—destroyed the statues. Again, this projected an image of Islam as an uncaring and insensitive religion. Mullah Omar actually did a great disservice to the religion that he holds so dear. It is all very well for us to say that Islam is nothing of the sort, that it is in fact a very progressive, moderate, and tolerant religion—which indeed it is—but why should the people of the world bother to go out of their way and spend their precious time to explore the authentic sources of Islam? They are going to judge Islam by the utterances and actions of Muslims, especially those actions and utterances that affect their lives directly, and not by the protestations of academics and moderates, no matter how justified.

After 9/11 I was absolutely clear in my mind that the only way to avoid the wrath of the United States against Afghanistan and the Taliban was to somehow get Osama bin Laden and his followers out. My foremost concern certainly was the direct adverse effect on Pakistan of the United States' military action against the Taliban. The key to

Afghanistan lay in negotiating a surrender or extradition of Osama. We initiated a dialogue immediately, realizing fully that the window of opportunity was very small. The United States and the world now realized how useful Pakistan's existing diplomatic relations with the Taliban were. My earlier strategy of maintaining diplomatic relations with the Taliban, in order to try to change them from within, was vindicated at that moment. Had there been numerous embassies in Kabul and had they put collective pressure on Mullah Omar against Osama, maybe we would have succeeded.

The impact of 9/11 was lost on Mullah Omar and the Taliban. "It was God's punishment for the injustices against Muslims," Mullah Omar said. God was on their side and Osama bin Laden was a superman. Thus, negotiating with Mullah Omar was more difficult than one can imagine. It was like banging one's head against a wall. We have two entirely opposite worldviews. Whereas I believe that one must exhaust every avenue to avoid war and the death and destruction it entails, Omar thinks that death and destruction are inconsequential details in a just war.

Like all those who believe in an afterlife and regard temporal existence as transitory, religious extremists like the Taliban and al Qaeda believe that death, the "right" death, is of little consequence. Dying then becomes martyrdom, with paradise guaranteed. The problem is how to agree on what is a just or holy war. People like me hold it as a cardinal principle that a leader's first duty is to protect his country and the lives and property of his people. People like Mullah Omar believe that worldly possessions, including life itself, are secondary to their principles and traditions. One of those traditions is the protection of anyone who has been designated a guest. Osama bin Laden and his followers were guests of Mullah Omar and the Taliban, and therein lay the difficulty.

Try as we did, we could not persuade Mullah Omar to let go of Osama in the window available before October 7, 2001, the deadline imposed by President Bush. We told him that his country would be devastated, but he did not understand. He really believed that American forces could be defeated. In this he was misled first by Osama bin Laden himself, but also by other misguided religious thinkers, even in Pakistan.

The United States started its massive carpet-bombing of Afghanistan on October 7, simultaneously with a land offensive with the Northern Alliance. After a brief organized resistance, the Taliban commanders fled to the countryside and the mountains, where they are best at guerrilla warfare. In the first week of December 2001, Mullah Omar, sensing defeat, escaped on a Honda motorcycle and went into hiding. Once when Prime Minister Koizumi of Japan asked me about the whereabouts of Mullah Omar, I told him that Omar had escaped on a Honda and added jokingly that the best advertisement for Honda would be an advertising campaign showing Mullah Omar fleeing on one of its motorcycles with his robes and beard flowing in the wind.

Mullah Omar has not been heard from since. I am very sure he must be in and around his original base at Kandahar, in southern Afghanistan. I say this with reasonable surety because of two facts. First, ever since he came into the limelight in 1994, Mullah Omar has not once visited Pakistan. How could he now be comfortable in our country? Second, today the Taliban strongholds are the southern provinces of Afghanistan. All rural areas and most cities there are under the influence of the Taliban. They also dominate most movement at night. Mullah Omar would find it most convenient and safe to live and hide with his followers in his own area, which he knows so well and where he is welcomed by the local population. It has been suggested by the senior leadership of Afghanistan that he may be in Quetta, Pakistan. This insinuation is ridiculous and may even be mischievous. Had he been in Quetta he would have been caught long ago, like so many other former Taliban officeholders. However, as the war progressed and the forces of the American-led coalition and the Northern Alliance pressed on against the Taliban and al Qaeda, many of them escaped and crossed the border into Pakistan's tribal regions and cities. This caused immense problems for us.

Because Mullah Omar is still alive and free and the Taliban are by no means finished, some romantics believe that Mullah Omar has inspired his people by refusing to bow to America. It is easy to think this on a full stomach and in the comfort of one's family and home, but if one were to ask an Afghan to choose between his family, home, and hearth on the one hand and his "self-esteem" on the other, I am sure he would choose the former.

• • •

The other famous fugitive from the mountains of Tora Bora, is, of course, Osama bin Laden. Although the world knows much more about Osama than about Omar, it is worth filling in a few details of his background. After the Soviet occupation of Afghanistan, Muslims from all over the world were encouraged by the United States and its allies to flock to Pakistan to join the Afghan mujahideen in the jihad against the Soviet Union. In 1982, a Palestinian—Dr. Abdullah Azzam—and a group of spiritual leaders established an organization called Maktaba al Khidmat in Peshawar, Pakistan. Osama bin Laden was Azzam's deputy. The organization provided financial, logistical, and other support to the mujahideen. Most of the financing came from Osama bin Laden, whose family is very rich. Of course, all this didn't happen in a vacuum; neither was it the private initiative of a few Arabs. The CIA and Pakistan's Inter Services Intelligence were encouraging and helping them along.

However, by the middle of the 1980s Osama bin Laden started disagreeing with his mentor, Azzam. He no longer wanted to be only a donor to the cause; he also wanted to fight and become a *mujahid*. Instead of joining an Afghan mujahideen group, he formed his own Arab force of a few hundred fighters. It was popularly called the "Arab brigade" among everyone involved in the jihad. Osama considered the Afghan fighters too pragmatic, the sort that would leave battle if they sensed defeat, to return to fight another day. Osama's Arab fighters were fired by greater zeal. They had come all this way to fight for God, so they embraced martyrdom happily. The Afghans, on the other hand, were much more likely to return to their villages to sow or harvest crops, to get married, to attend marriages or funerals. The Arabs had nowhere to go. But I suspect that, more than this, Osama bin Laden wanted to forge his own identity—separate and distinct from the Afghan mujahideen leaders.

In 1986, Osama set up his own base close to a Soviet garrison in eastern Afghanistan, near a village called Jaji, about ten miles (sixteen kilometers) from Pakistan. In a rare display of ego, he named it Masada—"Lion's Den"—I suspect after himself, for the name Osama means lion. In the spring of 1987, Osama bin Laden fought a pitched battle against Soviet forces in Jaji. The battle of Jaji was reported in the media worldwide, and extolled by many. This was Osama's first taste of fame, and he must have loved it. The Egyptian militants Abu Hafs and Abu Ubaidah fought along with him in this battle. Soon thereafter, he befriended an Egyptian medical doctor, Ayman al Zawahiri, who was working out of Peshawar tending to the wounds of mujahideen.

The name al Qaeda, "the base," was first used by Dr. Abdullah Azzam in April 1988, in an article in a magazine called *Jihad*. His idea was to form an organization that would offer social services to Muslims and would act as a base for the "Muslim awakening." He never meant for al Qaeda to be a base in the military sense of the word. In fact, the full name used by Azzam was al Qaeda al Sulbah, "the solid base."

Abdullah Azzam's view of jihad was to expel occupiers from Muslim lands. But Osama also wanted to topple governments in Muslim countries that he considered "apostate." This would cause conflict between Muslims, however, and Azzam wanted nothing to do with it. It led to a falling-out between them. Osama bin Laden took the name suggested by Azzam and formed al Qaeda, dropping "al Sulbah." A year later, on November 24, 1989, Abdullah Azzam was assassinated. It is suspected that Osama was behind his mentor's murder.

In February 1998, nine years after the formation of al Qaeda, Osama bin Laden formed an umbrella organization called the Islamic World Front. Its purpose was to struggle against the occupation of Palestine by Israel. Al Qaeda, on the other hand, is a multinational extremist organization whose members come from various countries but most particularly from Egypt. It has a worldwide presence and its purposes are the following:

1. To radicalize existing Islamic groups and to create new ones where there are none.
2. To proselytize.
3. To drive American forces out of Muslim countries.
4. To combat the designs of Israel and the United States in the Middle East.
5. To support Muslims' struggles for freedom everywhere.
6. To pool all Muslim resources for the common cause of jihad.

Al Qaeda comprises a consultative council or *shoora* under which there are four committees—military, media, finance, and religious affairs. Its operating cells are believed to exist in about forty countries, including the United States and Canada. It focuses primarily on operations in Afghanistan, Iraq, Saudi Arabia, Pakistan, Turkey, southeast Asia, North Africa, Europe, the United States, the United Kingdom and Canada. Its operations are decentralized, and its hard-core trained manpower is kept dormant until it finds an opportune moment to strike.

Today, after the many setbacks al Qaeda has received, mainly in Pakistan, its new base and training ground are said to be increasingly the Sahel region running through the middle of Africa from east to west. Al Qaeda is taking on a new shape with the killing or capture of its top leaders. Its reformation is a perpetual activity, except at the very top.

We have done everything possible to track down Osama bin Laden, but he has evaded us. Most recently, he has been using couriers instead of electronic communications to maintain contact. This obviously slows down the time it takes for a message to get into or out of the mountains along the Pakistan-Afghan border, to as much as thirty days in each direction. We have been able to intercept some of the courier traffic.

The location of Osama and his few close associates has been a mystery that we, more than anyone else, have been anxious to resolve. Clues to Osama's whereabouts have arisen during interrogations. Ramzi bin al Shibh, who was supposed to be the twentieth hijacker of 9/11, escaped from Tora Bora unhurt and was arrested by us after a shootout in Karachi along with two Burmese nationals: Sayyid Amin and Abu Badr. Under interrogation, Amin told us that he had met Osama bin Laden at an unknown location around June 2002.

Khalid Sheikh Mohammad (KSM), the third-ranking member of al Qaeda, whom we captured in Peshawar, denied having met Osama after 9/11, but he told us that Osama was alive and well and that they had been in touch. He said that the last letter he had received from Osama came through a courier. He also said that Osama had been helped before Operation Anaconda to move out of Tora Bora to Waziristan by Jalal ul Din Haqqani; two Afghans, Mohammad Rahim and Amin ul Haq; and the Iranian Baloch Ahmed Al-Kuwaiti. On March 4, 2003, KSM speculated that Osama was in Konar in Afghanistan.

Abu Faraj Al Libbi, KSM's replacement, told us as late as May 2005, after his arrest, that he was in contact with Osama through a courier and the last letter he had received from Osama was sometime in December 2004. We have been looking for the couriers intensely.

As we went into the mountains of Waziristan and smashed al Qaeda's communication network in Pakistan, we discovered that its courier system was very well established. It is four-tiered, with distinct layers for administration, operations, media support, and the top hierarchy. The first three are two-way communications; only that of the al Qaeda high command is one-way, top-down.

The administrative courier network deals with communication pertaining to the movement and shifting of families and other administrative activities and the flow of information from families to financiers and vice versa. A combination of Afghan and Pakistani couriers runs this network.

The operational courier network deals with passing operational instructions. Here, greater care is exercised in selecting couriers. The procedure ensures maximum security through a code word and cutout system; that is, unwitting couriers are substituted for knowledgeable people wherever possible.

The media support courier network is used for propaganda and motivation. These messages are mostly in the form of CDs, leaflets, videos, etc., often delivered to the television network Al Jazeera.

The fourth tier of the courier network is used only by the top leaders of al Qaeda, who try not to pass messages in writing, except where that is unavoidable, as with letters to KSM and Libbi. Normally, the leaders make their best, most trusted, die-hard couriers memorize messages to al Qaeda's operational hierarchy, and then convey them verbatim.

It is only a matter of time before bin Laden is caught. He does not have the sympathy or hospitality of all the tribes in Pakistan's tribal areas. If I had to guess, I would assume that he is moving back and forth across the Pakistan-Afghanistan border somewhere. The fact that so many Saudis are in the Konar area perhaps suggests that this is where Osama bin Laden has his hideout, but we cannot be sure.

I have said, half-jokingly, that I hope he is not caught in Pakistan, by Pakistan's troops.

CHAPTER 22

THE WAR COMES TO PAKISTAN

The United States was not the only casualty of 9/11. The attacks hit Pakistan differently, but with equally savage force. We feel the ramifications to this day. No other country has faced as many threats on as many fronts. We stood with the United States, and we stand with the entire world, in opposing terrorism. Yet we face threats from within and without. Afghanistan is our neighbor; we share a porous boundary and religious, ethnic, and tribal affinities as well as familial links. Many of our tribes originally come from Afghanistan, and there have been numerous intermarriages among them, across the border. We also have a large number of Afghan refugees who made Pakistan their home after the Soviets invaded their country in 1979. Twenty-five years later, we have 4 million Afghan refugees, the largest refugee population in the world. We have had to bear most of their economic and social cost, especially after the Soviet withdrawal and America's abandonment.

Yet another front was public opinion at home: whereas most Pakistanis condemned the 9/11 attacks, there was also a strong sentiment against the United States' reaction. That sentiment was encouraged partly by the religious lobby and partly by pre-existing anti-American feelings left over from the United States' abandonment of Pakistan after the Soviet withdrawal from Afghanistan.

Twenty-one years earlier it was natural for us to join the jihad against the Soviet occupation of Afghanistan, because we did not want the Soviet Union to consolidate its position and turn its attention toward our warm waters. In 2001 it was just as natural for us to join the war against terror because Pakistan had been a victim of sectarian and external terrorism for years, and certainly had no desire to be "Talibanized." In both instances, it was in our national interest to do what we did. Just as we could not tolerate Soviet hegemony, under no circumstances could we tolerate homegrown terrorism or extremists who try to indoctrinate our society with a radical and violent interpretation of Islam.

Ironically, once we started clamping down on terrorism, yet another front opened against us: militant extremist organizations around the world put a price on my head and unleashed foreign terror in our country. In 2002, terrorists attacked worshipers in a church in Islamabad, children in a Christian-run school in Murree, and patients in a Christian hospital in Taxila. French naval technicians and the U.S. consulate in Karachi were bombed, and the American journalist Daniel Pearl was kidnapped and murdered.

In this chapter and the following chapters, I will tell the stories of some of our most important victories in the war on terror. We have done more than any other country to capture and kill members of al Qaeda, and to destroy its infrastructure in our cities and mountains. Many of these stories have not been told in full before now.

On January 23 and 24, 2002, the world's media received e-mails saying that the journalist Daniel Pearl had been kidnapped. Pearl, a citizen of both the United States and Israel, was the South Asia Bureau Chief of the *Wall Street Journal.* The ransom demanded by the kidnappers was the release and return to Pakistan of Pakistani prisoners in Guantánamo Bay, the immediate end of the United States' presence in Pakistan, the delivery of F-16 planes that Pakistan had paid for but never received, and the release of Mullah Zaeef, the former Afghan ambassador of the Taliban regime to Pakistan. The e-mails also stated, "We assure Americans that they shall never be safe on the Muslim Land of Pakistan. And if our demands are not met this scene shall be repeated again and again."

I was incensed when I learned of this, disgusted that these criminals were distorting a religion of peace and beauty and using it as a cloak for their sins. Islam places the highest emphasis on the rights of the human being regardless of class or creed, and condemns murder and suicide as very great sins.

I immediately ordered all agencies to find Pearl's kidnappers and launch a rescue operation. The e-mails were traced to three men: Fahd Nasim, Suleman Saqib, and Muhammad Adil. We discovered that these e-mails had been sent not only to the media but also to the governments of Pakistan and the United States. They had been forwarded to someone else as well—a man named Omar Saeed Sheikh.

The *Wall Street Journal* informed us that Pearl, who had arrived in Pakistan on December 29, 2001, with his wife, Marianne, had come to interview Pir Mubarik Ali Shah Jilani in connection with the story of the so-called "shoe bomber," the Briton Richard Reed. However, the *Journal* was unaware what Pearl had been doing on the day of his kidnapping, or whom he was meeting. It is likely that Pearl was chasing a story and in doing so broke what journalists tell me is a cardinal principle of safety: informing someone beforehand of where they are going.

Our police detained and interrogated Jilani, who told them that Omar Sheikh had been very eager to meet the journalist. With this second mention of Omar Sheikh's name, it seemed clear that he was involved in the affair.

We had been looking for Omar Sheikh since the e-mails, but at first he could not be traced, although the police did manage to trace some of his friends and relatives, and we arrested them. It was only when a man named Adil Sheikh was arrested that the police obtained Omar Sheikh's phone number. Adil Sheikh confessed that he was an accomplice to Pearl's kidnapping, as was the elusive Omar Sheikh.

By tracing the e-mails sent by Omar Sheikh's accomplices to the media, the police had been able to capture some of his key accomplices and relatives, and his own family as well, including his eighteen-month-old son. Finally, on February 5, 2002, Omar Sheikh surrendered, presenting himself before the home secretary, of Punjab. Under interrogation Omar Sheikh revealed that when his family members were arrested he became desperate. He phoned an accomplice in Karachi named Hussein, and told him to release Daniel Pearl. He was then told that Daniel Pearl had been killed (or so he said). The next day Omar Sheikh called Amjad Faruqi, an important al Qaeda terrorist in Pakistan, to confirm the story. Faruqi confirmed that Pearl was indeed dead and had been killed by an Arab. This was the first time that we had heard of Amjad Faruqi. Later, we were to hear of him many times, in equally deadly circumstances. He was the planner of the attempts to assassinate me.

Ahmed Omar Saeed Sheikh's surrender was formalized on February 12, 2002. It was only after Omar Sheikh's arrest that we ourselves discovered that Daniel Pearl was dead. A gruesome video of Pearl's slaughter was mysteriously released on the Internet. Although Omar Sheikh confessed in detail to having masterminded and arranged the kidnapping, he was adamant that he had not ordered the murder and that Pearl had been killed against his instructions. The story that emerged from Omar Sheikh's confessions was chilling and sinister.

Omar Sheikh is a British national born to Pakistani parents in London on December 23, 1973. His early education was in the United Kingdom, although he also spent four years at Lahore's prestigious Aitcheson College. He then went to the London School of Economics (LSE) but dropped out before graduation. It is believed in some quarters that while Omar Sheikh was at the LSE he was recruited by the British intelligence agency MI-6. It is said that MI-6 persuaded him to take an active part in demonstrations against Serbian aggression in Bosnia and even sent him to Kosovo to join the jihad. At some point he probably became a rogue or double agent. On his return from Bosnia he came to Pakistan and met Maulana Abdul Jabbar, who guided him to Khost in Afghanistan to be trained not in religion but in guerrilla warfare.

In 1994, after one year of training, Omar Sheikh went to India on his British passport, along with a band of others, in an attempt to secure the release of Maulana Masood Azhar (associate of Maulana Abdul Jabbar). Azhar had been arrested for instigating conflict in Indian-held Kashmir in February 1994 and was imprisoned for seven years. The method Omar Sheikh and his associates used to pressure the Indian government was the abduction of three Britons (Rhys Partridge, Paul Benjamin Rideout, and Christopher Miles Crosten) and an American (Bela Joseph Nuss) in Delhi on September 29, 1994. All were later released. Omar Sheikh was arrested by Indian security from Uttar Pradesh in 1994. But he was released in 1999 along with Maulana Masood Azhar in exchange for the release of an Indian airplane that had been hijacked to Kandahar, Afghanistan.

After his release, Omar Sheikh settled in Lahore but visited

Afghanistan on four occasions to train operatives of a group called Harkat-e-Jehadi Islami Afghanistan. He claims that during these visits, he met Osama bin Laden and Mullah Omar and that although he was not a permanent member of al Qaeda, he helped finance it through ransom money generated from kidnappings.

In January 2002, Mohammad Hashim, a close friend of Omar Sheikh's from Harkat-e-Jehadi Islami Afghanistan, informed him that an American journalist named Daniel Pearl had turned up at the offices of extremist organizations in Rawalpindi and Islamabad to arrange meetings with Pir Mubarik Ali Shah Jilani. At first Omar Sheikh suspected that Pearl might be an agent of western intelligence agencies working against extremist organizations. He asked Hashim to arrange a meeting between him and Pearl. This Hashim did on January 10 and 11, 2002. Using a pseudonym, Omar Sheikh introduced himself to Pearl as a follower of Pir Mubarik Ali Shah Jilani. Pearl insisted on a meeting with Jilani, and Omar Sheikh promised to arrange it. The two exchanged telephone numbers and e-mail addresses.

It was at this meeting that an idea cropped up in Omar Sheikh's twisted mind. In what had become a habitual ploy to get the attention of governments, Sheikh would kidnap Pearl to pressure the U.S. government to change its policies toward prisoners held in Guantánamo Bay and force it to release a few. He thought first of carrying out the abduction in Rawalpindi but was unable to find a hideout. He then phoned his old colleague Amjad Faruqi, who was delighted to help but said that the necessary arrangements could be made only in Karachi. Omar Sheikh lured Pearl to Karachi by telling him that Jilani was in Karachi and could meet him on January 23, 2002. The trap was set.

Omar Sheikh then flew to Karachi. Once in Karachi, Amjad Faruqi directed him to a popular restaurant, Student's Biryani, where he would meet a man named Hussein. Omar Sheikh complied and was accompanied by two colleagues: Asim Ghafoor and Salman Saquib. The three men met Hussein, who took them to Aga Khan Hospital to meet yet another man, who called himself Ahmad Bhai. It was Ahmad Bhai whom Amjad Faruqi had enlisted to carry out the kidnapping.

When they met, it became apparent to Omar Sheikh that Ahmad Bhai had enough experience to handle the operation. He tested Ahmad Bhai by asking to be shown the location where Pearl would be held, but

Ahmad Bhai refused, saying that the site could not be compromised because it was also required for other operations. At Omar Sheikh's request, Ahmad Bhai agreed to arrange for an English interpreter.

That evening, Omar Sheikh went to a McDonald's with his friend Adil Sheikh, from whom we later obtained Omar Sheikh's contact numbers. He told Adil about his abduction plan. Adil, also trained in Afghanistan, became excited and expressed interest in joining the plot.

The final meeting between Omar Sheikh and Ahmad Bhai took place on January 22, 2002. Adil was also present, as was another accomplice of Ahmad Bhai's named Imtiaz. It was agreed that Ahmad Bhai would deliver photographs of Pearl in captivity to Omar Sheikh at a particular mosque, as confirmation of his kidnapping. They purchased a Polaroid camera and showed Ahmad Bhai and Hussain how to use it. Omar Sheikh then paid Ahmad Bhai 17,000 rupees and gave both men two messages—one typed in English and the other in Urdu—and instructed them to e-mail these to the media along with the photographs after the kidnapping.

All that was left to do now was to ensnare the victim. Omar Sheikh contacted Pearl by e-mail and informed him that a man named Iftikhar would receive him at the airport and take him to Pir Mubarik Ali Shah Jilani. Iftikhar, of course, was a fake name. The man who met Pearl was one of Ahmad Bhai's accomplices. Pearl arrived in Karachi on January 23, 2002, and was kidnapped the same day by Hussein, Adil, Ahmad Bhai, and Imtiaz near the Metropole Hotel.

Omar Sheikh flew to Lahore the same day. That evening Hussein informed him that the deed had been done. From then on, Omar Sheikh remained in constant telephone communication with Salman Saqib, Adil, Hussein, and Ahmad Bhai to supervise and guide them.

At first I could not understand why Omar Sheikh had surrendered to the police. Why didn't he escape? Only after all the pieces had been put together did I realize that Omar Sheikh had panicked because the situation had spiraled out of his control. He didn't expect the media backlash; he didn't expect the police to be so efficient in tracking him and his friends, family, and accomplices; he didn't realize that the people he had enlisted to help in the kidnapping were hard-core criminals who wouldn't necessarily take instructions from him. He was now trying to save himself, thinking that by surrendering he might be treated leniently.

On February 21, 2002, the horrifying videotape of Pearl's murder was released. It didn't show the faces of his murderers. In addition, we had nobody. Then, in May 2002, we arrested someone named Fazal Karim, an activist of Lashkar-e-Jhangvi, the militant wing of the Sunni sect known as Sipah-e-Sahaba. We had arrested him for other reasons, but when we interrogated him we discovered that he was involved in Pearl's slaughter. He also told us that he knew where Pearl was buried. He was asked how he knew. Chillingly, he replied—without remorse—that he knew because he had actually participated in the slaughter by holding one of Pearl's legs. But he didn't know the name of the person who had actually slit Pearl's throat. All he could say is that this person was "Arab-looking."

He led us to the small house in a neighborhood in Karachi where Daniel Pearl had been held captive. He then took us to a plot of land nearby and told us where he was buried. We exhumed the body and found it in ten badly decomposed pieces. Our doctors stitched the pieces back together as best as they could. I have seen the photographs. Needless to say, they are disturbing.

The man who may have actually killed Pearl or at least participated in his butchery, we eventually discovered, was none other than Khalid Sheikh Mohammad, al Qaeda's number three. When we later arrested and interrogated him, he admitted his participation.

In July 2002, an antiterrorism court in Pakistan gave Omar Saeed Sheikh the death penalty. The case is currently on appeal. Daniel Pearl's murder was one of many terrorist acts in Pakistan after 9/11, but it was particularly gruesome. War correspondents share something with soldiers: when they opt for this profession they know the dangers. May his soul rest in peace.

Unfortunately, Daniel Pearl wasn't the only foreigner killed on our soil by terrorists in 2002. There were several other incidents, though we did break all the cells involved.

On a warm Sunday morning—March 17, 2002—the prayers of worshippers at the Protestant International Church in Islamabad's diplomatic enclave were shattered when a man ran in and started hurling hand grenades. About seven or eight were thrown, of which three failed to detonate. Six people were killed and forty-two injured, including the Sri Lankan ambassador. Perhaps saddest of all was the tragic death of Kristen Wormsley, an eighteen-year-old American girl attending the International School of Islamabad. Although we arrested a large number of suspects, nothing could be established conclusively, because the terrorist had blown himself up, leaving no clues.

Five months later, in the idyllic hill resort town of Murree, which is about 6,500 feet (2,000 meters) above sea level and a popular destination for summer holidays, terror struck again in a Christian school. There are a number of very good schools in Murree, some of which are run by Christian missionaries, and many people from all over the country send their children there. On August 5, 2002, three masked men wearing tracksuits started to enter the school compound. The guard at the gate tried valiantly to stop them but was shot dead. The sound of the shot alerted the school staff to the imminent danger, and they quickly locked all the doors. The scuffle with the guard and the gunshot caused such a commotion that the terrorists were forced to abandon their mission and run into the forest.

It so happens that a police station and an army garrison are very near the school. So is the army's dog breeding center. So is a small village. Many people thus heard the shot and ran to the school. Finding the guard dead and his killers gone, soldiers of the Pakistan Army took tracker dogs and chased the terrorists into the forest. The villagers joined the chase. One of the villagers was a retired junior commissioned officer of the Pakistan Army. He actually spotted the three fleeing men and ran after them. He managed to corner them by a cliff above the Jhelum River and threatened to kill them if they didn't surrender. It was a tense moment. Suddenly, all three men climbed onto a boulder and without warning blew themselves up. Two fell headlong into the fast-flowing river. Only one body was recovered. Again, we had no useful evidence.

Four days after the attack on the school, the terrorists struck again. This time the target was a Christian hospital in Taxila, renowned for its humanitarian work. It also has a church. On August 9, 2002, just as people were coming out of a church service, three men forcibly entered the grounds and hurled two grenades at the worshippers. One man and four women were killed, and twenty injured. The attackers fled immediately. The police rushed to the scene and found one of the terrorists dead outside the gate, killed by a hand grenade. Nobody actually saw how this man died, though one assumes that he held the grenade in his hand too long. At the scene of this attack, unlike the previous two attacks, we found a helpful clue. The dead man had a photocopy of his identity card in his pocket. His name was Kamran Mir.

Two teams—one from the army and the other from the police— were assembled to carry out the investigation. They went to Kamran Mir's home and found vital clues there as to the identities of some of his accomplices and the terrorist group to which he belonged. They also found some addresses and phone numbers. They learned that Kamran Mir went by the alias Ali. One of his friends was a man called Mohammad Ayaz, who went by the name of Waqar. They managed to trace the whereabouts of Waqar through his cell phone and arrested him.

This was our first vital arrest in the bombings cases. Waqar confessed to supplying the grenades, explosives, and pistols to the terrorists. He also revealed the identity and whereabouts of twenty other members of his group. Most crucially, he revealed the identity of Saif-ur Rahman Saifi—the mastermind behind the three attacks. It was Saifi who had provided the grenades, explosives, and pistols to Waqar.

Saifi was arrested on August 14, 2002. Under interrogation he claimed that the motive behind the attacks was retaliation against the United States for its invasion of Afghanistan and the treatment meted out to Muslims in Afghanistan, Kashmir, and Palestine. Ironically, what Saifi perhaps didn't know at the time was that these attacks had been conceived earlier, by someone else, for an entirely different motive.

Saifi had been trained in terrorism at the Afghan camp of Maulana Masood Azhar (*maulana* means "cleric"). We had actually arrested this fake *maulana* in January 2002, when he was released by India as part of the bargain for their hijacked plane. Now he feared that we would hand him back to India. To preempt this, he instructed two more so-called maulanas, one of them his associate Abdul Jabbar, to unleash terrorist attacks in the country as a demonstration of his organization's power and to display their anger at the possibility that he would be handed over to India.

Abdul Jabbar contacted Osama Nazir, who along with Saifi had been trained in Masood Azhar's Afghan camp. He told Nazir to attack foreigners and Christians in Pakistan. But suddenly, just a few days before these attacks were due to take place, Masood Azhar ordered Abdul Jabbar to abort the plan. He claims that once he was satisfied he would not be handed over to India, he ordered the operation stopped.

Abdul Jabbar asked Nazir to abandon the plan, but perhaps because the disciple had become more fervent than the teacher, Nazir refused. Defiantly, he disassociated himself from Jaish-e-Mohammad and assembled about fifteen like-minded terrorists. He divided them into two groups: one headed by himself and the other by Saifi, who carefully planned the three attacks. The group headed by Saifi was called Fidayeen. It was Fidayeen that carried out these attacks.

Saifi was a highly indoctrinated person. Once he was arrested in Multan on August 15, 2002, he confessed that he also had links with Lashkar-e-Jhangvi, the militant wing of the Sunni sectarian Sipah-e-Sahaba, and also al Qaeda. Thus did the nexus of al Qaeda and our local extremist organizations become clear: al Qaeda provided the money, weapons, and equipment, and the local organizations provided the manpower and motivation to actually execute the attacks. Further investigations also revealed that Azhar Masood's brother-in-law, Yousuf Azhar, and Fazal Karim, who led us to Daniel Pearl's grave, provided funds for these attacks. As for Osama Nazir, the explosives expert, he was arrested in Faisalabad in 2004 on Eid day, which takes place at the end of the holy month of Ramadan during which Muslims fast between dawn and dusk.

One other attack in 2002 struck terror into one of our cities. Once again, we tracked down the perpetrators and brought them to justice.

At seven forty-five AM on May 8, 2002, terror struck in Karachi when a bus of the Pakistan Navy pulled out of the Sheraton Hotel and a car driven by a suicide bomber rammed into it. A huge explosion shattered the bus, the hotel, and another hotel opposite. The bus had been carrying French engineers and technicians who were working on a submarine project. Eleven French nationals and two Pakistanis were killed. Twenty-four people were injured. Many vehicles nearby were damaged. The New Zealand cricket team was staying in the same hotel and was just about to leave for the playing field at the time. Luckily, none of the players was hurt, but all of them were so traumatized by the event that they called off the tour and went home.

A joint investigation was initiated between Pakistani investigators and their French counterparts. The suicide car was traced to a showroom in Karachi. A salesman at the showroom recalled having sold the car to three persons, whom he helped us sketch, but still we were no closer to finding the culprits. Our next break came in September, when a man who was already in our custody told investigators that he knew of an activist by the name of Sharib who had been intent on attacking the French technicians. Sharib was arrested on September 18, 2002. He denied involvement, but said he knew who was responsible. Two men—Asif Zaheer and Sohail Akhtar of Harkat-ul-Mujahideen al-Alimi (HUMA)—had planned the attack.

Next we arrested Asif Zaheer on December 28, 2002. He immediately confessed to his involvement and told us the identity of the suicide bomber. Actually, Asif Zaheer claims that he was originally selected to be the suicide bomber but pulled out and offered a heavily indoctrinated man called Rashid instead. It was not until March 17, 2004, that his accomplice Sohail Akhtar was arrested.

Three of the terrorists received the death penalty and their property was confiscated by Karachi's antiterrorism court.

I was enraged by these heinous acts of barbarism—enraged that people who called themselves Muslims could launch an unprovoked attack on Christians or foreigners, enraged that through their vile acts these terrorists were perverting our faith, which tells us that Christians are among the "people of the Book," that we should show discernment when fighting for the cause of God and not fight those who have not harmed us, that murder and suicide are grievous sins.

I assumed that we would face more attacks at home. Little did I realize that the targets would include me, and later our finance minister Shaukut Aziz, in addition to Lieutenant General Ahsan Saleem Hayat, our Karachi Corps commander. Although I am getting slightly ahead of our story, the latter two attacks are worth describing here, because they show once again that even a serious attack, with deadly power, can miss its target because of the smallest details of the moment.

•   •   •

Early on the morning of June 10, 2004, I was informed that there had been a serious attempt to assassinate our corps commander in Karachi, Lieutenant General Ahsan Saleem Hayat (who is now the vice chief of the army staff). This was most disturbing. The attempts against me, I believe, targeted me as the president of Pakistan more than as the chief of the army staff. This was the first attack on a senior serving army officer. In the war against terrorism, another threshold had been crossed.

I immediately telephoned Ahsan and found him well composed, considering that seven of his guards and his driver had been killed. He gave me the story.

The general was on his way to work. Just as his car reached the bridge that connects the wealthy neighborhood of Clifton, near the Arabian Sea, to downtown Karachi, it was met with a hail of bullets. The military police jeep ahead of him bore the brunt of the attack, but kept moving. Sadly, all seven men in the jeep behind the corps commander's car were killed. So were two innocent bystanders. The corps commander's driver was shot in the head and seriously injured, while his co-driver was also shot, and died on the spot. Yet as luck would have it, even with the injury his foot stayed pressed hard on the accelerator, and the car did not stop. If it had stopped, the general would have been killed. Because of the attack, the traffic in front had disappeared, so there was nothing to stop the car. At first it started moving in a zigzag pattern, but Ahsan's aide-de-camp, seated right behind the driver, leaned forward and got hold of the steering wheel.

The general's assassins had planned the ambush carefully and carried it out meticulously. What went wrong had all to do with luck. His would-be assassins had placed an improvised explosive device on the road, which was to be triggered by a cell phone the moment his car went over it, the idea being that the car would come to a halt and they would let loose with their guns from two directions. But fate had its own plans. The phone call to activate the explosive device never connected, and Ahsan's car went safely by it. In a panic, the assassins let loose their barrage of fire from the bridge, in front of the car, and also from the side, where they were hidden in an open lot. A failed phone connection, a dead driver's foot on the accelerator, and the presence of mind of the aide-de-camp, who finally managed to jump in front and take control of the car, robbed the attackers of their goal. This is how the plans of rats and terrorists come to naught.

Yet again our investigators found the cell phone. The terrorists had made a few calls on it before trying to activate the explosion. Given our previous experience, we quickly traced the calls to a particular house. When our investigators got there, they found that it was the house of the main planner of the assassination operation. He was there, and was arrested, but obstinately denied complicity, even in the face of the evidence from the cell phone's call data. But his mother was there too, and she persuaded her son to cooperate. So one by one he called all the terrorists involved in the plot to his house, and one by one they were arrested. It all happened on the night following the attack. This is how the terrorist group Jundullah was smashed. It was a great breakthrough, because this very group had been involved in several other high-profile terrorist attacks in Karachi.

On July 30, 2004, Shaukat Aziz had finished addressing a by-election rally in his constituency, about an hour's drive from Islamabad. There is always a crowd of people at successful political rallies, and this was no different. It's uncanny, but a day earlier I had a hunch about Shaukat's safety and had given him a bulletproof car from my pool. However, it had a left-hand drive, as in the United States, whereas most of our cars have right-hand steering. So the driver was sitting on the left side and Shaukat Aziz was sitting behind him. Just as the car started to move, a suicide bomber came through the milling crowd, placed himself a few feet from the front left door of the car, raised his right arm, and blew himself up, causing a massive explosion.

A television cameraman fell to the ground, and his camera dropped from his hand. He got up and ran for his life, leaving behind the camera, which, understandably, must have been the farthest thing from his mind. But the camera kept running, pointing in the right direction and recording everything, but sideways, because it was lying on its side. We saw the suicide bomber's head get torn off his shoulders, literally flying off like a kicked soccer ball. After it fell to the ground it looked like a coconut. The rest of his body was blown to pieces—a leg here, an arm there, the torso somewhere else.

Shaukat Aziz later told me that he had turned to his right to talk to the person seated next to him in the backseat. The suicide bomber was to his left, so Shaukat didn't see him. Since the car was armor-plated, all he heard was a thud, just as I did in the first attempt to assassinate me. Hot air hit his left side, as if from a hair dryer, and the left side of his open jacket moved upward and down. The bomb had made a hole in the window of the driver's door, and it was through this that the hot air from the bomb came in. Shaukat Aziz saw that his driver was slumped over and thought that he had fainted, so he caught the driver's shoulders from behind and shook him to bring him back to his senses. But to his horror he discovered that the poor man was dead. A small piece of shrapnel from the bomb had penetrated the glass of the window and killed him.

When Shaukat Aziz escaped from his car, a police officer told him to run for cover, as in all likelihood a second assassin was around to either shoot him or attempt another bombing. That was the usual pattern. The police officer was right: there was indeed a second suicide bomber, although he abandoned his mission and ran away.

We came to know that there was a second bomber because before undertaking the operation, both assassins had recorded a video statement, which was obviously meant for us but also the world at large. From the video, it seems as if the one who actually blew himself up was the weaker personality—the gullible kind. It could well be that he had been indoctrinated to undertake this mission out of misplaced religious zeal. The runaway, on the other hand, looked smug and far too clever for his own or anyone else's good. It seems that he was in the plot for the money; and when he saw his accomplice blown up, he left. He has still not been found.

Inter Services Intelligence and the police jointly undertook the investigation. The body parts of the suicide bomber had been scattered all over the place, but as is often the case, his head and face were mostly intact. On the inside of his shirt collar was a label that read "Arif Tailor" from a place called Attock (Campbellpur). The police traced Arif the tailor and took him and his workers into custody. Measurements were taken of various parts of the assassin's dismembered body, and these matched the specifications in the tailor's register for one of his customers. The suicide bomber's thumb impression was also taken from his hand, given to our national database organization, and matched with 67,000 thumb impressions of people from Attock. The list was soon narrowed down to one individual: a twenty-two-year-old Pakistani named Irfan who, we soon found out, went by the pseudonym Zeeshan.

Our suspicions were soon confirmed when an activist of Jaish-e-Mohammad who was already in our custody gave us some valuable leads. On the basis of these leads a number of activists from Jaish were arrested and interrogated. It turned out that Maulvi (a variation of *maulana*) Imtiaz Ahmed had spearheaded the operation. Although Maulvi Imtiaz Ahmed was a member of Jaish, he also had links with al Qaeda. A day before the assassination attempt, Maulvi Imtiaz brought the two would-be assassins to the house of yet another purported *maulvi* called Nisar and gave them their final instructions. The next day, the two of them tied explosive belts to their bodies and each took one hand grenade as well. The second suicide bomber was a twenty-five-year-old, Sultan Sikandar. Having fled the scene after Zeeshan had blown himself up, Sikandar went to Maulvi Nisar's house and returned the belt and hand grenade. He spent the night there, then shaved off his beard, left, and disappeared. We later recovered his belt and found that it was an improvised device fitted with about fifteen pounds (seven kilograms) of explosives wrapped in tinfoil and put into synthetic packets.

I was impressed by the way Shaukat Aziz conducted himself during and after the attempt on his life. A general of the Pakistan Army is trained to face bullets and bombs, but Shaukat Aziz was a banker in New York before he came to Pakistan. Yet he handled himself with great equanimity and self-control, and my already high regard for him went up even more. "Welcome to the club," I said to him when I phoned him after he reached home. We are still a club of two in Pakistan, and hopefully its membership is closed.

CHAPTER 23

MANHUNT

Since shortly after 9/11, when many members of al Qaeda fled Afghanistan and crossed the border into Pakistan, we have played cat and mouse with them. The biggest of them all, Osama bin Laden, is still at large at the time of this writing, but we have caught many, many others. Some are known to the world, some are not. We have captured 689 and handed over 369 to the United States. We have earned bounties totaling millions of dollars. Those who habitually accuse us of "not doing enough" in the war on terror should simply ask the CIA how much prize money it has paid to the government of Pakistan. Here, I will tell the stories of just a few of the most significant manhunts.

Abu Zubeida, a Palestinian national whose real name is Zain-ul-Abideen, was the first high-ranking member of al Qaeda caught after the 9/11 attacks, which he had helped plan. He was the chief recruiter and trainer of al Qaeda operatives. The CIA had offered a $5 million reward for his capture.

After 9/11, Abu Zubeida came to Pakistan but remained elusive by continually moving among thirteen sites in three cities—nine in Faisalabad, one in Karachi, and three in Lahore. Nonetheless, we learned about his movements by catching lower-level operatives and proceeding on human intelligence. All thirteen sites were raided simultaneously by Pakistani intelligence agents supported by our law enforcement agencies, on the night of March 27, 2002. Agents from the CIA assisted in the location of sites through technical intelligence. The mission was successful: Abu Zubeida was caught and arrested along with twenty-seven of his al Qaeda associates, all of them foreigners—thirteen Yemenis, three Saudis, three Libyans, three Palestinians, one Russian, one Moroccan, one Sudanese, and two Syrians, one of whom was killed and the other injured. Abu Zubeida was handed over to the United States on March 30, 2002.

The policy followed by Pakistan on the extradition of foreigners has been first to ask their countries of origin to take them back. If a country of origin refuses (as is normally the case), we hand the prisoner over to the United States.

This was our single biggest catch at that time, not just numerically but in terms of importance. Those were the early days, when al Qaeda operatives were still fleeing from Afghanistan into Pakistan. After Abu Zubeida's arrest, they thought twice about this and started coming in smaller numbers.

Khalid Sheikh Mohammad (KSM) was the object of our next manhunt. He was one of the most sought-after terrorists and featured prominently on the FBI's "most wanted" list. A Kuwaiti-born Iranian national, KSM had most of his schooling in Kuwait and then attended college in North Carolina in 1984. From there he transferred to North Carolina Agricultural and Technical State University.

Khalid Sheikh Mohammad was a member of what is known as the "Afghan alumni" terrorist network. Its sole reason for existence was to kill as many Americans as possible, anywhere, anyhow. In 1993 KSM spearheaded the attempt to blow up New York's World Trade Center, along with his nephew Ramzi Yousef. Next, they plotted to blow up about a dozen airliners flying from southeast Asia to the United States on the same day. They also planned to dispatch a suicide pilot to crash into the CIA headquarters in Langley, Virginia. This was called the Bojinka Operation. None of these plans materialized, however, because Ramzi Yousef was arrested in Pakistan in 1995 and handed over to the United States, shortly before he could pull off the operation. Other conspirators were arrested too, but KSM managed to get away.

When KSM started his life as a terrorist he was not with al Qaeda; he had his own network. During much of the 1990s, KSM first tried to maintain his operational autonomy and resisted swearing allegiance to any terrorist leader, because he thought of himself as being in the same mold as Osama bin Laden. But after the failure of the Bojinka Operation and the arrest of Ramzi Yousef, he canceled his network and decided to develop closer ties with al Qaeda. He wanted to meet Osama bin Laden in 1996, but bin Laden was too busy moving his own family and organization from Sudan to Afghanistan. However, KSM remained in touch with the al Qaeda leaders Abdul Rehman Muhajir and Abu Aziz Al-Masri in order to develop contacts with key operatives.

Finally, in 1996, after Osama bin Laden had moved back to Afghanistan, KSM met him for the first time in Tora Bora. He told Osama about his role in the bombing of the World Trade Center in 1993 and the abortive Bojinka Operation. Then KSM presented the idea of 9/11 to Osama bin Laden, but Osama vetoed it, asking KSM to join al Qaeda first. Insisting that he wished to retain his independence, KSM refused.

At the same time, and in order to get money for his operations, KSM developed relations with the Libyan Islamic Fighting Group (LIFG) and also with Abu Zubeida.

In 1998 or 1999, perhaps persuaded by Abu Hafs Al-Masri—now known to the world by his alias, Mohammad Atef—Osama bin Laden approved the plan for 9/11, though of course at that time the exact date could not have been determined. As soon as KSM learned that Osama was on board, he brought his family from Qatar to Kandahar in Afghanistan. The plan for 9/11 was kept secret between Osama bin Laden, Atef, and KSM. Intelligence sources indicate that by 2000, Mullah Omar probably had a fair idea that large-scale operations on American soil were planned, but he did not know any details. It is also said that he was not happy about it but apparently could do nothing.

Mohammad Atef and Osama bin Laden short-listed the operatives for 9/11 and asked KSM to select the best of them. Al Qaeda's *shoora* council, or consultative committee, approved the plan in August 2001. All the main operatives, including Mohammad Atef, Nawaf Al-Hazmi, and Khalid Al-Mihdhar, were trained and dispatched to the United States by KSM. Two people—Mustafa Ahmed Hawsawi and Ammar Al-Balochi (another nephew of KSM)—provided money to KSM and provided logistic support to the hijackers from Dubai.

On the fateful day, KSM and four of his fellow terrorists—Ramzi bin Al-Shibh, Mustafa Ahmed Hawsawi, Ammar Al-Balochi, and Jaffar Al-Tayer—witnessed the attack on the first of the twin towers from an Internet café in Karachi. Then they rushed to a safe house, where they watched the rest of their murderous plan unfold; KSM says that he was amazed at his handiwork when he saw the towers collapse. On September 21 or 22, 2001, Osama bin Laden recalled KSM to Afghanistan, even though KSM wanted to stay where he was. After analyzing the suicide hijackings, they both got involved in the defense of Afghanistan and the transfer of their families to Pakistan.

Having been tipped off, our intelligence agents spotted an associate of KSM at Islamabad International Airport on the morning of February 28, 2003. He was scheduled to meet KSM that evening. Our source informed us that they would be using two houses on Peshawar Road, Rawalpindi. A plan was immediately drawn up to arrest them alive. The problem was that our source was unfamiliar with the area and knew the houses only by sight. But by sheer ingenuity, coupled with a deep familiarity with the area, our agents were able to identify the houses on the basis of simple descriptions. At one forty-five the next morning, they surrounded the houses. The entrance doors were broken down, and our agents rushed in, brandishing weapons and shouting. In one of the houses a man on the ground floor, taken by surprise, immediately pointed upward and said, "They are up there." Without breaking their momentum our agents ran upstairs and found KSM and his accomplice Mustafa Al-Hawsawi with loaded Kalashnikov beside them. When KSM managed to pick up his Kalashnikov, one of our officers tried to wrest it from his hand; the gun then went off, and a bullet hit and injured the officer. But before KSM and Mustafa could do further damage, they were overpowered and arrested. It had been a smooth, quick operation. We kept KSM in custody for three days, during which time we interrogated him fully. Once we were done with him and had all the information we wanted, we handed him over to the United States government.

Abu Zubeida and KSM are well known to most readers. There are other people, less well known, whom we have also captured. Of all these, one story in particular reveals just a hint of the vast amounts of intelligence that we have acquired—and some of the dreams and plans of the terrorists that we shattered.

This story concerns a Pakistani national. He was born in Karachi and earned a bachelor's degree in computer engineering in 2002.

He had actually been recruited by KSM in March 2002. In August 2003 he was sent to Wana in Pakistan's tribal belt to meet Hamza Rabbiya, Hamza Al Jawfi, Abu Faraj Al Libbi, and Abu Hadi Al Iraqi. He also fought in Afghanistan on the Kara Bagh front during 2000–2001 and carried prize money of $5 million on his head. From December 2003 he had based himself in Lahore and was designated information technology chief of al Qaeda in Pakistan, which after the arrest of KSM was headed by Hamza Rabbiya. He was also a member of a group based in the United Kingdom and assisted the al Qaeda media committee.

After two top al Qaeda leaders—Ammar Al Balochi and Khallad bin Attash—were captured, this man became the point man in Karachi. Given al Qaeda's desire to hit American interests the world over before the presidential elections of 2004 in the United States, he was considered the best person to train a twelve-member suicide squad. He did this in Shakai, North West Frontier Province, and then sent them to Karachi. During this time he remained closely associated with the who's who of al Qaeda, including KSM, Hamza Rabbiya, Faraj al-Libbi, Hadi Iraqi, Hamza al-Jawfi, Hambali "Gun Gun" (brother of Hambali) and Abu Musaab Al-Balochi (another nephew of KSM, and brother of Ramzi Yousef).

Our American friends were, quite understandably, very anxious to terminate his activities. They too had been tracking him and gave us vital leads as to his whereabouts. Based on these, our Intelligence Bureau tracked him from Lahore and arrested him on July 21, 2004. He (and his laptop computer) proved to be a gold mine of information.

We had learned from KSM that al Qaeda's planners were thinking seriously about, and discussing, bombing Heathrow Airport in London, the busiest in the world, as well as London's subway system. The suspect had been told by KSM to carry out reconnaissance of, and prepare a plan to attack, Heathrow Airport. After initial planning, he also suggested Canary Wharf and London's subway system as additional possible targets.

One cannot say that KSM did not have big plans, the biggest of which, 9/11, he carried out with clockwork precision.

The laptop gave us vital information, because it contained plans for a terror attack in Britain. We not only gave this information to the British authorities but also gave them direct access to its owner. Later this would reveal a link with Siddique Khan and Shehzad Tanveer. Siddique and Tanveer were two of the people who were to carry out the suicide bomb attacks on London's underground system on July 7, 2005, a date that has come to be known as 7/7. This information about Siddique and Tanveer was not shared with us until July 28, 2005, twenty-one days after the attacks in London and despite the fact that Siddique and Tanveer had first been spotted seventeen months earlier.

Before the subway operation, however, al Qaeda planned to use the airports and national airlines of the Czech Republic, the Slovak Republic, Croatia, Poland, Romania, and Malta to attack Heathrow, because security at these airports and in their aircraft was lax. Al Qaeda also decided not to use too many Arab hijackers, to avoid suspicion. Instead, it planned to use hardened European Muslim veterans of the Bosnian jihad, and even Afghans. It asked Hazim Al Shair (killed in Saudi Arabia in 2004), the head of al Qaeda in Saudi Arabia, to recruit the pilots who would take over the hijacked airliners. Failing that, he should send students to flying schools. They would select flights that landed at Heathrow at about the same time. The signal for the hijackers to act would be the "fasten seat belts" sign when it was switched on before landing. For weapons they would use the stainless steel cutlery on the plane as well as broken alcohol bottles. They hoped to crash the aircraft into the various buildings of Heathrow. (According to KSM, another important al Qaeda operative, Khallad bin Attash, suggested at a later stage in the planning that they change the target from Heathrow to someplace in Israel, but KSM did not agree.)

All this information was passed on to the British authorities and fortunately the attack on Heathrow never came to fruition. This was one of our many hidden successes.

This source also led us to a group of fifteen terrorists in Gujrat, Punjab, one of whom was the computer wiz Ahmed Khalifan Ghailani, a thirty-year-old Tanzanian national who had been indicted by the United States for the bombings of August 7, 1998, at the American embassies in Dar es Salaam and Nairobi. His real expertise lay in making incredibly well-forged travel documents. He had the visas and entry and exit stamps of many countries on his computer. Ghailani also trained terrorists and made improvised explosive devices. So important was he to the United States that it had offered a reward of $25 million for any information leading to his arrest. We handed him over to the U.S. authorities on September 4, 2004.

His interrogation also revealed an al Qaeda network operating in the Punjab. This network was finished off when, acting on information from him, we arrested fifteen more people comprising al Qaeda operatives and their families (including a newborn baby), apart from the fifteen arrested earlier from Gujrat.

The foregoing is just a kaleidoscope of some of our operations against al Qaeda and its associated terrorist organizations in Pakistan, but it gives a very good idea of the intensity and extent of the war we have successfully fought against them in our cities.

For a full story of what it is like to fight the war on terror in Pakistan, we must return to December 25, 2003, just after I survived the bombing of my motorcade.

CHAPTER 24

TIGHTENING THE NOOSE

A blown-off face, a half-burned ID card, and a destroyed cell phone were all that we had to go on after the second attack. They led to success beyond our wildest expectations. It often happens in science that some of the greatest discoveries are made when researchers stumble onto something completely different from what they are looking for. Similarly, in criminal investigations, significant findings come from the most unlikely breaks, and can lead to dramatic events. It was these three crucial pieces of evidence—the face, the ID card, and a "subscriber identification module" (SIM) card from the cell phone—that led to a major victory in the war on terror in Pakistan.

After the first attempt to assassinate me, on December 14, 2003, I asked the Rawalpindi corps commander, Lieutenant General Ashfaq Parvez Kayani, to take charge of the investigation, since the crime had been committed in his jurisdiction. This was no ordinary criminal act that the police alone could handle. This was an attempt at destabilizing Pakistan by killing its head of state. As you can imagine, we threw everything we had into the investigation.

There were several competing agencies involved under Kayani's command: Inter Services Intelligence (ISI), Military Intelligence (MI), the Intelligence Bureau (IB), the Special Branch of the Criminal Investigation Department (CID), the police, and relevant elements of the army.

Kayani told them to forget about rivalries over turf and work as one unit, sharing all information. He also told them that if they thought any information was very sensitive, all they had to do was to come directly to him; they would find his door always open. He assigned tasks so that the three principal investigating agencies—ISI, MI, and CID—would not run after the same things and duplicate one another's efforts. He himself was hands-on, leading from the front.

It was easier said than done. Intelligence agencies within any country compete with each other and jealously guard their turf and information. This situation has led to many lapses in intelligence, and Pakistan is no exception. But when Kayani got tough, the problems of coordination disappeared and the agencies started working like a well-oiled machine. He told them that they had to investigate three things: one, find all the evidence at the site of the attacks; two, discover how the explosive had been prepared and activated or triggered; and, three, locate the network responsible for masterminding, planning, and execution.

In the first attempt, the attackers had placed explosives under the bridge so that they would detonate at its farthest end, throwing steel and concrete in the direction of the oncoming motorcade. My car was supposed to ram into the bared steel rods protruding like spears, or fall through the gaping six-foot lateral that would be cut in the bridge. That would have been my end. Thank God, as it happened, no one actually lost his life in that attack. The explosive charge was to be activated through a telephone call made to a receiver attached to the explosives. Luckily, the terrorist who had to make the call situated himself in such a manner that he could not clearly see the position of my car when it entered the bridge, and could not time the explosion accurately. This gave us a crucial two to three seconds to escape.

The key break in the first investigation would be from the old-fashioned dark arts of interrogation. But first there was a forensic lead. Our investigators found a small piece of the keypad of a telephone at the bridge. It looked peculiar and didn't seem to belong to a cell phone. They discovered that it was from a Chinese-made long-range cordless phone. In a documented economy—for instance, in Europe or America—it would have been a simple matter to trace the importer of the phone and the distributor and outlets that had helped sell it. Not so when a lot of goods are smuggled and no such record is available.

Still, we learned some things. Such long-range cordless phones have a base unit and a handset, with pager buttons on each. If one presses the pager button on the base unit it generates a call on the handset, and vice versa. The pager button on the handset was ingeniously used as the trigger device. Our investigators found that it worked over a distance of about three or four miles (six or seven kilometers), even in a heavily built-up area. They expanded their search to a radius of four miles (seven kilometers) from the bridge in order to look for the base unit, but found nothing. Then they spread their search out to Chaklala Air Force Base, where my plane had landed. They faced a dead end there, too. They looked at the transmission nodes along the route that pick up telephone signals and pass them on to the next node; this is the arrangement that makes mobile and cordless phones operate. Still nothing.

While this investigation was proceeding, a clue came by chance from the Quetta corps commander. He telephoned Kayani to say that his intelligence people had learned that a terrorist named Mushtaq had links with Quetta and air force personnel based in Peshawar. If there were terrorists or sympathizers in the air force at Quetta and Peshawar, why not at Chaklala? A coordinated intelligence operation was launched that finally led to the arrest of Mushtaq. This was what began to unravel the puzzle. Under interrogation, Mushtaq gave clear leads about who was involved in the first assassination attempt, and to what extent. He gave very specific information on all the conspirators, almost all of whom were from the Pakistan Air Force. Kayani contacted the air chief at midnight and said what he had discovered. Four of the conspirators from the air force were arrested. The air force personnel involved in the attempted assassination were all very junior—warrant officers and below—who had been recruited either for money or for ideological reasons.

From these men we learned how the job had been accomplished. About 551 pounds (250 kilograms) of explosives were hidden under the bridge, having been brought there bit by bit. The design of the bridge made it possible to hide them for a long time. Five steel-and-concrete reinforced beams under the road rested on abutments at their ends, creating six compartments of six feet by eight feet (1.8 by 2.4 meters), completely concealed from view. It is in these rooms that the explosives were initially stored over several nights and then laid in a circuit, without being detected.

Under interrogation, the suspects revealed that they had been using one house in Jhanda Chichi, a locality near the bridge, and another house in Islamabad to hide the explosives. They had been operating from bases in Nowshera and Peshawar in the North-West Frontier Province. The explosives were first brought to the house in Islamabad and then shifted piecemeal to the house in Jhanda Chichi. From there they were gradually shifted to the bridge over several days.

Mushtaq was the only civilian involved in the operation. He was the one who triggered the explosive. He finally turned out to be the planner for an organization of between 150 and 200 people who owed allegiance to Mullah Omar, leader of the Taliban, and had taken an oath to work for Omar's cause. Though they had no direct link with al Qaeda, they were sponsored by the terrorist organization Jaish Mohammad, headed by Maulana Masood Azhar. Not only did Jaish sponsor this organization but Maulana Masood Azhar's brother also helped train its people in the use of explosives and weapons.

Mushtaq had stationed himself in a slight depression about 200 yards (180 meters) upstream from the bridge. This position obscured his sight of the motorcade when it passed over the bridge, and so he mistimed the action and inadvertently allowed us all to escape unhurt.

The terrorist group involved in bombing the bridge knew nothing of the cell assigned to carry out the second attack. The two assassination attempts were totally compartmentalized from each other, and the people involved were entirely different. In fact, the second set of attackers had actually geared itself up on December 14, by sheer coincidence. When the bridge exploded, they were completely taken aback and were forced to temporarily abort their own plan.

When the minivan bombs of December 25 exploded, they were so powerful that Kayani heard the blasts in his house, nearly two miles (three kilometers) away. The memory of the explosion from the first attempt was still fresh in his mind. He jumped into his car and rushed to the scene as fast as his escort of military police could take him. The first thing he did was to seal off the area. Personnel from Inter Services Intelligence, Military Intelligence, and the police were already at the site.

Having secured the site, Kayani rushed to Army House, where he found me still standing in the porch. I instructed him to add this investigation to his responsibilities.

Again, small pieces of evidence proved crucial. There is a two-story police station opposite the second gasoline pump, where the second vehicle struck my motorcade. Our first clue was found in the inner compound of this police station, in the form of the sheered-off face of the first suicide bomber. It had been propelled over and across the building. It was like a mask made of human skin, like something in the movie *Face/Off.* The skin had been peeled off the facial bones and the skull. It was gruesome. It looked as if someone had done a very fine job of surgery. It was lying flat on the ground, faceup. The face was taken to a very able plastic surgeon at the Combined Military Hospital, who did an excellent reconstruction job in order to show us the true appearance of the attacker.

We also found a partially burned identity card near the first explosion. The reconstructed face matched the photograph on the ID card perfectly. Investigators took the card to the National Database and Registration Authority (which has issued over 50 million identity cards and maintains an up-to-date database of Pakistani nationals above age eighteen and their minor dependents) and found information on the person. His name was Mohammad Jamil, and he came from a village in Rawalakot in Azad (Independent) Kashmir. He was the first of the two suicide bombers.

By three thirty PM that same day, instructions went out to the army in Rawalakot to raid Jamil's house and seal it. Before nightfall, the house had been raided and swept, all its occupants had been taken into custody, and crucial evidence had been gathered and flown to Rawalpindi by helicopter. By far the most important evidence came from Jamil's diaries, which contained code names, real names, addresses, and many phone numbers. It took some effort, but our people broke the code within hours, and we got a lot of information, including a great deal of material on terrorist activities.

Jamil's relatives said that he was working with an extremist religious organization and would sometimes disappear for months. He had received training from a terrorist organization in the Kotli area of Independent Kashmir and had gone to Afghanistan to participate in the jihad against the American-led invasion in 2001. There he had been arrested and imprisoned for nearly two years, until his father paid money to obtain his release. When he came back to Pakistan he was very bitter about the outcome of the war there. He was not the only one to take an oath to avenge the United States' attack on Afghanistan by assassinating me.

The mutilated body of the second suicide bomber had flown off and fallen quite some distance away, in front of the entrance to an apartment complex. We also found his partially burned ID card. It had his photograph, but a false name and address. Still, we managed to establish his identity. The card had its registration number, which led us to the office of issue. The complete application form of this individual for a national identity card was dug out. It had the name of the person who had verified his identity. The sponsor was reached, and it was he who gave the bomber's real name and address. The real name was Khaleeq (the name on the ID card was Shafiq). One wonders how people who can plan an operation so meticulously can be so careless as to take their identity cards along with them, unless they think that they will gain fame through martyrdom. Little do they realize that the discovery of their identities can compromise their entire organization. But then, without such egotistical lapses, investigators would never get lucky. The bombings of July 7, 2005, in London followed much the same pattern: more than sufficient evidence was found at the scenes of the crimes to help establish the identities of the suicide bombers without any doubt.

We also discovered a cell phone on the roof of the same police station where Jamil's face mask was found. The instrument had been destroyed, but a meticulous search of the area helped to find the SIM card. Surprisingly, it was intact.

As noted earlier, SIM stands for "subscriber identification module," and as the term implies, it identifies the person in whose name the phone has been purchased. Even if it is a prepaid phone, the record of the calls made to or from the number can be traced. The chances that the terrorist's SIM was still functional seemed dim, but to our surprise, when we put it in another phone, it worked. Thus we not only obtained a lot of phone numbers from the SIM itself, but were able to get many more from the call record at the cell phone company. That actually became the starting point of an investigation that led to the entire network.

After the first assassination attempt, we had worked out the calls made from cell phones along the entire route of the motorcade, from anyone nearby. Similarly, after the second attempt, we discovered from the call records that there was a person acting as a spotter. He had reported to somebody located at the center of the route, acting as the controller, who in turn gave instructions to the suicide bombers. The spotter had stationed himself at the boundary of responsibility between the police forces of Islamabad and Rawalpindi where the motorcade had the option of taking one of two routes. It was only after my motorcade took one particular route that the controller told the suicide bombers that the operation was a "go."

After the second assassination attempt Kayani was confronted with a maze of telephone calls from different numbers. At first, it was a daunting mass of data. He was quick to assemble a team of army officers who were computer experts by hobby. They developed a software program that was able to sort through all the calls, arranging them chronologically up to the moment of the attack. It allowed him to extract a tangible network pattern of the terrorists' calls. This was a major technical breakthrough and subsequently led to the clear separation of the terrorist planners and executors.

He could see which numbers belonged to the planners and which to the executors. The planning group had been talking earlier, before and after a two-hour window on either side of the blasts. The execution group had been talking only just before the time of the first blast. We would see an accelerating series of very brief calls, just a few seconds long. I can imagine the words: "He's approaching"; "He's within a mile"; "Fifty yards."

Faced with the vast number of calls and telephone numbers, Kayani and his investigators soon ran into another maze. They discovered that the terrorists had changed SIMs, or simply exchanged SIMs among themselves in order to confuse investigators and avoid detection. But again, a chance breakthrough solved the problem.

One day Kayani mentioned his problem to Nadeem Taj, my military secretary. Nadeem said that his son Nomi worked for a cell phone company and had told him that even if a SIM is changed, a caller who continues to use the same instrument can still be traced. Our investigators had been told the opposite by the cell phone companies. But they had been talking to senior management, people who are often unaware of the minutiae of their own operations. When Kayani asked his people to contact the hands-on staff of the companies, they were told, yes, it was possible to trace the user of the same instrument even if the SIM is changed. What happens is that every phone has its own specific code number and every SIM has its own code number. When the phone is used, they both get transmitted and recorded. So even if the SIM is changed, the code of the instrument remains the same and the caller can be traced.

Now the investigators had another method for analyzing the available data. It became a great help in breaking into the terrorists' telephone networks.

At one point Kayani became frustrated because he couldn't ascertain the modus operandi of al Qaeda. He asked ISI to give him the reports of the interrogation of al Qaeda's top brass, Khalid Sheikh Mohammad (KSM) and Abu Zubeida. He received ten thick folders. Scanning them, he saw that al Qaeda liked to work on any given objective with two separate and independent cells that were unaware of each other. He also realized that they had a few highly specialized makers of improvised explosive devices (IEDs). Those few men would prepare IEDs, hand them over to the executor of any given plot, and then detach themselves. The bomb makers did not know when, where, or for what purpose the bombs would be used, or by whom. So it was essential that we find and arrest al Qaeda's IED maker or makers.

Our next break came when Kayani's men traced the dealer who had sold the Suzuki van that Jamil used in the suicide attack on me. The dealer gave them descriptions of the buyers. One description matched Jamil. We also matched Jamil's DNA with samples taken from his parents.

The second bomber, Khaleeq, belonged to a village in the North-West Frontier Province. He turned out to be an orphan living with uncles and aunts. His family said that he had been involved in the Afghan jihad and would sometimes be away from home for six months at a time. When he was home, strange people would sometimes visit him. He ignored his family's warnings that he was falling into the hands of the wrong people, who would get him killed. The family appeared quite dysfunctional.

This was a common feature we found among all the suicide bombers: they had personality disorders and came from broken homes or dysfunctional families. Some were of an uninformed religious bent; others became terrorists just for the money. For example, Jamil was religiously motivated but the second suicide bomber was not. Many either were illiterate or had only a very basic education. Some came from very poor backgrounds and large, disjointed families that couldn't make ends meet. They were ripe for indoctrination and molding.

At about the same time that we traced the vehicle used in the attack, we arrested someone named Salahuddin who was close to people high up in al Qaeda's hierarchy. We got him through the good work of the Criminal Investigation Department of the Punjab provincial government. This was a very important breakthrough. Salahuddin was arrested in Jhanda Chichi, the same locality from which the bridge bombers were operating.

We discovered that Salahudddin had actually recruited the people involved in the second assassination attempt. We also discovered that he had gone to Afghanistan to join the war there. He knew Abu Faraj al-Libbi and Hadi al-Iraqi, two prominent members of al Qaeda. After Salahuddin returned from Afghanistan he got married, took a house in Jhanda Chichi, and had children. Now he had additional needs and responsibilities. Making money was high on his agenda.

He had contacted Hadi al-Iraqi and said that he wanted to meet him, but Iraqi could not meet him personally, and arranged instead for Salahuddin to meet Abu Faraj al Libbi. They met twice, in Hasan Abdal, twenty-eight miles (about forty-five kilometers) from Rawalpindi and not far from Peshawar, the capital of the North-West Frontier Province, which had also been the capital of the mujahideen during the jihad against the Soviet Union during the 1980s. Salahuddin claimed that Abu Faraj gave him money.

Under interrogation, Salahuddin claimed that two noncommissioned officers of the Special Services Group of commandos (SSG), to which I also belong, were helping him. One was named Arshad and the other Dogar. This was a surprise but not a complete shock—it is almost impossible to guard against extremists' indoctrinating the lower ranks in any armed forces.

We arrested Arshad—of all places—from the security detail of the vice chief of the army staff. Arshad was from a village in Kahuta near Islamabad. But it is appalling nevertheless how close the terrorists could get to us.

I was initially shocked by the apparent involvement of Dogar, because he was one of my close personal guards and was actually in the front seat of my car on December 25. Happily, he turned out to be innocent. It was a different Dogar, who had been in my security detail at one time, but no longer. We also picked up the bad Dogar.

Arshad started divulging a lot of information. We found that he had been part of this terrorist group for a long time. He had met Omar Saeed Sheikh, the person involved in the kidnapping and murder of Daniel Pearl, when Omar Sheikh was contemplating the abduction. Arshad also told us that some rockets had been brought to Islamabad a year earlier and were supposed to be used to assassinate me and others in the high command of our government during our Republic Day Parade on March 23, 2003. This was reminiscent of the assassination of President Anwar Sadat of Egypt. We had heard about this at the time but didn't know for sure where the rockets had come from or where they were. Arshad told us that they were in his village, close to Kahuta. His home was raided by Military Intelligence at midnight that very day, and three powerful rockets were found. There were watches as well, to be used as timers for bombs. Everything needed for suicide bombing, including bomb-making kits and detonators, was discovered. The activation kits for the bombs were highly sophisticated.

Like the second suicide bomber, Arshad was hardly religious. He was just a mercenary, working for money.

On January 2, 2004, our investigation led to the discovery of the third suicide vehicle in Shakrial, a neighborhood of Rawalpindi. January 2 was just a few days before a summit of the heads of government of the South Asia Association for Regional Cooperation was to take place in Islamabad. It was on the sidelines of this summit that Prime Minister

Atal Bihari Vajpayee of India and I would sign the famous Islamabad Declaration that commenced the composite dialogue between Pakistan and India. When we found the vehicle, it was fully prepared for an assault. There was a large cylinder in it, the sort that is used for compressed air or natural gas. The terrorists had drilled a hole in the cylinder and filled it with a large amount of explosive. The detonation cord was visible through the hole. We also discovered a lot of explosives at the house where this vehicle was found, secreted in an overhead water tank. The terrorists were all set to attack the summit meeting.

After all the arrests and investigations, we were finally able to begin to define the structure of the network. There was a definite link between Salahuddin and Abu Faraj al-Libbi (al Qaeda's number three), as well as between Salahuddin and Arshad. Salahuddin's role was that of a go-between for the mastermind, Libbi. Al Qaeda's style is decentralized: once the mastermind identifies a target, he gives it to the go-between, who in turn hands the operation over to a planner. After the planner has planned the operation, he hands it over to an execution team for implementation. The execution cell then executes the operation on its own. There is no timetable for execution. The timing is left to the executers.

For the second attack, Abu Faraj al-Libbi was the mastermind. Salahuddin was just a mailman—a courier who took Libbi's plans and gave them to the planner. But who was the planner? We were told that the air force personnel and the commandos of the Special Services Group whom we had arrested were relatively small players. We were still missing a link. It was then that the interrogators came across the name of Amjad Faruqi.

Faruqi and Libbi had met in Afghanistan. Faruqi turned out to be the main planner of al Qaeda in Pakistan. Not only did he plan and direct the second attempt to assassinate me, he was also in the vicinity when the attempt was carried out. Faruqi had gone to Afghanistan many times. He was very highly regarded in the al Qaeda hierarchy, from its high command downward, as well as in extremist sectarian circles, for his operational capabilities, leadership qualities, and professionalism.

We started searching for Amjad Faruqi. We knew he had the capacity and resources to arrange the second assassination attempt and that it was he who put together the entire operation. Could Salahuddin help us find him?

During all this time, many offers kept coming from our American friends to help us in our investigations. One day Kayani invited them to his headquarters and asked for their technical help with the explosives. The Americans said that they needed to see the site, and he allowed them to see it. He then asked them how much time they needed. They said four weeks. After four weeks they presented him with their report. Kayani was surprised to find that there was nothing in it that he did not already know. It merely contained the type of explosive used. He asked the Americans whether there was anything he was missing. They said no, this was all they had. Kayani thanked them and said that we had already achieved significant breakthroughs, made many arrests, and completed our investigations. That was the help we got from our friends.

Abu Faraj al-Libbi was the biggest fish in this pond. As I have said, he was al Qaeda's number three, who now filled the shoes of KSM. We desperately wanted to find him. Yet I was equally interested in the arrest of Amjad Faruqi. If we got both, that would be ideal, for with the mastermind and the main planner in Pakistan out of the way, a very big blow would be dealt to organized terrorism in our country and we would have some peace. And so it came to pass, at least in our cities.

As it transpired, we bagged Amjad Faruqi first. We were able to track him thanks to our analysis of all the phone calls on December 25, 2003. We started by tracking Faruqi's phone. He kept changing numbers and would often go quiet for some time. But we kept at it. He could not keep quiet for too long. In September 2004, we found that he was talking to two people in particular, in the Punjabi dialect of Faisalabad, the third largest of our cities in central Punjab. Their conversations were always very brief. It soon became apparent that he was the most important person in the trio, for he was usually giving the instructions. Libbi's name came up in some of those conversations.

Two parallel, independent investigations were going on at the same time—one by Kayani's men in Rawalpindi and the other by the commanding officer of the Inter Services Intelligence detachment in

Karachi. As it turned out, the commanding officer's information was better and more accurate than that of Kayani's team. Both sides had recorded some of Faruqi's phone calls. Kayani took the recordings of the telephone conversations from the commanding officer and compared the voice samples with his own team's recordings. He found that all three voices matched.

On September 25, 2004, Major General Zaki, director general of Counterintelligence, called Kayani and informed him that Faruqi was on the move. His destination was Nawabshah, in the province of Sindh, about 100 miles (160 kilometers) north of Karachi on the Arabian Sea. Both teams started tracking Faruqi constantly, and in coordination with each other.

Faruqi was heading south, starting out from Dera Ismail Khan and then going on to Lakki Marwat, both in the North-West Frontier Province. When he reached Nawabshah, our agents were hot on his heels. He holed up in a house with his accomplices. Our men surrounded the house. When they rang the doorbell and someone came out, they grabbed him. Our agents climbed onto the roof. Inside the house, Amjad Faruqi realized that he was surrounded. This was a traditional eastern-style house with a courtyard at the back. At one end of the courtyard was a solitary room. Faruqi took a woman and child from inside the house, ran into the room, and bolted the door. Our agents climbed onto its roof and asked him to come out. Faruqi replied that he would not and insisted that their commander speak to him. We were very anxious to take him alive, so our agents cut a hole in the roof (which was not made of concrete) and fired in a tear-gas canister, smoking Amjad Faruqi out. Faruqi came running out toward our agents, but instead of firing pistols from both hands, he had something that looked even more lethal and deadly—a thick shawl wrapped around his body, like a poncho. He might have been hiding a weapon or wearing an explosive belt. Our agents shouted at him to stop, but he kept moving toward them. Fearing that he would blow everyone up, they shot and killed him. When they pulled back the shawl, they saw that he was not only carrying a loaded submachine gun but also wearing an explosive belt. When a person is determined to go down fighting, it is very difficult to take him alive.

Now the problem was to positively identify him, because he had changed his appearance by shaving off his beard. We flew in a man named Khalid Fauji, who was in our custody and who knew Amjad Faruqi very well. He had been Faruqi's "shadow" when they operated together. When he saw the body he confirmed that this was indeed Amjad Faruqi. Of course we followed up this visual identification with DNA testing.

"I have good news for you," I said to General John Abizaid, commander in chief of CENTCOM, when he came to visit me in May 2005. "We have Libbi."

I consider Abizaid an able general and also a good friend.

"Really? When?" asked the surprised American.

"A few days ago," I replied.

"Where is he now?" asked Abizaid.

"Oh, he's here in Islamabad," I replied nonchalantly. "Please tell President Bush—or should I?"

"It would be better if you informed him." said Abizaid, his excitement growing.

"I don't know," I said. "You tell President Bush."

"No, I can't. You please tell him."

I said that I would. That evening I phoned President Bush and gave him the news. "You've got Libbi?" he exclaimed in excitement. The one al Qaeda operative whose name Bush knew, apart from Osama bin Laden and Dr. Ayman al-Zawahiri—the one man he had asked me to arrest if I could—was Abu Faraj al-Libbi.

His real name is Mustafa Muhammad, but he is better known as Abu Faraj al-Libbi. His capture was as significant as the capture of KSM, and is worth telling about in full. It began in the old-fashioned way: we nabbed three men who told us what we needed to know.

Abu Faraj al-Libbi came to Afghanistan to fight in the early 1990s, after the Soviet Union had withdrawn and the jihad was over. He became a pioneer member of al Qaeda. After the arrest of KSM on March 1, 2003, Libbi took his place in the al Qaeda hierarchy. He became prominent, and his name became known to the public after the two attempts to assassinate me.

After Kabul fell to the American-led coalition in 2001, Libbi came to Karachi. He kept on the move, shifting from Karachi to Gujranwala in the Punjab and then on to Abbotabad and the Bajour Agency in the North-West Frontier Province. He was chief of al Qaeda's operations in Pakistan and received funds from al Qaeda abroad.

Truth to tell, Libbi led us a merry chase, even though he was easy to recognize, owing to leukoderma on his face, a condition that makes white albinolike blotches on the skin. We came very close to arresting him twice before we finally managed to get him. The first time was as early as April 2004, about four months after the second attempt to assassinate me. We had arrested many people, one of whom was Libbi's driver. He gave us a lot of leads to work on.

One of those leads caused us to arrest someone from Gujranwala, Punjab, who had kept Libbi in his house and was Libbi's courier. Under interrogation he revealed that he had rented a house in Abbotabad, and that was where Libbi was living right then. This man had also kept his family there to provide cover for Libbi. What he did not tell us is that there were actually three houses in Abbotabad that Libbi used. At that time Libbi was in the third house. Our people raided the first one, and Libbi escaped.

The second miss was again in Abbotabad. We were tipped off that someone important in al Qaeda was living in a house there, and that someone else, also very important, someone we were looking for, was supposed to come and meet him. We did not know that the second someone was Abu Faraj al-Libbi, but we had enough information to attempt an interception. Our team members stationed themselves around the house in Abbotabad. When the expected visitor turned up, the person in the house came out to meet him. But as he approached, the visitor acted suspicious and tried to run away. There was an exchange of fire, and he was killed. The visitor was not Libbi. Later, after we arrested Libbi and interrogated him, we discovered his pattern: he would always send somebody ahead as a decoy while he himself stayed behind to observe. He was undoubtedly watching his decoy perform the fatal pantomime that day.

We had to start afresh. We managed to "turn" one of Libbi's important accomplices, of course without Libbi's knowledge. Our agents made the captive accomplice arrange a meeting between himself and Libbi. The accomplice tried to arrange the meeting in Bannu, but Libbi stayed away. He had said he would appear, but he intended only to send a courier. Then he even canceled the courier. Our lead, the captive accomplice, was next told that a new meeting would take place in Mardan, again in the North-West Frontier Province, at four thirty on the afternoon of May 1, 2005.

Pakistani intelligence planned its operation. We knew from informants that Libbi traveled on a motorbike as a passenger, while somebody else drove. Our people were camouflaged, hiding and ready, with three men on motorbikes. As four thirty approached, Libbi kept calling, asking the captive accomplice in code whether everything was OK. The accomplice assured him that everything was fine. Our men took their informant to a bazaar so that Libbi would hear the background noise and be assured that he wasn't in custody. We played other such games with him. But still, he did not appear at four thirty. Then the line went dead.

Early the next morning a call came that Libbi would be at the meeting place at nine thirty, thus reducing the warning and preparation time. Not all our men were there, but they still decided to go ahead with the operation. The meeting place was a dark graveyard where there is also a shrine that has a lot of visitors, who come and go all day long. Three of our people put on burkas, the robes that women wear to cover themselves, including their faces. Abu Faraj al-Libbi got there at nine thirty on the dot. At some distance from the meeting point he got off his bike. For some reason, he broke with his usual procedure of sending in a decoy first, and simply started walking toward our man. Though he was wearing big sunglasses and a cap, our people had no doubt that it was he, because of the leukoderma on his face. His driver stayed on the bike while a gunman followed at a distance. The moment Libbi came close to one of our burka-clad "women," "she" jumped up and embraced him. It was quite a scene. In a place as conservative as the North-West Frontier Province, a woman in a burka embracing a man in public is unthinkable.

The moment this happened, Libbi's gunman (later identified as Ibrahim, a Pakistani courier) opened fire aimlessly and then ran and hid in a house some distance away. Our agents chased him and surrounded the house. They asked him to come out. When he wouldn't, they fired a tear-gas canister into the house, forced him out, and arrested him.

Meanwhile, the bike driver ran off at high speed. We tried to hit him and capture him, without killing him, but he managed to escape. Nonetheless, the capture of Abu Faraj al-Libbi is one of the greatest victories in our terrorist manhunts.

With Amjad Faruqi's death and Libbi's capture, the story of the attack of December 25, 2005, on me reached closure. The mastermind was in custody; the chief planner was dead; Salahuddin, the go-between, was also captured, as were all the major operatives in the case. A few minor players are still at large. Kayani, who by now had become director general of ISI, was able to bring the case to a successful conclusion. He was not the only happy man.

There was one final twist: Mushtaq, the man who had played a key role in the first attempt to assassinate me, on December 14, 2003, escaped from a base of the Pakistan Air Force in Rawalpindi, where he had been kept in custody. Not being a regular prison, the air base had slack security. An opportunity to escape came at six AM on November 25, 2004, when Mushtaq asked the guard on duty to let him take a shower. When he came out of the shower, he found the guard asleep. They were in a gallery where off-duty air force technicians leave their overalls. Mushtaq put on a pair of overalls and slipped past the sleeping guard and out through a window. He then managed to hoodwink the guards at the main gate, since he was in Pakistan Air Force overalls and they did not suspect that he was one of their prime prisoners. Then the situation went from the stupid to the ridiculous. To get away fast and undetected, Mushtaq asked a bicycle rider who was also wearing an air force uniform to give him a ride to the Daewoo intercity bus stop. From there he went to Peshawar, over 100 miles (160 kilometers) away, where he phoned a man named Mubashir, who directed him to one Noor Jehan, with whom he stayed till January 2005. (Noor Jehan is normally a woman's name, but not in this case.)

From Peshawar, Mushtaq went to Lahore, where he met up with Mubashir's cousins, who told him to go and work in a poultry farm owned by two brothers, Naukhez and Javed, in a nearby small town named Bhai Pheru. He told them that the intelligence agencies were looking for him. At a later date Mushtaq met up with a man named Kaleem, and the two discussed killing foreigners in Islamabad, and even started planning some operations.

Mushtaq then changed course. Along with Naukhez and Mubashir, he started planning another attempt to assassinate me, in the area of the Islamabad Highway, which leads from the capital to Rawalpindi. In fact, they had made all the necessary arrangements and Mushtaq left Lahore for Islamabad on April 19, 2005, to carry out the assassination attempt on April 20, 2005. But by now the ISI was on his heels and he was arrested on the highway near the Salem intersection.

How the ISI traced Mushtaq is another interesting story. His escape deeply shook our authorities. Searching for him would be like looking for a needle in a haystack, but the ISI was assigned to catch him, come what may. A special exclusive unit was set up within the ISI to find Mushtaq. A number of his family members were already either in custody or under strict watch. We also had a lot of data concerning his friends and associates and the places he used to visit or hide out in. The ISI paid special attention to three phone numbers and addresses. The first was Mushtaq's mother's number in Karachi, the second was his girlfriend's in Gujrat, and the third was Mubashir's in Peshawar.

When Mushtaq made the first phone call to Mubashir after reaching Peshawar on the day he escaped, we were still not onto him. But after about four weeks he called his mother from a public call office in Bara near Peshawar, so we knew that he was there. A few days later he called his girlfriend in Gujrat from a cell phone and joyfully told her, "I have escaped, and they will never be able to catch me again." Unfortunately for him, his girlfriend told him that she had written him off after he had been arrested and had taken on another boyfriend. This infuriated him so much that he threatened to travel to Gujrat immediately and kill his rival. However, instead of going to Gujrat he remained in Peshawar. Later he went to Lahore and then to Bhai Pheru in January 2005. By now the ISI had his cell phone number and the codes of his SIM, as well as the phone itself.

After these two telephone interceptions, the ISI was able to establish Mushtaq's movement pattern and identify his associates in Peshawar. Mushtaq knew that his phone could get him into trouble, so he kept changing SIMs. Eventually he was using different SIMs for different people, including his girlfriend in Gujrat. The ISI knew all this, and was on his heels when he got onto the highway from Lahore to Islamabad.

That is how he was arrested at the Salem interchange. He was found fast asleep in his seat in the last row of a bus, with a switched-on cell phone in his pocket. When the ISI officer asked him to identify himself, Mushtaq replied, "You know exactly who I am."

Hopefully, Mushtaq's saga has finally come to an end.

CHAPTER 25

AL QAEDA IN THE MOUNTAINS

In part to be nearer to Afghanistan, in part because of the success of our campaign against them in the cities, in part to be in a remote area with natural defenses, many members of al Qaeda relocated to the mountains—specifically to the Federally Administered Tribal Areas (FATA) in the North-West Frontier Province. The border with Afghanistan is a stretch of 850 miles (1,360 kilometers) and is home to seven main tribes, which on the Pakistan side are organized into seven tribal agencies: Khyber, Bajaur, Mohmand, Orakzai, Kurram, and the North and South Waziristan agencies (see Map 4). The terrain is inhospitable and inaccessible—rugged and mountainous, with heights ranging from 8,000 to 15,000 feet (2,400 to 4,500 meters), subject to harsh winters and burningly hot summers and largely devoid of roads. During the colonial period the British were restricted to transit on just a few roads in this region, and many of those were rarely open.

Under our constitution, FATA enjoys a semi-autonomous status. It is home to some 3.2 million tribal folk. It is spread over 10,600 square miles (27,220 square kilometers) and is largely governed by age-old tribal customs, with *maliks,* or chiefs and elders, wielding political and military influence and authority over their tribes. Although the tribes are religious, the role of the mullahs is restricted to mosques. The federal government is represented by "political agents" who exercise control through levies and through a local police force called *khassadars.*

Pakistan's border with Afghanistan cuts across tribes, dividing people with deep ethnic and social bonds. A clause in the Durand Line agreement of 1893 separating India and now Pakistan from Afghanistan, commonly known as "easement rights," allowed cross-border social and commercial interaction for the tribes in the late decades of the British Empire. The practice continues to this day. Historically reputed to be fierce fighters who carry weapons and maintain their own arsenals, the tribesmen of FATA have always been profoundly patriotic in their attitude toward Pakistan. They actively participated in the Kashmir war of 1948 and also contributed armed tribesmen to the Pakistan Army in its wars with India.

Yet they are fiercely independent as well. It was only in 2000 that the Pakistan Army was allowed to enter all the tribal agencies for the first time ever, to build roads and to foster economic development. Our ultimate goal is to integrate the tribal areas politically into the North-West Frontier Province.

After 9/11, the army's strength was increased and a network of human intelligence was created in the area. When we received initial reports of al Qaeda's presence there, we did not take them very seriously, and in any case the magnitude of the threat was unknown. The truth dawned on us only gradually, with increased intelligence.

In December 2001, when Operation Tora Bora caused many al Qaeda and Taliban fighters to flee to Pakistan, I established a net for apprehending them. Our regular forces and the paramilitary Frontier Corps were dropped in by helicopter, as the area is quite inaccessible from the ground. We even gathered mules from all parts of the country and formed them into animal transport battalions to sustain our troops in this extremely inhospitable area, most of which has no communication infrastructure at all.

The Tora Bora net led to the capture of 240 al Qaeda operatives belonging to twenty-six different nationalities, the majority from Afghanistan and the Arab countries. It remains the largest catch in a single antiterrorist operation conducted anywhere in the world since 9/11.

Since then, we have engaged in a number of operations of varying size. They have been recounted in the press in only bare outlines. The full stories, and results, show that we have made far more progress than most people know.

The first big operation after Tora Bora was a real eye-opener. We called it Operation Kazha Punga, after the name of the place. It was conducted in the South Waziristan agency on the night of June 25, 2002. We received information about the presence of thirty to thirty-five al Qaeda operatives and their families in Kazha Punga. A force of 500 comprising elements of the Special Services Group (SSG), the regular infantry, and the Frontier Corps was immediately dispatched to search the area. The infantry and the Frontier Corps traveled by road through the night, over the most rugged terrain. They stopped at a distance from Kazha Punga and then marched there using local guides. The SSG was dropped at dawn using some of our scarce helicopters. We learned later that the terrorists had deployed lookouts and knew that our force was approaching.

Once a cordon was established, the terrorists inside the compound started to plead innocence, saying that there were only two men and four women, one of whom was pregnant. It was a bluff. Still sounding innocent, they invited our troops to search the compound. Our troops fell for the pretense, thinking that our intelligence must have been faulty. They entered the compound without taking precautions and were met with a spray of bullets. Ten soldiers lost their lives, and two terrorists were killed. The remaining terrorists managed to escape.

This operation was a turning point, because it highlighted the magnitude and seriousness of the threat. It also confirmed the presence of foreign terrorists beyond the Tora Bora area; it confirmed, too, that they were receiving local assistance. Our men also learned, the hard way, just how disarmingly "innocent" this vicious enemy could be.

Operation Kazha Punga made us realize that we needed a special, fast-reacting, hard-hitting force for the mountains. In coordination with the United States' CENTCOM and intelligence agencies, a helicopter-borne Special Operations Task Force (SOTF) was created. It was composed of a battalion from SSG made helicopter-mobile, thanks to assistance from the United States. We demanded and were assured of night-flying and firing capabilities. We also established technical intelligence centers in cooperation with U.S. intelligence. Unmanned aerial vehicles were to be made available to us on demand, flown by American handlers. This completed a triad of intelligence—human, technical, and aerial. The human responsibility was ours; the other two were under the control of the United States.

Unfortunately, assistance did not materialize as promised from the

United States. Its assets and intelligence took a lot longer to arrive than we were told to expect. While we trained our new force and established an intelligence network on the ground, dozens of minor operations were conducted against identified al Qaeda targets. Unfortunately, most of them were inconclusive. Our information was deficient or delayed, and our forces were much slower than al Qaeda. We simply had to have night-flight helicopters, but the promised equipment still did not come. In order for us to reach our targets, we had to traverse a very difficult terrain. The terrorists always had agents among the villagers and their own lookouts, with excellent communications, and would thus be warned in time to make their getaway.

In 2002 we made hectic efforts to establish an effective intelligence network and to strengthen the operational effectiveness of SOTF. On the intelligence side there were occasional misunderstandings between the Pakistan Army and the agencies, both American and Pakistani. The army blamed the intelligence agencies for inaccurate intelligence, while the agencies blamed the army for its slow reactions. There was truth in both claims. On many occasions our intelligence was inadequate or delayed, and often the army was slow to react. Our intentions were firm and determined, but we needed the helicopters. The United States was extremely slow in providing the promised equipment, especially helicopters, to SOTF. The Pakistan Army had to scrounge from its own limited helicopter resources from all over, and to commit its very precious helicopter gunships from its limited military operational reserves.

It took more than a year to get the American helicopters for SOTF, and these were for day operations only; it took approximately another year to train and equip some of the pilots for the conduct of night operations. Gunships have still not been provided. This has led to much finger-pointing among Pakistani operatives and our American facilitators. Eventually, Pakistan did manage to get substantial military assistance for SOTF, and by late 2003 we were able to score some telling victories.

The first operation conducted by the newly raised SOTF was called Operation Baghar China. It was launched in the first week of October 2003 in the area of that name. It was supported by regular infantry elements, which established blocks at the likely entry and exit points of the target compounds. While our cordon was being established, the terrorists started firing. Intense exchange of fire continued an entire day, until the resistance was finally overcome. A total of eight terrorists were killed, including a Jordanian named Samarkand, who was a senior al Qaeda member with a bounty of $5 million on his head; and a Chinese named Hassan Masoom, who was the leader of the East Turkistan Islamic Movement. Nineteen others were arrested, of whom eight were foreigners. This operation confirmed the presence of large numbers of foreign terrorists operating in an organized manner in the South Waziristan agency.

Five months later, from March 16 to 28, 2004, a major counterinsurgency operation was conducted in the Wana valley in the South Waziristan agency. We had reports of activity by al Qaeda there. We approached the local population through their tribal councils or *Jirgas,* asking them to surrender all foreigners. Amnesty was promised to those who surrendered. In fact, they were offered not only amnesty but also the chance to live peacefully in the tribal agencies. The response of the
Jirgas was positive, and they passed our offer to the terrorists. But the foreigners refused to comply. This clearly showed that al Qaeda terrorists were very much in command of themselves and not under the dictates of the locals.

So we decided to launch an operation through the Frontier Corps. When the troops reached Wana, they found themselves trapped in a cleverly laid ambush. Our forces were in a low-lying area while the terrorists had occupied the surrounding hills and mountains. There was a hail of fire from the mountains, and our troops suffered heavy casualties in men and matériel. A pitched battle ensued, with the terrorists dominating the area. The army was called in to break the ambush and retrieve the trapped men of the Frontier constabulary. Nearly 6,000 troops were immediately moved in, including 600 lifted by helicopters from a distance of approximately 190 miles (300 kilometers). These troops, in conjunction with SOTF, immediately threw a cordon around the ambush site and launched a search operation. Unfortunately, an adjacent ridge occupied by the terrorists remained outside the cordon. The army drew heavy fire from this ridge and suffered sixteen dead.

We launched an attack on the ridge to clear it, and finally won the battle. Wana was cleared of al Qaeda. This operation led to the elimination of a major command and communication center of the terrorists. We found a network of tunnels containing sophisticated electronic equipment, including a telephone exchange. All told, during the operation sixty-four soldiers lost their lives and fifty-eight were injured. The terrorists' casualties were sixty-three killed, thirty-six foreigners and twenty-seven locals.

The Wana operation proved to be a watershed in counterterrorism. It displayed our firm resolve and commitment despite the intensity of the opposition we faced. Nonetheless, it also exposed our continuing inadequacies in terms of night flying and insufficient helicopters, and it caused further tension in our relations with the United States. We were even denied the use of helicopters provided to our Ministry of the Interior by the United States government's Drug Enforcement Agency during this very critical operation. It would have also been very helpful to have unmanned aerial vehicles for real-time information, but we were out of luck there too.

The Wana operation was the first large-scale operation by the Pakistan Army in South Waziristan. We reinforced the local division of our Peshawar Corps with two additional brigades. The troops had the task of keeping the Wana valley under control, establishing checkpoints on main roads and walking tracks to deny free movement to the terrorists, and chasing the terrorists beyond Wana.

After two additional months of operations by the Pakistan Army along our western border with Afghanistan and the Wana valley, some fleeing foreign terrorists took refuge in Shakai valley. There they began to reorganize and train themselves. We received reports of more than 200 to 250 Chechens and Uzbeks, along with a few Arabs, and 300 to 400 local supporters. On June 10, 2004, we launched the Shakai valley operation in response. It was massive, involving 10,000 regular troops combined with SOTF and Frontier constabulary troops.

After nearly 3,000 soldiers established an outer cordon and secured the approaches leading to Shakai, the Pakistan Air Force struck at dawn, using precision weapons against nine compounds. Indirect artillery fire and precision rocket attacks by helicopter gunships were also brought to bear. At the same time we used helicopters to drop in SOTF personnel to search the compounds. Simultaneously, infantry troops launched an operation to clear the valley and link up with SOTF. Later, an additional force of 3,000 men was brought into the area to clear more of the valley up to Sangtoi, Mangtoi, and the watershed of Bosh Narai.

During the operation four soldiers were killed and twelve injured; over fifty terrorists were killed. We eliminated a major propaganda base and stronghold of the terrorists, which also included a facility for manufacturing improvised explosive devices. The haul from a large underground cellar in one of the compounds included two truckloads of television sets, computers, laptops, disks, tape recorders, and tapes. It proved to be a turning point with the local tribesmen. The myth of the invincibility of the terrorists was broken and the local population withdrew its support from them. Thereafter, the local people helped the Pakistan Army to establish the authority of the government in the area. The successful conduct of this operation also forced the Waziri tribe to sign the famous Shakai Agreement with the government, after which we started development work in the area. We are concentrating on infrastructure, schools, health care facilities, and water projects for irrigation.

From a bird's-eye view, our mountain campaigns have been something like a landlocked version of Douglas MacArthur's island-hopping campaign in the Pacific during World War II. We had cleared two "islands," but our hopping was not finished. After fleeing Shakai and the border areas of South Waziristan, most of the foreign terrorists next took refuge in the Mahsud tribe's area, where they found support. Some sixty to seventy foreigners were reported to be in the Dila Khula area. It was said to have become a major training and logistical base of the terrorists.

The complex there had three distinct operational and administrative bases. On September 9, 2004, an air strike was launched in which over seventy foreign and local terrorists were killed. The army launched a ground operation with approximately 10,000 regular troops, with aerial support, against all three strongholds. Resistance was stiff, and forty-two soldiers were martyred and 124 injured, including five officers. Over seventy terrorists were killed. It was costly, but it was a victory. Another island was cleared.

This was a major operation, indeed the culmination of military operations in the South Waziristan agency. With the destruction of their main command, training, logistical, and propaganda bases, the terrorists lost the ability to operate as a cohesive, organized body. Those who survived fled into the mountains in small groups. Their local sympathizers were badly discredited, and most of them decided to cooperate with the government. All told, the casualties suffered by the terrorists included 350 dead and 800 arrested. On our side, approximately 300 soldiers laid down their lives in the war against terrorism. They will always be remembered for their supreme sacrifice.

The battle continues. Al Qaeda, though defeated in the South Waziristan agency, is now reported to be in the towns of Mir Ali and Miranshah of North Waziristan agency. Our focus has thus shifted to these towns.

After all the military operations against al Qaeda, we have developed a fairly good picture of its characteristics. At its peak strength in Pakistan, its core comprised up to 300 battle-hardened fighters of Arab, Uzbek, Tajik, Chechen, and Afghan origin. Though we have eliminated its command, control, communication, and propaganda bases in the South Waziristan agency, it is still operating in North Waziristan. The terrorists are very well trained in hit-and-run tactics and are adept at raids and ambushes. Most of their actions are intense and swift. They are capable of putting up stiff, last-man-last-bullet resistance. They are equipped with sophisticated weapons and high-tech communications, which they use efficiently for effective command and control.

Al Qaeda appears financially secure. It has attracted Pakistani followers by a combination of religious indoctrination and more straightforward monetary incentives, including the renting of local compounds at exorbitant rates. At times, it has forcibly coerced people into supporting it.

Gathering intelligence about al Qaeda is harder than conducting physical operations against it. All antiterrorist operations are intelligence-driven, but also require swift mobility by day and night and effective firepower. Unfortunately, despite our best efforts, we were not given timely access to modern technology for intelligence gathering, surveillance, and target acquisition. Our army operations remain dependent on technical intelligence provided through U.S. resources.

One very effective theme used by al Qaeda in its propaganda has been to depict its members as the true followers of Islam, and the Pakistan Army as infidels operating under the spell of the United States and the West. Countering this vicious propaganda was crucial, because al Qaeda's message seemed very convincing to gullible illiterates. Commanders of our army have had the critical task of countering the effects of such propaganda among their own rank and file. I feel proud that our army officers have kept their troops fully motivated, ingraining in them the truth that they are dealing with anti-Pakistan elements, and that religion is not an issue in the conflict.

It is often said that Pakistan is not doing enough in the war on terror. Such remarks can be made only by those who have no knowledge of the truth on the ground. Pakistan's decision to support the global war on terror was based on its own interests. There is no reason why we would not do enough for ourselves. In fact, Pakistan is the one country in the world that has done the maximum in the fight against terrorism. We have also suffered the maximum casualties. Pakistan has made enormous sacrifices in the war on terror. We have deployed approximately 80,000 troops in antiterrorist operations, and we occupy nearly 900 posts along the Pakistani-Afghan border. It is disappointing that despite our deep commitment and immense sacrifices, some people continue to tell tendentious stories casting aspersions on our counterterrorism operations and on the contributions we have made. We have lost more men than any other country—and we fight on.

The other common accusation against Pakistan is that most of the terrorist acts inside Afghanistan are emanating from the tribal areas of Pakistan. A negative perception is growing that Pakistan abets and provides sanctuary to terrorists. This propaganda is linked with efforts to create anti-Pakistan sentiment in Afghanistan. The world at large and countries involved in the war on terror have to take a realistic view of such malicious propaganda. Pakistan's own stability is linked with peace in Afghanistan. The Afghan government needs to focus more on improving security inside its own country instead of blaming others.

The base of the Taliban is Kandahar, in southeastern Afghanistan. Most of the terrorist operations launched against the coalition forces are conducted deep inside Afghanistan, in places that cannot be accessed from Pakistan. While it is unavoidable, because of the terrain and the length of the border, that some terrorists—members of al Qaeda and the Taliban—must be sneaking across to Afghanistan from the Pakistan side, it is mendacious to put the blame for all of this on Pakistan. Moreover, although al Qaeda operatives are recognizable, being foreigners, the Taliban are from Afghanistan and come from the same Pathan ethnic stock as the Pakistani Pathans. To identify friend or foe is often impossible, unless someone commits a hostile act. The reality is that most of the terrorist activity in Afghanistan is indigenous, even though some groups from Pakistan also sneak across. We need to cooperate with each other to fight this scourge, instead of getting involved in the blame game and weakening our common cause.

Another misperception Pakistan has to contend with is that the leaders of al Qaeda and the Taliban are operating from Pakistan. This is nothing but conjecture, without any evidence. The mountainous terrain of the border belt does afford an opportunity to hide, but this is the case on the Afghan side of the border as well, because the terrain is similar there. Whereas we have an effective security mechanism on our side of the border, no such arrangement exists on the Afghan side. In large areas of the Afghan countryside, there are no military operations. Hence it is easier for anyone to hide on the Afghan side than on the Pakistan side.

All these accusations, misperceptions, and differences notwithstanding, we have covered a long distance in our joint fight against terrorism. Pakistan has developed a fairly good working relationship with its coalition partners in Afghanistan, and especially with the United States. We now have effective strategic, operational, and tactical coordination through effective intercommunications and the suitable placement of liaison officers.

The key question that remains is, of course, the whereabouts of Osama bin Laden and Ayman al Zawahiri. They could be in one of the tribal agencies, hiding with the help of sympathetic locals. But they could just as well be on the Afghan side enjoying the hospitality of Mullah Omar. Or they could, cleverly, be moving close to the border, alternating between Afghanistan and Pakistan, to confuse those looking for them.

Pakistan has shattered the al Qaeda network in the region, severing its lateral and vertical linkages. It is now on the run and has ceased to exist as a homogeneous force, capable of undertaking coordinated operations. Now we need to sustain the pressure, denying al Qaeda the opportunity to regroup. I can say with surety that in Pakistan we are winning the war against the terrorists. I am proud of my army for all the sacrifices its officers and soldiers have made and for the results they have produced in the defense of their nation. This war can, and will, be won.

CHAPTER 26

THE SYMBIOSIS OF TERRORISM AND RELIGION

Several times in the quiet of the night, sitting alone in my study, I have pondered over what has happened to Pakistan. What has caused the deterioration in our national fabric? We were once a perfectly normal, religiously harmonious society, with only occasional tension between the Sunni and Shia sects of our religion. How did we reach the present-day epidemic of terrorism and extremism?

The trauma started in 1979 with the invasion of Afghanistan by the Soviet Union. The Russians all along had the ambition of reaching Pakistan's warm waters of the Indian Ocean through the Arabian Sea. We suddenly realized that we were faced with a two-front threat—India from the east and the Soviet Union and its Afghan puppet from the west. Pakistan's security was gravely threatened. The nation and the military were in a quandary. Fortunately for us, the West, led by the United States after the election of Ronald Reagan, considered Afghanistan an important arena in which to check the Soviets' ambitions. A jihad was launched in Afghanistan, with Pakistan as the inevitable conduit and a frontline supporter because of its contiguity to Afghanistan. Afghan warlords and their militias were armed and financed to fight the Soviets. Alongside 20,000 to 30,000 mujahideen from all over the Islamic world, students from some seminaries of Pakistan were encouraged, armed, financed, and trained to reinforce the Afghans and confront the Soviet war machine. Before 1979, our madrassas were quite limited and their activites were insignificant.

The Afghan war brought them into the forefront, urged on by President Zia ul-Haq, who vigorously propounded the cause of jihad against the Soviet occupation.

The entire decade of the 1980s saw religious extremism rise, encouraged by Zia. It is undeniable that the hard-line mullahs of the Frontier province were the obvious religious partners in this jihad, because the Afghan Pukhtoons adhere to their puritanical interpretation of Islam. Actually, Zia, for his own personal and political reasons, embraced the hard-line religious lobby as his constituency throughout Pakistan and well beyond, to the exclusion of the huge majority of moderate Pakistanis. Fighting the infidel Soviet Army became a holy cause to the jihadis, and countless Pakistani men signed up.

This jihad continued for ten years, until the Soviets were defeated in 1989. They withdrew in a hurry, leaving behind an enormous arsenal of heavy weapons that included tanks, guns, and even aircraft, with abundant stocks of ammunition. The United States and Europe were also quick to abandon the area, as the Berlin Wall fell and the Soviet threat dimmed. The sudden vacuum in Afghanistan led first to the toppling of the puppet government that had been installed by the Soviet Union, and then to mayhem and bloodletting among warlords jostling for power. Afghanistan was ravaged by a twelve-year internal conflict, from 1989 to 2001.

The effect of this upheaval, from the Soviet occupation of Afghanistan to the internal mayhem, was threefold. First, it brought 4 million refugees into Pakistan. Second, it sparked the emergence of the Taliban in 1995. Third, it led to the coalescing of the international mujahideen into al Qaeda, with reinforcements coming from the newly independent Central Asian Republics, the discontented Chechens, and several Arab countries.

Then came 9/11, the catastrophe that changed the world. Even before Secretary of State Colin Powell called me to ask for help, even before President Bush announced in a public speech that all nations were either "with us or against us," I knew that Pakistan was at a crossroad. Here was an opportunity for us to get rid of terrorism in our midst in our own national interest, and we must not falter. The extremists were too well armed, and too numerous, for us to manage quietly. Yet after the United States' angry invasion of Afghanistan and the con-

tinuing turbulence and guerrilla warfare there, many al Qaeda operatives shifted to the cities and western mountains of Pakistan. Our situation, before the attacks on me, had worsened.

As if this were not enough, the struggle for freedom that erupted in
Indian-held Kashmir in 1989 had a major impact on Pakistani society.
The struggle was initiated through an indigenous intifada, with public
demonstrations in the streets of Srinagar. The Indian law enforcement
agencies were ruthless in crushing the movement for freedom. Massive
army reinforcements were brought into the Srinagar valley to nip the
movement, then largely political, in the bud. The movement reacted in
self-defense, went underground, and took up arms. From then on it
became militant, confronting Indian forces with guerrilla warfare. The
Pakistani people are emotionally and sentimentally attached to their
Kashmiri brethren. Dozens of support groups sprang up all over the
country, prepared to join the jihad against the Indian army.

For twenty-six years now on our western borders, and for sixteen
years to our east in Kashmir, we have been in turmoil. A culture of militancy, weapons, and drugs now flourishes in Pakistan. A deadly al
Qaeda terrorist network entrenched itself in our major cities and the
mountains of our tribal agencies on our western border with
Afghanistan. A culture of targeted killing, explosives, car bombs, and
suicide attacks took root. The attempts on my life and that of Prime
Minister Shaukat Aziz were part of this story.

This is what Pakistan has gone through in the last twenty-six years
and what still causes us suffering, albeit somewhat less after our many
successes against the terrorists. I shudder to think what the situation
would have been like if we had not decided to take action when we did.
What hurts us, in addition, is the lack of understanding from some in
the West of our suffering, and of Pakistan's contribution. Had we not
joined the jihad against the Soviets, and had they not pulled out of
Afghanistan, would the Cold War be over yet? We did what Napoleon
and Hitler could not do; we defeated Russia, with the help of our
friends in the jihad. If you take Pakistan out of the picture, the jihad
would never have been won. On the other hand, if you take the United
States out, one never knows. I say this to give you an idea of the size of
our contribution to the Afghan jihad and of our critical and pivotal role.
It was some consolation when I read an inscription on a plaque on a

piece of the Berlin Wall presented by a chief of German intelligence to the chief of Pakistan's intelligence: "To the one who struck the first blow."

Our major successes in smashing al Qaeda's Pakistani network are a good start toward reclaiming Pakistan—but the extremists are far from defeated. We must continue to confront them and to reharmonize Pakistan and its emotionally wounded society.

At our core, the people of Pakistan are religious and moderate. Pakistan is an Islamic state created for the Muslims of the subcontinent. Only a small fringe of the population is extremist. This fringe holds rigid, orthodox, even obscurantist and intolerant views about religion. A problem arises when it wants to impose its rigid, dogmatic views on others. This fringe not only is militant and aggressive but also can be indoctrinated into terrorism.

Leaving the extremist fringe aside, the moderate majority can be divided into three broad categories. On one side are the semiliterate de facto clerics (Islam recognizes no church or clergy) with a very orthodox, ritualistic understanding of Islam. On the other side is an educated, enlightened group that understands religion in its true sense and focuses on character, values, and responsibilities to society. In the center lies the vast mass of less literate poor people of Pakistan, living largely in rural and semiurban areas. They too are moderates who adhere to a philosophy of "live and let live." They love visiting the shrines of Sufi saints and listening to the hypnotic beat of devotional mystical music, but because of their illiteracy, poverty, and desperation, the extremists try to recruit them and often succeed, especially among the semiliterate de facto clerics.

However, there are extremists in our midst who are neither poor nor uneducated. What motivates them? I believe it is their revulsion at the sheer pathos of the Muslim condition: the political injustices, societal deprivation, and alienation that have reduced many Muslims to marginalization and exploitation. This accounts for the likes of Osama bin Laden, Dr. Ayman al Zawahiri, Khalid Sheikh Mohammad, and Omar Saeed Sheikh—all rich and educated, two of whom attended school and college in the United States and Britain and one of whom was British-born. More recently, we saw terrorists from this class in the bombings of 7/7 in London.

Unfortunately, the enlightened class has abdicated its responsibility of teaching true Islam to the central masses, leaving them in the hands of the semiliterate clerics. People from the enlightened class tutor their children in every subject under the sun, but when it comes to religion they relinquish this crucial responsibility to their neighborhood clerics. The educated class had not thought it important to get involved in religious controversies. They never predicted 9/11 and the impact it would have on the Muslim world. Now they are faced with a catastrophe.

Today, the central masses are confused about where Islam actually stands on various serious issues facing the world in general and the Muslim world in particular. They need to be drawn away from the clerics' obscurantist views, and toward the enlightened, progressive, moderate message of Islam. The challenge is great, no doubt, but it is eminently achievable.

As I have said earlier, our experience has taught us that foreigners in al Qaeda have almost invariably masterminded terrorist acts in Pakistan. The masterminds find local planners. The planners penetrate into bands of religious extremist organizations, or they indoctrinate groups of selected fanatics to take on specific terrorist tasks. Such attackers are mere pawns. They are not always religiously motivated, yet this is how terrorism in Pakistan has been mixed with religion.

If I were to make a comparison between the terrorist tiers and a tree, I would call the attackers mere leaves of the tree. Leaves will keep growing, or even multiplying, as long as the tree lives. The entire al Qaeda network, including masterminds and planners, I would equate with a branch of the tree. By eliminating al Qaeda we will have chopped off only one branch of the tree, even though it is a large branch. The tree of terrorism will continue to flourish as long as the roots remain intact.

What drives a person to kill innocent fellow human beings? What drives a person to the extreme act of wasting his own life to take the lives of others? It must certainly be a powerful urge. I strongly believe that the one factor pushing a person to extremes is a sense of hopelessness, powerlessness, and injustice, arising from political deprivation— these are the roots of the terrorist tree. The tree must be destroyed root and branch, and it can be destroyed only if it is uprooted first. The only way to do this is to remove the sense of injustice and the actual political deprivation. Feelings of powerlessness and finally hopelessness will develop if the roots of the tree are not destroyed. The roots are the prime cause, the original sin that eventually grows into a terrorist tree.

Such a feeling, when combined with illiteracy and poverty, makes for an explosive mix. This is what the Muslims in many parts of the world are suffering from today—an acute sense of loss, with nothing to look forward to. When a person with such a mind-set is illiterate enough to believe that a key hung around his neck is the key to paradise (this is actually what some suicide bombers believe), and if he is leading a miserable, impoverished life that holds nothing for him, he is easy prey for recruiters. Why not contribute something toward one's political cause and then leave this miserable world for a more joyous and bountiful hereafter?

The bombers involved in London on 7/7 were not politically deprived, uneducated, or poor. Quite clearly, their motivation came from the socioeconomic deprivation of their community. Being unassimilated into the society they lived in, facing unequal treatment, and seeing atrocities meted out to their coreligionists—these could be the reasons for their resorting to terrorism.

All this has to be combated today. We need a holistic understanding, approach, and strategy. I prefer to separate the response against terrorists into short-term and long-term strategies.

The terrorist has to be faced with full force in the short term. He needs to be physically eliminated. But that isn't enough to root out the menace. The issues that spawn terrorism must be addressed at three levels: the international community, the Muslim world, and the domestic situation within each country, in accordance with its own particular environment.

Internationally, we must resolve key political disputes. Within the Muslim world we must reject extremism and terrorism and concentrate our energies on socioeconomic development. Domestically, I will confine myself to what needs to be done in Pakistan. Without doubt, we have to fight terrorism frontally and with full force until we root it out completely from our country. The strategy that Pakistan has followed is to strike at the masterminds and planners at the top tiers of the terrorist hierarchy. This has met with great success in breaking the back of terrorism in our country, though more needs to be done. We have to sustain the pressure and keep the terrorists on the run. The bigger success lies in the elimination of their top leadership. But ultimate success will come only when the roots that cause terrorism are destroyed: that is, when injustices against Muslims are removed. This lies in the hands of the West, particularly America.

Dealing with extremism requires prudence. It involves addressing religious and sectarian extremism. It is a battle of both hearts and minds. Mind-sets cannot be changed by force. They must be transformed through superior logic and action. We have to facilitate this transformation. It involves mobilizing the silent moderate majority to rise and play a positive role. The following areas that we have addressed will, I am sure, produce positive results.

We have banned all extremist organizations, denying them any access to funds, while remaining alert to their reemergence in some other garb. This effort needs to be vigilantly sustained.

We banned the writing, publication, printing, sale, and distribution of hate material in the form of books, pamphlets, magazines, newspapers, or handbills.

We modified school curricula to eliminate all materials promoting sectarian or religious hatred or confrontation, and replaced them with teachings of the real values and spirit of our religion, focused on the emancipation of self and society.

We began monitoring the misuse of loudspeakers in mosques to spawn hatred and disharmony.

We began mainstreaming madrassas to teach standard educational subjects in addition to religion, and to offer examinations developed by the boards of education so that their students become equipped for professions other than the clergy.

Last, we are initiating a national discourse on Islam, with enlightened Islamic scholars, to influence the minds of the masses in the right direction. This may be the start of a Muslim renaissance, as it were, from Pakistan.

There is a great commonality in the cultural, intellectual, and emotional environment of most Muslim countries. We have a lot to learn and adopt from each other's experience. We have a lot of work to do, but we will succeed if only we remain focused and determined.

PART SIX

PAKISTAN AT HOME
AND ABROAD

CHAPTER 27

NUCLEAR PROLIFERATION

South Asia is the nuclear flashpoint of the world. Before the end of the Cold War, the rivalry between America and the Soviet Union, both armed with thousands of powerful nuclear weapons, transfixed the world. When those countries rattled their sabers, as in the Cuban missile crisis, the world held its breath.

Now, ever since Pakistan followed India into the nuclear club, the world holds its breath at our every confrontation. This situation is much worse than the Cold War, which was fought at a distance, mostly by proxy. When your enemy is your neighbor, when you have fought open wars repeatedly, when you are in dispute over a large piece of territory, and when your historical memory is rooted in mutual slaughter from the founding of your nation, you face not a cold war, but a deadly embrace, with guns drawn and fingers on the triggers.

The nuclear status of this standoff was confirmed when India exploded five nuclear devices on May 11 and 13, 1998, and Pakistan responded in kind on May 28 and 30 with six nuclear devices. The world was shocked, far more so than in 1974, when India unilaterally exploded its first nuclear device. India described its test of 1974 as a "peaceful detonation," and the world swallowed this explanation after some token show of disapproval. Yet that "peaceful" bomb initiated not only a nuclear arms race in south Asia but also nuclear terror, for the neighboring states experienced tremendous fear and anxiety.

The much stronger condemnation by the world in 1998 was surely because Pakistan was the first Muslim state to go nuclear. This is perceived in Pakistan as very unfair. Surely any state whose chief rival has the bomb would want to do what we did. After all, we knew we could not count on American protection alone.

Pakistan has always pursued a balance of power and forces with India. Deterrence demands it. Until 1974, this military balance involved conventional forces only. Once India went nuclear, our deterrent became untenable. We had to rectify this situation, come what may. Remember that this was only three years after the war of 1971, when India severed East Pakistan from us.

Ironically, the years between 1974 and 1998 were relatively peaceful along our border with India. We had fought bloody conflicts in 1947–1948, 1965, and 1971. During the twenty-four years of nuclear imbalance, we had continued to fight semi-wars, along the Line of Control in Kashmir and Siachen, but they were of much lower intensity. Since 1998, although we haven't approached anything comparable to the conflicts of 1965 and 1971, we have mobilized significant forces twice, in 1999 and 2002. It may be that our mutual deterrent has stopped us from plunging into full-scale war. We must never let a situation reach the point of no return. We must resolve the dispute over Kashmir, for the sake of world peace.

In this chapter, I will explain how Pakistan achieved its nuclear status and then discuss the dangers of proliferation beyond our borders.

Dr. A.Q. Khan, a metallurgist by profession, working in a uranium enrichment facility called URENCO in the Netherlands, offered his services to the government of Pakistan in 1975. He was asked to return to Pakistan. He brought drawings of centrifuges along with him. We assembled working centrifuges according to his blueprints at our nuclear enrichment facility. In the years that followed, we obtained all the other materials and technology we needed through an underground network based mainly in the developed countries of Europe. India was also developing its nuclear arsenal during these years. Perhaps we were both being supplied by the same network, the non-state proliferators.

Why did India acquire nuclear, and later missile, capability? Quite clearly, it had grandiose ambitions of projecting its power regionally and even globally and achieving hegemony over the Gulf and in south Asia and southeast Asia. Why did Pakistan opt to go nuclear? Quite obviously, and contrary to world opinion, we needed to defend ourselves against the Indian threat. India's intentions were offensive and aggressive; ours were defensive. The world and its powers relentlessly pressured us to desist, without similarly pressuring India. I never found this logical; in fact, I always considered it unjust. If the world were serious about avoiding a nuclear arms race in the subcontinent, it was restraining the wrong horse. The great powers should have stopped India from going nuclear. Pakistan would never have done it if India hadn't done it first. Instead, south Asia became the flashpoint of nuclear proliferation and black-market technology transfers.

Pakistan kept its nuclear program top-secret. In the 1970s the program was managed by Prime Minister Zulfikar Ali Bhutto, who was dealing directly with Dr. A.Q. Khan. Funds were placed at A.Q.'s disposal, no audits were carried out, and security was left to A.Q. himself. Later, when President Zia ul-Haq took over, the same direct link was maintained between the president and the scientists. After Zia's death in 1988, Ghulam Ishaq Khan took over as president. Since he was a civilian, he brought the army chief into the loop. From then on the chief of the army staff started managing our nuclear development on behalf of the president, dealing directly with A.Q.

This arrangement continued, but the chain lengthened. It ran from the prime minister to the army chief to a major general appointed as director general of combat development (DGCD), to whom A.Q. reported. No other government department was involved, nor was anyone else from the army. I say this about the army with full authority because I became the director general of military operations (DGMO) in 1992, an appointment that involved dealing with all sensitive military planning and operational matters, but I was kept totally out of the nuclear circuit. This was the right thing to do if the program had to remain under wraps. Everyone in Pakistan wanted us to have the bomb. A.Q. Khan was not, in fact, the sole scientist in charge of the entire effort, yet he had a great talent for self-promotion and publicity and led the public to believe that he was building the bomb almost single-handedly. Furthermore, our political leaders were intentionally ambiguous in public about our capabilities, for strategic reasons. I did not know the facts (at what stage of development we were); and as we would all discover, they didn't either, thanks to the complete trust and freedom of action given to A.Q. Nobody ever imagined how irresponsible and reckless he could be.

I took charge of the army as chief of the army staff on October 8, 1998. This was five months after we had conducted our first nuclear test, and by then A.Q. was a national hero. In May, he had instantly become the "father of the Islamic bomb" to our public and to the world—as if a bomb could have a religion. I find this description pejorative and offensive. No one else's bomb is called Hindu, Jewish, Christian, capitalist, or communist, yet somehow our bomb becomes "Islamic," as if that makes it illegitimate. The idea is illogical and essentially racist. This is an example of how Muslims continually feel unjustly singled out and alienated.

At any rate, A.Q. was now my responsibility. One of my very early recommendations to Prime Minister Nawaz Sharif was to bring our strategic organizations and nuclear development under custodial controls. We made a presentation to him at the GHQ, and I even submitted a written plan calling for a National Command Authority and a new secretariat within the government that would take charge of operational, financial, and security controls, which so far had been left to the discretion of A.Q. I had suggested this because I saw complete lack of coordination between the several scientific organizations involved, primarily the Khan Research Laboratories (KRL) and the Pakistan Atomic Energy Commission (PAEC). Unfortunately, the proposal remained unapproved and did not see the light of day during Nawaz Sharif's term in office.

Nevertheless, in early 1999 I decided to informally put in place, in at least a rudimentary version, the proposed secretariat of Strategic Plans Division (SPD) within the GHQ. By then the Combat Development Directorate had been wound up. Immediately, I started seeing the first signs of some suspicious activities by A.Q. Pakistan had contracted a government-to-government deal with North Korea for the purchase of conventional ballistic missiles, including transfer of technology for hard cash. It did not—repeat, not—involve any deal whatsoever for reverse transfer of nuclear technology, as some uninformed writers have speculated. I received a report suggesting that some North Korean nuclear experts, under the guise of missile engineers, had arrived at

KRL and were being given secret briefings on centrifuges, including some visits to the plant. I took this very seriously. The chief of general staff, the director of our Intelligence Service, and I called A.Q. in for questioning. He immediately denied the charge. No further reports were received, but we remained apprehensive.

When I took the helm of the ship of state on October 12, 1999, I was solely in charge of all our strategic programs. I soon realized that I could not devote as much time to them as they required. I decided to implement the system that I had proposed earlier. In February 2000, our strategic weapons program came under formalized institutional control and thorough oversight, duly approved by my government.

At the top of the new structure was (and remains) the National Command Authority (NCA), comprising the president, the prime minister, key federal ministers, military chiefs, and senior scientists. This is the apex body responsible for all policy matters including the development and employment of our strategic assets.

A new secretariat called the Strategic Plans Division (SPD), under a director general from the army, assists the NCA in the implementation of plans and oversight of strategic assets. All financial and security controls for the scientific organizations were taken over by this secretariat.

Further, army, navy, and air force strategic force commands were created to handle all strategic assets in the field, while retaining centralized operational control with the NCA.

Two things happened as a result. First, we soon began to get some more information, though sketchy, about A.Q.'s hidden activities over the preceding months and years. Second, we were in a better position to learn about his ongoing activities, some of which were clearly problematic and potentially dangerous.

So far, he had been used to going abroad without permission. I now insisted that we should be informed of his visits and their purpose. Even then, I would learn that he had visited countries other than those he had requested.

We were once informed that a chartered aircraft going to North Korea for conventional missiles was also going to carry some "irregular" cargo on his behalf. The source could not tell us exactly what the cargo was, but we were suspicious. We organized a discreet raid and searched the aircraft before its departure but unfortunately found nothing. Later, we were told that A.Q.'s people had been tipped off and the suspected cargo had not been loaded.

On another occasion, I was informed that A.Q. had requested clearance of a chartered cargo flight coming from a third country to Islamabad, "including refueling stops both ways at Zahedan in Iran." This raised suspicions again. When I asked why, I was told that some conventional artillery ammunition was being brought in. But that of course didn't explain why the aircraft had to land in Iran "both ways." I approved the ammunition but disallowed permission to land in Iran. Some days later, I was informed that the aircraft had never come to Pakistan after all. Evidently, the ammunition was probably a cover for something else.

There were other similar incidents, and I became reasonably convinced that A.Q. was up to mischief, which could be extremely detrimental to Pakistan's security. Since A.Q.'s expertise was in nuclear weapons applications, the possibilities were frightening. Because he had been severely cautioned, and thereby alerted, he apparently became careful. He started taking steps that indicated he was trying to cover up some of his past activities.

It was becoming clearer by now that A.Q. was not "part of the problem" but "the problem" itself. In his presence, we could never get a firm grip on KRL; the only way to do so was to remove him from his position. Therefore, in 2000 I decided in principle to retire him when his contract ended in March 2001. How to "manage" his retirement was the question. He was a hero to the man on the street. In the past, his contract had been renewed automatically on several occasions. This time I decided not to extend it. I did the same with the chairman of the Pakistan Atomic Energy Commission, Dr. Ishfaq Ahmed, who was a highly respected, honorable, and capable senior scientist. The sad truth is that Ishfaq became a decoy to forestall the impression that A.Q. was being singled out. I felt sorry about Ishfaq because he still had much left to contribute. On March 30, 2001, Dr. A. Q. Khan was retired as chairman of KRL, effectively cut off from his base. To soften the blow, I appointed him an adviser with the status of a federal minister. Practically, however, he had no further role to play in our weapons program. There were some adverse comments in the media, but then things calmed down and I was content with my decision.

When A.Q. departed, our scientific organizations started functioning smoothly, with mutual and integrated cooperation that had never been possible while he was around. He was such a self-centered and abrasive man that he could not be a team player. He did not want anyone to excel beyond him or steal the limelight on any occasion or on any subject related to our strategic program. He had a huge ego, and he knew the art of playing to the gallery and manipulating the media. All this made him a difficult person to deal with.

After 9/11, we were put under immense pressure by the United States regarding our nuclear and missile arsenal. The Americans' concerns were based on two grounds. First, at this time they were not very sure of my job security, and they dreaded the possibility that an extremist successor government might get its hands on our strategic nuclear arsenal. Second, they doubted our ability to safeguard our assets and prevent them from falling into the hands of freelance extremist groups or organizations. I took pains to disprove both of these suspicions. I was sure of the nation's support for me and my decision to join the coalition against terrorism. I was also sure of the efficacy of the custodial command and control system that we had instituted. I was concerned that A.Q. might have been involved in illicit activities before March 2001, but I strongly believed we had now ensured that he could not get away with anything more, and that once he was removed, the problem would stop. I was wrong. Apparently, he started working more vigorously through the Dubai branch of his network.

The concerns of the United States mounted. Every American official from the president down who spoke to me or visited Pakistan raised the issue of the safety of our nuclear arsenal. Colin Powell, whom I consider not only a friend but also a very balanced, clearheaded, able person, sought assurances from me. My response was that I had full confidence in Pakistan's environment and our custodial control system. Still, at official-level meetings, some time after A.Q.'s retirement, the United States continued to raise questions about proliferation that had originated in Pakistan at some point in the past—but, like us, they had no concrete evidence. We kept denying the allegations, because we did not have any conclusive evidence; we had only suspicions.

Very significant and alarming revelations kept surfacing from 2002 onward, all having to do with A.Q.'s activities. The United States' concerns were focused on North Korea. We denied the allegations again—again in good faith—and explained that we did cooperate somewhat with North Korea in the development of conventional weapons, but not at all in the nuclear weapons. This was absolutely true as far as the government of Pakistan was concerned. In late 2002, during official talks between the United States and North Korea, the Koreans disclosed that they had "even more sophisticated technology" (perhaps implying enrichment technology) of which the United States was unaware. The United States took this as a hint about centrifuge technology from Pakistan. The suspicion against Pakistan grew to such an extent that the U.S. government was obligated, in accordance with its laws, to impose sanctions against us. Such sanctions would have been disastrous for us. Fortunately, by this time I had developed a relationship with President Bush based on trust and common interests. President Bush imposed sanctions only on KRL, A.Q.'s institute. Nonetheless, the pressure on us to investigate A.Q.'s illicit nuclear transfers continued. We did try, covertly, to learn more, but we did not get anywhere.

Then came another bombshell. In the middle of 2003, during inspections in Iran by the International Atomic Energy Agency (IAEA), signs of nuclear proliferation surfaced when nuclear contamination at high levels was detected on the premises of Iranian facilities. In our minds, this immediately gave rise to the possibility of a link with A.Q. In my gut, I was getting more and more suspicious of him. I was convinced that we needed to get to the bottom of this, even if that implied a formal investigation.

Then came one of my most embarrassing moments. After I met with President Bush in September 2003 at the UN Summit, he drew me aside and asked me if I could spare some time the next morning for the CIA director, George Tenet. "It is extremely serious and very important from your point of view," he said. I agreed.

Tenet arrived at my hotel suite the next morning. After initial pleasantries, he drew out some papers and placed them before me. I immediately recognized them as detailed drawings of Pakistan's P-1 centrifuge, a version that we were no longer using but had developed in the early stages of our program under A.Q. The papers amounted to a blueprint, with part numbers, dates, signatures, etc. I did not know what to say. I have seldom found myself at a loss for words, but this time I was. My first thought went to my country—how to protect it from harm? My second thought was extreme anger toward A.Q.—he had endangered Pakistan. There could be no doubt that it was he who had been peddling our technology, even though Tenet did not say so and the papers did not include his name. His past behavior left me in no doubt. I pulled myself together and told Tenet that I would like to take the papers and start an investigation. He obliged. I must say that he showed complete trust and confidence in me. The trust that President Bush and his entire state department team had in me by this time was to prove our saving grace.

The whole ugly episode leaked out and blew straight into Pakistan's face. Later, the IAEA's inspectors also detected some contamination in the centrifuges in Iran, which Iranian officials conveniently deflected to the "outside source" providing the centrifuges. Pakistan was all over the media. As if this were not enough, in late 2003 a ship named *BBC China* was seized in the Mediterranean carrying sensitive centrifuge components from Malaysia to Libya. The facility in Malaysia also turned out to have links to A.Q. Libya named Pakistan as its source for technology and centrifuges. We stood before the world as the illicit source of nuclear technology for some of the world's most dangerous regimes. I had to move quickly and decisively to stop any further activity and to find out exactly what had happened.

We launched our investigations in early November 2003. Revelations began to flow. Our investigations revealed that A.Q. had started his activities as far back as 1987, primarily with Iran. In 1994–1995 A.Q. had ordered the manufacture of 200 P-1 centrifuges that had been discarded by Pakistan in the mid-1980s. These had been dispatched to Dubai for onward distribution. Overall, the picture that emerged was not pretty: A.Q. was running a personal underground network of technology transfers around the world from his base in Dubai.

One branch of his network was based at KRL. It included four to six scientists out of the thousands working there. Most of them proved to be unwitting participants, working on A.Q.'s orders without comprehending the real purpose or outcome.

The other branch of the network was based in Dubai and dealt with procurement and distribution. It included several shady individuals and various European businesses.

On the basis of the thorough probe that we conducted in 2003–2004, and on the basis of the information that has since been collected (and fully and truthfully shared with the IAEA and international intelligence agencies), I can say with confidence that neither the Pakistan Army nor any of the past governments of Pakistan was ever involved or had any knowledge of A.Q.'s proliferation activities. The show was completely and entirely A.Q.'s, and he did it all for money. He simply lost sight of the national interest that he had done so much to protect. Contrary to some perceptions, he is no fall guy for anyone. There is absolutely no evidence to the contrary.

The unearthing of A.Q.'s involvement in nuclear proliferation was perhaps one of the most serious and saddest crises that I have ever faced. The West in general and United States in particular wanted his scalp, but to the people of Pakistan he was a hero, a household name, and the father of Pakistan's pride—its atom bomb. The truth is that he was just a metallurgist, responsible for only one link in the complex chain of nuclear development. But he had managed to build himself up into Albert Einstein and J. Robert Oppenheimer rolled into one.

Perceptions are sometimes far more important than facts. I had to act fast to satisfy international concerns and yet also avoid inflaming the masses of Pakistan in support of their hero. Sadly, our opposition parties were more interested in attacking me over this scandal than in displaying unity at a time of national sadness and adversity.

I assured the world that the proliferation was a one-man act and that neither the government of Pakistan nor the army was involved. This was the truth, and I could speak forcefully. The more difficult issue, however, was to avoid an open trial of A.Q. The public would be sure to protest any prosecution, no matter what the facts were. I needed a solution that would be accepted by all.

I wanted to meet A.Q. myself and talk to him. When we met and I confronted him with the evidence, he broke down and admitted that he felt extremely guilty. He asked me for an official pardon. I told him that his apology should be to the people of Pakistan and he should seek his pardon from them directly. It was decided that the best course of action would be for him to appear on television and apologize personally to the nation for embarrassing and traumatizing it in front of the entire world. I then accepted his request for a pardon from trial but put him under protective custody for further investigation and also for his own sake.

Since then, we have isolated A.Q. and confined him to his house, primarily for his own security, and interrogated him at great length. We have learned many details of his activities, which we have shared truthfully with international intelligence agencies and the IAEA. They have proved extremely helpful in dismantling the network, internationally and in Pakistan.

There is little doubt that A.Q. was the central figure in the proliferation network, but he was assisted over the years by a number of money-seeking freelancers from other countries, mostly in Europe, in manufacturing, procuring, and distributing to countries like Iran and Libya materials and components related to centrifuge technology. According to A.Q., these people included nationals of Switzerland, Holland, Britain, and Sri Lanka. Several of these individuals based in Dubai and Europe were simultaneously also pursuing their own business agendas independently. Ironically, the network based in Dubai had employed several Indians, some of whom have since vanished. There is a strong probability that the Indian uranium enrichment program may also have its roots in the Dubai-based network and could be a copy of the Pakistani centrifuge design. This has also been recently alluded to by an eminent American nonproliferation analyst.

In his interactions with the Libyans, A.Q. suggested that they should build centrifuge plants that would look like goat and camel farms and sheds. He went on to convince them that such camouflage was fairly easy to create. Interestingly, because A.Q. knew full well that Libya had a very weak technological base, the components of centrifuges, less the all-important rotors, were arranged through various sources, while the Libyans were asked to develop rotors themselves. Under this arrangement, while the Libyans purchased a lot of equipment and everybody in the network benefited, they would not have been able to operate a centrifuge plant, as they could not have made the rotors indigenously. The deal with Libya is estimated to be in the region of $100 million. The recklessness of A.Q. can be gauged from the discovery in Libya of a nuclear weapons design provided by him in the shopping bag of a tailor based in Islamabad.

Doctor A. Q. Khan transferred nearly two dozen P-1 and P-II centrifuges to North Korea. He also provided North Korea with a flow meter, some special oils for centrifuges, and coaching on centrifuge technology, including visits to top-secret centrifuge plants. To the Iranians and Libyans, through Dubai, he provided nearly eighteen tons of materials, including centrifuges, components, and drawings. All this information has been shared with concerned international agencies.

When, in November 2003, we started our investigations into A.Q.'s proliferation activities, our intelligence agencies intercepted two letters written by him. The first was being carried by a courier, a business partner of his; and in the letter A.Q. advised some of his friends in Iran not to mention his name under any circumstances to the IAEA. He also advised them to name dead people during investigations, just as he was naming dead people in Pakistan. Naively, he also suggested that the Iranians should put the blame for the contamination found in Iran on IAEA's inspectors, "who could have spread it surreptitiously." He recommended that Iran renounce the NPT and finally promised more assistance after this event had passed.

The second letter was addressed by him to his daughter, who lives in London. The letter, besides being critical of the government for the invesigation, contained detailed instructions for her to go public on Pakistan's nuclear secrets through certain British journalists.

For years, A.Q.'s lavish lifestyle and tales of his wealth, properties, corrupt practices, and financial magnanimity at state expense were generally all too well known in Islamabad's social and government circles. However, these were largely ignored by the governments of the day, in the larger interest of the sensitive and important work that he was engaged in. In hindsight, that neglect was apparently a serious mistake.

CHAPTER 28

INTERNATIONAL DIPLOMACY

Before 9/11 my focus was mainly on internal consolidation and socioeconomic uplift. But 9/11 changed the world. It became so very violent. Suicide bombings became commonplace. I never favored the invasion of Iraq, because I feared it would exacerbate extremism, as it has most certainly done. The world is not a safer place because of the war in Iraq; the world has become far more dangerous. With westerners arguing about a possible "clash of civilizations," is it any wonder that some Muslims fear a new age of the crusades?

I have given considerable thought to the present violence in Pakistan, the unstable conditions in our region, the destabilized condition of the Muslim world, and the violence around the world. Most unfortunately, all the violence is centered on the Muslims. These thoughts haunt me frequently.

The idea of "enlightened moderation" dawned on me in my study one night when I was meditating on all this. To stop violence, we need a global solution. The turmoil in the Muslim world arises primarily because of unresolved, long-standing political disputes that have created a sense of injustice, alienation, deprivation, powerlessness, and hopelessness in the masses. This situation is aggravated by the fact that by any measure, the Muslim countries have the least healthy social conditions in the world. Political deprivation, combined with poverty and illiteracy, has created an explosive brew of extremism and terrorism. Muslim societies must shun terrorism and extremism if they ever hope for emancipation and a release from these conditions. But at the same time their demand for a just resolution of certain political disputes must also be addressed.

Enlightened moderation is a two-pronged strategy that I sincerely believe is also a win-win strategy. One prong, to be the responsibility of the Muslim world, is the rejection of terrorism and extremism in order to concentrate fully on internal socioeconomic development. The other prong, to be the responsibility of the West in general and the United States in particular, is to put their full weight behind finding a just resolution of all political disputes afflicting Muslim societies. Justice for Muslims around the world must not only be done, but seen to be done. The Palestinian dispute lies at the core of international turmoil, as does the nuclear flashpoint of Kashmir, which needs urgent resolution if there is to be permanent peace in south Asia.

I have tried my utmost to promote this idea around the world. While many people have responded positively, actual progress has been slow in coming. My diplomatic efforts continue on two fronts. First, I am urging the world's powers to exert the maximum pressure to resolve the Israeli-Palestinian dispute and the dispute over Kashmir. I believe both are ripe for a final resolution. Second, I am trying to move the Islamic world forward toward the implementation of as much of its prong as possible, even before the United States and the West produce tangible, just results in their prong. If we all agreed—the western and Muslim governments—this could become a coordinated pincer movement, instead of merely two prongs that either side may or may not implement or for which either side may do its part in its own good time and at its own pace.

I am very glad, and proud, that my proposals for enlightened moderation were adopted at the Islamic Summit of 2004 in Malaysia. This summit also rejected terrorism and extremism. My idea of restructuring the Organization of Islamic Conference (OIC) to make it potent and dynamic enough to redress our collective socioeconomic problems was also adopted. Accordingly, a group of "eminent persons" nominated from nine member countries worked on restructuring the OIC. Further, at the Special Ka'aba Summit in Mecca in December 2005, this team was given the task of redoing the charter of the OIC. Thus the second prong is definitely progressing, however slowly. It is the pace of progress on the first prong that worries me, because the moment for resolving disputes is on us. If all concerned do not seize it now, the moment will pass and a great opportunity to bring peace and harmony to the world will have been lost—a loss for which neither God nor history will forgive us.

Some detractors misunderstand and misquote the essence of enlightened moderation, criticizing it as a flawed interpretation of traditional Islamic thought. It certainly is not. I have no pretensions to being an Islamic scholar, but I am a Muslim and I understand in my soul the essence and spirit of Islam even if I am not, intellectually, entirely familiar with its minutiae. (But then, who is?) In any case, enlightened moderation has nothing to do with Islam and its teachings. It has more to do with Muslims and their emancipation.

Peace in south Asia is crucial to pursuing the cause of peace in the world, including and especially the Islamic world. I have taken what can justifiably be called bold steps toward a rapprochement with India. The Indo-Pakistan dispute is a hindrance to socioeconomic cooperation and development in south Asia. As someone has aptly remarked, "When two elephants fight, the grass gets trampled." I have thought very deeply about our hostile relationship over the past half century and more: our wars, Siachen, Kargil, and the struggle for freedom in Indian-held Kashmir. The collective effect of all these military actions has been to force both sides back to the negotiating table—but from this point forward, military actions can do no more. There is no military solution to our problems. The way forward is through diplomacy. I believe India has also realized that it can no longer use military coercion against Pakistan. As early as 2001, I believed the time had come to turn over a new leaf.

I saw the first opportunity for a thaw when India suffered a massive earthquake in Gujrat in early 2001. I telephoned Prime Minister Vajpayee to offer my sympathy, and Pakistan sent relief goods, including medicines. This broke the ice and led to an invitation for me to visit India. I landed in Delhi on July 14, 2001.

I generally perceived the mood in India to be upbeat. Wherever Sehba and I went, there was a strong show of warmth and affection, be it among the hotel employees we encountered, the officials we met, or the ordinary Indians and the several families now living in my ancestral home, Nehar Wali Haveli. There was a discernible air of expectancy. We reciprocated with equal warmth. I had gone to India with an open mind and in a spirit of optimism and accommodation.

After all the protocol and pleasantries on our arrival in Delhi on July 15, 2001, were over, Prime Minister Vajpayee met me in the historic city of Agra the next day. Agra is the site of the Taj Mahal, the famous Mughal monument to love, one of the wonders of the world because of its perfect symmetry and ethereal beauty. We began our formal dialogue on the morning of July 16, 2001. What followed was initially quite encouraging, but ended on a disappointing note. During two prolonged interactions, before and after lunch, initially one-on-one but then joined by our respective foreign ministers, we drafted a joint declaration. This declaration contained a condemnation of terrorism and recognition that the dispute over Kashmir needed resolution in order to improve bilateral relations. The draft, I thought, was very well worded: balanced and acceptable to both of us. The signing ceremony was scheduled for the afternoon in the Hotel J. P. Palace where Prime Minister Vajpayee was staying and where we had held our dialogue. Preparations in the hotel were complete, down to the table and two chairs where we would sit for the signing ceremony. The hotel staff and all the delegates were truly exuberant.

I took leave of the prime minster to return to Hotel Amar Vilas, where we were staying, to change into my traditional *shalwar kameez*. After the signing ceremony I planned to pay a visit to the shrine of a highly revered Sufi saint in Ajmer Sharif. I found the hotel staff at the Amar Vilas equally cheerful and happy. We were approaching the climax of our visit. Instead, it was an anticlimax, when after barely an hour my foreign minster and foreign secretary informed me that the Indians had backed out. I could not believe my ears. "How could that be? Why?" I asked.

"The cabinet has rejected it, sir," was the answer.

"Which cabinet?" I asked. "There is no cabinet in Agra." I became very angry, and my impulse was to leave for Islamabad immediately. The two diplomats cooled me down, asking for some time to try a redraft. I allowed it, and reluctantly canceled my evening visit to Ajmer Sharif.

The redrafting took another two to three hours of intense haggling over words and sentences. But ultimately my team returned, signaling success. They showed me the new draft, which I approved. I thought it still carried the essence of what we wanted, except that now the language was different. They returned to the other hotel to make fair copies of the draft. I assured my wife, saying that the "Agra declaration" would hit the headlines the next day.

Yet this too was not to be. Just as I was about to leave for the signing ceremony I received a message that the Indians had backed out again. This was preposterous. I decided to leave immediately, but my foreign minister now persuaded me to call on Prime Minister Vajpayee before leaving. I consented to fulfill this diplomatic protocol, though much against my wishes. At the same time I sent word to the media that I would hold a press conference at the hotel. I later found that this was disallowed. No one from the media was allowed to enter either Vajpayee's hotel or mine. So much for freedom of expression in "the largest democracy in the world."

I met Prime Minister Vajpayee at about eleven o'clock that night in an extremely somber mood. I told him bluntly that there seemed to be someone above the two of us who had the power to overrule us. I also said that today both of us had been humiliated. He just sat there, speechless. I left abruptly, after thanking him in a brisk manner.

There is the man and there is the moment. When man and moment meet history is made. Vajpayee failed to grasp the moment and lost his moment in history. As my wife and I left, we could clearly see dismay and despondency on the faces of the hotel staff. When our car took the turn on the road just outside the hotel, I was surprised to see hundreds of media people lining both sides of the road, restrained by baton-wielding policemen. We went through this crowd for about 200 yards (180 meters), as flashbulbs went off continuously to capture my mood, which was anything but normal. This sad and ridiculous episode ended our first attempt toward normalization of relations.

We went through a period of extreme tension throughout 2002, when Indian troops amassed on our borders during a hair-trigger, eyeball-to-eyeball confrontation. We responded by moving all our forces forward. The standoff lasted ten months. Then the Indians blinked and quite ignominiously agreed to a mutual withdrawal of forces.

I tried another diplomatic maneuver at the Kathmandu South Asian Association for Regional Cooperation (SAARC) Summit in Nepal, in January 2002. All of the region's leaders were seated behind a long table on a stage, taking their turn to make speeches. As I finished my speech, and on the spur of the moment, I moved to the front of the table, confronting Prime Minister Vajpayee head-on, and extended my hand for a handshake. He was left with no choice but to stand and accept it. A loud gasp of awe (and I daresay admiration) went through the hall, full of stuffy officialdom, that the prime minister of "the largest democracy in the world" had been upstaged. But upstaging him was not my intention at all; unlocking the impasse that had developed at Agra was. I was pleased when this handshake had the desired effect. Prime Minister Vajpayee decided to visit Pakistan for the SAARC Summit in January 2004. We had a happy meeting and this time agreed on a written joint agreement, which has now come to be known as the Islamabad Declaration. We also decided to move the peace process forward through a "composite dialogue," which includes the dispute over Jammu and Kashmir. Again, however, it was not to be. Before the composite dialogue could gain momentum, there were early elections in India and Prime Minister Vajpayee's party, the Bharatia Janata Party (BJP), lost. A new coalition government was formed by Sonia Gandhi's Congress Party, with not her but Manmohan Singh as prime minister. That changed the entire scenario of the peace process. I wished we had not lost this opportunity, one year after Agra.

I put out diplomatic feelers with congratulatory telephone calls to the new prime minister and to Sonia Gandhi. I felt they were received very positively. I also thought it appropriate to telephone Vajpayee to urge him to continue supporting the peace process, which we had initiated, even from the opposition benches. He promised to do so.

I had my first meeting with Prime Minister Manmohan Singh during the UN Summit in New York when he called on me at my hotel on September 24, 2004. It was an extremely pleasant encounter. I found the prime minister to be a very positive and genuine person with a desire to resolve disputes with Pakistan and establish good relations with us. Our joint statement after the meeting reflected a common desire to take the peace process forward.

My next meeting with Manmohan Singh occured when the Pakistani cricket team toured India and he invited me to one of the games. I accepted the invitation and went to a one-day match in Delhi on April 18, 2005. I traveled via Ajmer Sharif—the visit that I had missed after the Agra summit. This, I thought, was an auspicious beginning.

April 18, 2005, began with the cricket match. Unfortunately for my hosts, the match turned out to be an embarrassment for India because one of Pakistan's star batsmen, Shahid Afridi, clobbered virtually every ball that the Indians bowled at him. Many of his hits headed straight for our VIP enclosure. Like any normal cricket fan I wanted to jump out of my seat shouting and clapping, but I had to control my enthusiasm in deference to my hosts. Before the match was over, we left for our discussions. It goes without saying that I was dying to get back to the exciting match. So during our official one-on-one meeting I suggested to the prime minister that we go back to see the last hour of the match and also distribute the prizes. I made him agree in spite of his concerns about security. But then, as the meeting continued, my staff kept sending in notes informing me about the collapse of the Indian team when its turn came to bat. India's entire team got out long before the end of the game. Tightly repressing any outward signs of my inner joy, I had to inform Manmohan Singh that the Indian team's batting had been wasted and there was no point in another visit to the stadium. "Boys will be boys," some might say, but they obviously don't know cricket, or the importance of a match between Pakistan and India.

Still, our one-on-one dialogue was most productive. We discussed Kashmir in depth. We both agreed that we had to resolve the dispute and that we needed to find a solution "outside the box." The prime minister did say that he could not agree to any redrawing of borders, while I said I could not agree to accepting the Line of Control as permanent. We had to find a solution satisfactory to both sides, and to the people of Kashmir especially. This meeting ended in a very positive joint declaration, which the prime minister read out to a gathering of the media. We decided to carry forward the peace process with all sincerity.

Prime Minister Manmohan Singh invited me to dinner at his hotel in New York on September 14, 2005, during the UN General Assembly. The occasion started on a down note, with the Indians very upset at the tenor of my speech to the General Assembly. I thought they were being unnecessarily sensitive. The dialogue heated up quite a bit, perhaps because of my military gruffness, but our respective foreign ministers soon cooled the situation down. Dinner was served after about three hours of discussion, still in a tense atmosphere. The atmosphere improved after dinner, however, and we did manage to draft a bland joint statement. The media were fast to pick up the tense mood of the opposing sides and concluded that the meeting had not gone very smoothly. Still, I invited Manmohan Singh to Pakistan and he accepted readily. As I write this in June 2006, we are still awaiting his visit. The Indian cricket team toured Pakistan in early 2006. This gave India's prime minister an opening but he didn't take it, apparently because Indian officialdom felt that our discussions were far too serious to be mixed with something as "frivolous" as cricket. As it turned out, India won four out of five one-day international games. Prime Minister Manmohan Singh could have attended one of the games that India won, and we would have been even!

Such intricate diplomacy with India has produced results. Our bilateral relations are better than they ever were. I have said repeatedly that the time for conflict management has passed and the time for conflict resolution has come—and come urgently, because such moments do not occur often or last long. We are moving on two parallel tracks: one track is confidence-building measures (CBMs), and the second is conflict resolution. My preference has always been to move along them simultaneously; but the Indians, it seems, want to move quickly on CBMs while only crawling forward on conflict resolution.

The initial signs of sincerity and flexibility that I sensed in Manmohan Singh seem to be withering away. I think the Indian establishment—the bureaucrats, diplomats, and intelligence agencies and perhaps even the military—has gotten the better of him. I feel that if a leader is to break away from hackneyed ideas and frozen positions, he has to be bold. He has to dominate the establishment, rather than letting it dictate to him. I am still waiting for Manmohan Singh's "outside the box" solution. In the meantime, I have initiated many new ideas. We await responses or any counter ideas to solve the dispute over Kashmir, without which I strongly believe permanent peace in the region will remain elusive.

I have myself spent hours on many a day pondering a possible "outside the box" solution. The idea that I have evolved—which ought to satisfy Pakistan, India, and the Kashmiris—involves a partial stepping back by all. The idea has four elements and can be summarized as follows:

1. First, identify the geographic regions of Kashmir that need resolution. At present the Pakistani part is divided into two regions: Northern Areas and Azad Kashmir. The Indian part is divided into three regions: Jammu, Srinagar, and Ladakh. Are all these on the table for discussion, or are there ethnic, political, and strategic considerations dictating some give and take?

2. Second, demilitarize the identified region or regions and curb all militant aspects of the struggle for freedom. This will give comfort to the Kashmiris, who are fed up with the fighting and killing on both sides.

3. Third, introduce self-governance or self-rule in the identified region or regions. Let the Kashmiris have the satisfaction of running their own affairs without having an international character and remaining short of independence.

4. Fourth, and most important, have a joint management mechanism with a membership consisting of Pakistanis, Indians, and Kashmiris overseeing self-governance and dealing with residual subjects common to all identified regions and those subjects that are beyond the scope of self-governance.

This idea is purely personal and would need refinement. It would also need to be sold to the public by all involved parties for acceptance.

Let me now say a few words about Afghanistan, another of our neighbors, and another source of tension in the region and around the world. Landlocked Afghanistan is dependent on Pakistan for access to the world. The Central Asian Republics (CARs) are also looking to the world for trade and commercial activity. This whole region will gain economically if Afghanistan stabilizes and allows free transit for trade and commerce through its territory. Pakistan would be a major beneficiary because all trade into or out of Afghanistan and beyond to the CARs would be dependent on Pakistan's outlets and inlets—its roads, railways, and seaports.

I am convinced that a peaceful, sovereign, integrated Afghanistan is in the interests of Pakistan, our region, and indeed the whole world. We therefore wholeheartedly support the Bonn Process and are in favor of massive reconstruction in Afghanistan. We support President Hamid Karzai and his policies for bringing peace and a democratic dispensation to his war-ravaged country. Our combined fight against terrorism and extremism has to be fought with full vigor, perfect coordination, and complete cooperation.

Historically, Pakistan has always championed the Arab and Palestinian cause. Our stand against Israel has been confrontational. Interaction with Jews or the Jewish state has been taboo. We have been more pious than the pope on the subject of the Palestinian-Israeli dispute, given that we are not Arab and that quite a few other Muslim countries, including Arab countries, have recognized Israel, at least to some degree.

I have always wondered what we stand to gain by this policy. It is a given that Israel, besides being the staunchest ally of the United States, has a very potent Jewish lobby there that could wield influence against Pakistan's interest. Moreover, if the intention is to strengthen and promote Palestinian rights, I thought more could be contributed through joining the dialogue rather than remaining on the sidelines. The change that has occurred in the political realities of the Middle East and the world after the end of the Cold War, and after 9/11, suggested to me that it was time to reconsider our policy toward Israel. I am aware of the sensitivity of this issue, domestically and in the Arab world, and I realize that we must tread carefully.

I tested the domestic ground first, by giving a careful statement that if Israel moved forward toward the creation of a viable state of Palestine—a state acceptable to the Palestinians—then Pakistan would reconsider its diplomatic stance toward Israel. As I expected, the media and the intelligentsia reacted very positively, whereas the man in the street could not have cared less. I was then approached by some representatives of the American Jewish community led by Jack Rosen, president of the American Jewish Congress, to address the Jewish community in New York. It didn't take me long to agree. Simultaneously, we saw discernible changes in the attitude of Israel's prime minister, Ariel Sharon, toward the Palestinian dispute. He started the forced removal of Jewish settlements from Gaza. When I saw this on television, I immediately sensed an opportunity. I thought the foreign ministers of Pakistan and Israel could meet overtly. We considered Turkey the best venue for such a meeting and also thought that the good offices of the Turkish prime minister could be used to arrange it. It took just one day to organize all this. The Israeli's eagerness to respond was very clear. My gratitude went to my friend the prime minister of the brotherly host country, Turkey.

The historic, groundbreaking meeting of the foreign ministers of Pakistan and Israel took place on September 1, 2005, in Istanbul. It was positive and was followed by my address to the American Jewish Congress in New York on September 17, 2005. The atmosphere was electric, and the reception given to me was very warm and welcoming. All the prominent figures in the American Jewish community were on hand. I met every one of them before the formal ceremony. This was a very big first: a Pakistani leader mixing with and then addressing the American Jewish community. The ceremony started with the Jewish ritual of breaking bread. Jack Rosen praised me in his opening speech. Congressman Tom Lantos read out and then presented me with a framed copy of the Congressional Record of the House of Representatives titled "Tribute to President Pervez Musharraf of Pakistan." My own speech was emotional, and I think it had the desired impact. New ground was broken. The domestic reaction was all positive, and the international response euphoric.

Following the PLO's recognition in its charter of Israel's right to exist, Pakistan now accepts Israel as a Jewish state and a de facto reality, but at the same time stands by its commitment to support a viable and independent Palestinian state that is acceptable to the Palestinian people. I think now we will be able to play a more effective, proactive role in a resolution of the Palestinian dispute and the creation of a state for the long-suffering Palestinians.

In our attempts to bring peace to the world, within the Muslim *ummah,* and to our region, I have followed a policy of peaceful coexistence with all. I believe in nurturing bilateral relations with countries with whom we have interests, unaffected by their relations with other countries. I have especially tried to get away from Pakistan's Indocentric approach to relations with other countries. China remains our time-tested and sincere friend, irrespective of its developing economic relations with India. We are simultaneously developing broad-based and long-term relations with the United States, free from the effects of the warming up of relations between India and the United States.

In the Gulf, besides maintaining cordial relations with all states, Pakistan has always been very close to Saudi Arabia and the United Arab Emirates (UAE). These very special relationships continue. I have strengthened them through my personal contacts with the leaders of both countries.

Iran is our important neighbor. Our effort has always been to have close, cordial relations, but in reality we continue to have our ups and downs. The nuclear standoff between the United States and Iran, our separate relations with India, and our stands on Afghanistan do create complications in our bilateral relationship. Quite clearly we have to understand each other's sensitivities in order to forge the strong friendship that our geography and our history dictate.

The twenty-first century will be driven by geoeconomics more than by geostrategy or geopolitics. Relations between countries are based on economic bonds—interaction in trade, joint ventures, and investment. Our foreign missions, I believe, ought to promote trade, especially Pakistani exports and investment in Pakistan. These are two areas that were virtually ignored in the past.

An attitudinal change had to be introduced in our diplomats to make them conscious of their new orientation. Our ambassadors had also to be made to work in unison with their own Ministry of Foreign Affairs plus the ministries of Commerce, Industries, and Investment, and the Export Promotion Bureau. Only a coordinated effort could produce results.

We launched this effort aggressively in 2000. We posted able commercial councilors in our missions abroad. I made it clear to the ambassadors that their performance would be judged by their success in generating commercial activity. We decided to diversify our market from our traditional focus on the United States and Europe to South America, Africa, Eastern Europe, Southeast Asia, and China and within our own region of south Asia. We used all diplomatic efforts to enter into preferential trade agreements and even free trade agreements. With our old and good friend China we achieved an "Early Harvest" program to give a special boost to trade. Such momentum was generated that our exports increased to $18 billion in 2006—an increase of 125 percent in five years.

I expected our ambassadors to sell Pakistan as a destination for foreign investment. They have started to deliver. Wherever I go, I have a dual agenda: to enhance political relations and to interact with the business community to attract it to Pakistan. A strong business delegation from Pakistan always accompanies me. As a result of such measures, investment has started flowing into Pakistan.

CHAPTER 29

THE SOCIAL SECTOR

In 1999 I was on the horns of a dilemma, made worse by limited financial resources and by an economy in extreme distress: should our strategy be to allocate maximum resources to education and health, or to development projects that would boost the economy? I decided on the latter because we needed a revived economy in order to increase funds for the social sector. This strategy worked well, and in two to three years we had reached such a healthy position that we could greatly increase funds for health and education, especially the latter.

We took a holistic look at the education sector, which had decayed pathetically. We decided to address every level of it. At the bottom of the education ladder, we decided to improve literacy, which was at a shameful 48 percent. We decided to universalize education, especially for girls, and also focus on adult literacy.

The second rung of the education ladder is primary and secondary education. To improve these we decided to modify the curriculum, introduce a better examination system, and emphasize the training of teachers. I created a public-private partnership organization that I called the National Commission on Human Development to assist in health, education, and building capacity at the grassroots level. This commission, with a plan to access all 110 districts of Pakistan by December 2006, is delivering on its mandate. It has opened "feeder" schools with the assistance of local villagers (no brick and mortar involved), employing local girls and boys as teachers, and 20,800 adult literacy centers. I give all credit for this to Dr. Nasim Ashraf, a dynamic expatriate

Pakistani-American medical doctor who gave me this idea and is now spearheading the effort.

Augmenting these efforts are the provincial governments. In Punjab, for example, all state schools have been made free, as have textbooks. A computer program has tagged every school, identified what each lacks, and plugged the holes. In eighteen districts of southern Punjab, where the dropout rate for girls was highest between classes five and eight, 200 rupees a month are given to any girl whose attendance rate is 80 percent or more. Not surprisingly, the dropout rate has decreased dramatically.

The top rung of the education ladder, which we tackled separately, is higher education. We completely dismantled the decayed University Grants Commission and from its remains created a new Higher Education Commission (HEC) headed by a most able and dynamic scientist and educationist, Dr. Atta-ur-Rahman. Besides formulating a new University Ordinance, HEC introduced revolutionary changes in the universities and improved their quality. Funds for higher education were increased from a paltry $10 million to $350 million per annum, an unprecedented increase of 3,500 percent. An ambitious program has been launched to produce 1,500 PhDs annually in engineering and science by 2010. In the past, only a dozen or two dozen PhDs were awarded annually. By 2008 six new engineering universities meeting international standards will have been opened. The HEC has initiated a distance learning program linking fifty-nine existing universities all over Pakistan and has also brought in 16,000 expensive science journals on the Internet, making them available to students all over the country. These measures are having a salutary effect on higher education.

In the past, we have grossly ignored technical education. Therefore, certain technicians, and skilled manpower in general, have been in short supply. We have now created a National Vocational and Technical Education Commission (NAVTEC) to develop technical schools and vocational centers around the country in an organized manner. Thus technical education has now been taken away from the Ministry of Education, where it was languishing. The overall idea is to create linkages between our universities producing engineers, the technical schools producing skilled technicians, and the requirements of our present and future industry. This will not only enhance our technical expertise but also create jobs.

The last thorny issue that we are tackling is madrassa education. We have approximately 14,000 madrassas in Pakistan with about 1 million poor students. Eighty percent of these madrassas fall under five Wafaq ul Madaris ("trusts for madrassas"). Their strength lies in the fact that they generally provide free board and lodging to their students. In that sense they are very strong providers of human welfare. Their weakness, however, is that they generally impart religious education only, and a few of them get involved in terrorism and extremism. In general, most are characterized by religious rigidity and intolerance of other sects. Such a system generates thousands of young men annually who can become only clerics in a mosque. We need to change this situation through a dialogue with the Wafaq ul Madaris. We have been trying to mainstream madrassas into our normal education system.

First, we now require madrassas to register with the government and to teach all the normal subjects specified by the board of education and administer the related exams, instead of restricting themselves to merely a religious curriculum. The government has decided to fund only those madrassas that comply with these requirements. All five Wafaqs are generally accepting this. While they accept the teaching of subjects in accordance with a syllabus provided by us, however, they have opposed joining the system of our board of education." We are making progress toward a compromise, despite a lack of trust on both sides. I am sure we will reach an agreement soon, and that it will go a long way toward harmonizing relations between Pakistan and its madrassas.

Of the 20 percent or so madrassas that are not part of the Wafaq ul Madaris, only a small and decreasing number are in the hands of extremists. It bears repeating that among Pakistan's 150 million Muslims, only a small fraction are extremists. The problem, here as elsewhere in the world, is that extremists are so vocal and do such drastic things that they receive a disproportionate share of attention, whereas the peace-loving, moderate majority is so silent and meek that it gives the impression of being a minority. The overwhelming majority of Pakistanis are firmly on the side of enlightened moderation. It bears repeating that Islam in India was spread by the Sufis, not by the sword. This is why the majority of our Muslims are tolerant and peace-loving.

Eventually, as a result of board examinations and standardized curricula, madrassa students will be eligible to apply to colleges or universities on merit. There are many countries around the world that intertwine religious and public schools successfully, and there is no reason why Pakistan cannot do the same.

CHAPTER 30

THE EMANCIPATION OF WOMEN

Mukhtaran Mai become a household name internationally. It is most unfortunate that her traumatic experience—a rape—propelled her to fame. Much has been heard, said, and written about this rape, yet it bears telling as an example of some of the challenges faced by women in Pakistan

Mukhtaran Mai, a woman of the Gujjar tribe, was born in 1969 in the village of Mirwala in south Punjab. She is divorced—or at least was at the time of the incident. Her brother, Abdul Shakoor, was believed to be in a relationship with a woman named Naseem, of the Mastoi tribe, which considers its status higher than that of the Gujjar. Abdul Shakoor and Naseem were supposedly caught together by Abdul Khaliq and Allah Ditta, both brothers of Naseem. Abdul Shakoor was overpowered, sodomized, and then handed over to the police. The villagers decided to convene a *panchayat* (a traditional forum of local elders) to resolve the dispute. The *panchayat* decided that Abdul Shakoor was to marry Naseem, and that Mukhtaran Mai should marry one of the brothers of Naseem.

Naseem's brother Abdul Khaliq and a few others did not agree with the decision. Mukhtaran Mai was dragged into a room by Abdul Khaliq and Allah Ditta (another brother) and two others. According to the testimony of witnesses, Mukhtaran Mai came out visibly ruffled and partly undressed. Needless to say, Mukhtaran Mai was not to blame nor should she have been punished for her brother's indiscretion with Naseem.

Islam forbids both fornication and punishing an innocent person for someone else's crime. It also forbids giving girls from one family away in marriage to someone in an aggrieved family as reparation. This is un-Islamic, illegal, inhumane, and uncivilized; it is, however, one of the regrettable age-old customs of some of our rural areas that have imposed their beliefs onto both Islamic and secular law. This does not mean that state should not use all the means at its disposal to root out such customs. It is indeed the duty of the state to protect the weak, the disadvantaged, and those at the margins of society. That is what the state is all about. However, rooting out old customs is easier said than done in a country of 160 million that occupies a vast area, where education is limited, especially in the rural regions. Still, we are trying.

The *panchayat* and the incident in the room took place on June 22, 2002. A report was lodged with the police on June 30. The hue and cry raised in newspapers caught my attention, and I immediately moved in favor of Mukhtaran Mai. I sent her the equivalent of about $10,000 and assured her of my full support. No amount of money, however, can ever compensate for the trauma of rape. The case was tried in an antiterrorist court in Dera Ghazi Khan, and the court gave a death sentence to the two brothers of Naseem and their four accomplices on August 31, 2002. The convicted men appealed to the Lahore high court, which acquitted all except Abdul Khaliq, whose death sentence was reduced to life imprisonment, owing to insufficient evidence. This judgment was passed on March 3, 2005.

The judgment by the high court led to an extensive campaign by the media, human rights groups, NGOs, and women's rights activists. A petition on behalf of Mukhtaran Mai was filed in the Supreme Court of Pakistan on June 26, 2005, against the verdict of the Lahore high court. Arrest warrants were issued against all the released men, and they were put behind bars again, bail having been disallowed.

Throughout this saga I remained discreetly on the side of Mukhtaran Mai. The government facilitated the establishment of a school, a police post, and a women's crisis center in her village, at a cost of approximately $300,000. Innumerable NGOs, ambassadors, and women's rights activists visited the village, invited her to various functions, and gave her financial and moral support. She was awarded the Fatima Jinnah Gold Medal by an adviser to the prime minister for social welfare on August 2, 2005.

Mukhtaran Mai traveled extensively all over the world. She went to Spain on February 2, 2003; to Saudi Arabia on August 12, 2004; to India on January 10, 2004; to the United States in October 2005, January 2006, and May 2006; and to France in January 2006. She has been interviewed on many television channels and by the print media and has also been given innumerable awards the world over.

Mukhtaran Mai is very well known now, a celebrity of sorts, though because of her tragedy I am cautious about using that word. She runs schools and a women's crisis center, and has a Web site and a secretary to assist her. If there is a silver lining to her mis-treatment, it is that she has been able to bring attention to the plight of women in many parts of Pakistan.

Rape, no matter where it happens in the world, is a tragedy and deeply traumatic for the victim. My heart, therefore, goes out to Mukhtaran Mai and any woman to whom such a fate befalls.

It is also not easy for a woman victim to prosecute her oppressors. That is an experience which is at times no less harrowing than the crime itself. Any woman who takes this road deserves credit and our respect for her courage. Mukhtaran Mai is indeed such a woman. Her fortitude also has helped focus the debate and indeed our attention on the need for speedy and effective corrective measures.

The women of Pakistan suffer. They are often denied justice—and in a civilized society that is inexcusable. Violence against women, including rape, is not uncommon in Pakistan. We have to take focused measures to rectify this sad malady.

Rape and violence against women are a universal phenomena, but this does not justify their presence in Pakistan. We need to set our own house in order. I only object when Pakistan is singled out and demonized.

When a case of female victimization in Pakistan comes to light, sometimes the first casualty is the truth. Why does this happen? The media is usually the first source and attention for such cases. This is helpful because it gives prominence to the issue and generates a sense of urgency in the government. But some irresponsible outlets broadcast their opinions and write their own versions of event without complete knowledge of the facts. People with only half-baked knowledge make statements that become gospel truth. The official agencies are slow to react, sometimes through sheer callousness and sometimes because they do not want to reveal certain facts for fear of affecting the case or weakening the investigation. Politicians, especially those in opposition, are fast to enter the fray and distort the facts to malign the government. NGOs also join in, mostly with good intention, but they become victims of the hundreds of unsubstantiated stories. The truth thus keeps getting buried deeper and deeper. Last but not the least, so much money sometimes gets involved in the story that facts get further submerged.

The government must take cognizance of and practical measures to undo the tragic and shameful condition of women in our society. The authorities must be the first to reach out and to react when injustice occurs. They must be the ones to get all the facts out. They must not be overly concerned about the secrecy or confidentiality of the evidence. We are now trying to adopt this line of action.

The emancipation of women mattered to me even before I took office. As an army officer, I saw the situation faced by women in many parts of the country. It always felt wrong to me. We have to do something about it.

The debate, however, must take place within Pakistan's political and social landscape. Domestically, I am prepared to discuss and address any and all gender issues affecting our society. Through this book I declare my total support of and commitment to the cause of women in Pakistan.

The views of our local champions of women's right are consonant with mine. Perhaps where we differ is over the methodology for achieving our shared goals. When one demands equal rights for women, one needs to assess in which areas women can work better than men, in which they can work like men, and in which they need protection and affirmative action for when they cannot work like men. I personally feel that we have to adopt a graduated, incremental approach, taking measures simultaneously to develop capacity in women in areas where they need help and improvement.

My first aim has been the political empowerment of women. Empowering them politically gives them a way to shape their own future. Through empowerment, they gain an opportunity to fight for women's causes themselves in the highest governmental bodies. (Earlier, I discussed what I have done to empower women politically at all levels of government—local provisional, and national).

We established a women's political school at a cost of $4.3 million to help train women for political offices. By 2006 about 27,000 had been trained.

We established a National Commission on the Status of Women, to oversee women's rights; and a Gender Reform Action Plan, fully funded by the Government of Pakistan, to ensure enhanced representation of women and their overall emancipation. These efforts have helped women make great strides. Today women are serving in public office at every level: seven in the federal cabinet, six provincial ministers, ten parliamentary secretaries, and twelve chairpersons of standing committees of the senate and National Assembly. Besides all this, for the first time a women has been appointed to the prestigious and powerful position of governor of the State Bank of Pakistan; one major general in the army is a women; two women for the first time, have been appointed as judges of the Sindh High Court, a woman has been appointed a deputy attorney general, again a first, and women have been inducted in the army and also as pilots in the Pakistan Air Force.

Major initiatives are being taken to encourage education among girls through increased facilities and special incentives. These are all bearing fruit. Girls in cities are now much more committed to higher education than boys. In fact, their overall performance is far better than that of boys.

Efforts are also being made toward the economic empowerment of women. Several skills—training projects backed up by micro credit facilities have been launched. A Women's Chamber of Commerce and Industry has been launched. A huge exhibition showcasing products for women was recently held in Karachi; I had the privilege of helping to launch it. Over 100,000 women participated.

We have to confront the curse of violence against women and fight against laws that discriminate against them. The National Assembly passed legislation banning "honor killing," or *Karo Kari,* as it is locally called. This however, is not the ultimate answer. Honor killing is an evil practice, which has the sanction of custom in certain backward areas of Pakistan. It is repugnant to Islam, but it has been practiced by some Pakistani Muslims for a very long time. Only education and enlightenment—not just legislation—can eventually bring it to an end. A big step has been taken by the government, but its implementation will take time. To support the legislation and provide solace to women who have been treated violently, a National Committee on Violence against Women has been formed, a chain of well-equipped crisis centers and shelters have been opened, and special complaint phone lines for women have been established at police stations.

The trickiest of all issues, and the most sensitive, is the Hudood law that was enacted in 1979 under General Zia, who openly courted religious extremists. The word hudood means "limits," and the Hudood law pertains to the transgression of those limits. It sets punishments for such crimes as adultery, theft, and rape. The religious lobby and especially its political parties consider this law to be in accordance with Islamic tradition; but most women and intellectuals and many enlightened religious scholars think that the law misinterprets our religion and that it discriminates against women. This law has tarnished our image immeasurably. It is now under review by the National Commission on the Status of Women, and the results will be presented to parliament. The Ministry of Women's Development is trying to develop a consensus for its repeal. The issue needs deft political and constitutional handling, but I believe we should be bold enough to correct past wrongs.

On the whole, I believe we have set in motion an irreversible process toward the emancipation of women. I say it is irreversible because I see it gradually gaining momentum. Women themselves have risen to fight for their rights, and many men now realize that they cannot, and should not try to, stop the process.

CHAPTER 31

THE SOFT IMAGE OF PAKISTAN

I t is unfortunate that Pakistan's image abroad has been tarnished so badly that the world associates it only with terrorism and extremism. Many people think of our society only as intolerant and regressive. However much we plead that the vast majority of Pakistan is moderate and that only a fringe element is extremist—and that our national fabric has been damaged by the turbulence to our west in Afghanistan and to our east in Kashmir, not by anything inherent within our borders and society—the message does not get across. I have therefore tried to project a truer image of Pakistan, which I call a soft image, through the promotion of tourism, sports, and culture.

We have arguably the best and certainly some of the highest mountains in the world, as well as a virgin coastline with beautiful beaches stretching all along our south, mighty rivers and stark deserts, dense forests, and historic religious sites for Buddhists, Hindus, and Sikhs. We have many other historic monuments and excavation sites and museums, going back to ancient times. Yet we have hardly any tourism. What a pity! Even before 9/11 we failed to market ourselves effectively, and we failed to develop the infrastructure needed to facilitate tourism. Now, of course, our grim reputation for extremism and the many travel advisories against us hinder tourism.

I have been conscious of our strengths and weaknesses. We have improved our telephone networks and completed a beautiful coastal highway stretching from Karachi in the east to the newly built Gwadar Port in the west. This links all the coastal towns and numerous picturesque sites along the route. We have also linked all four major valleys in our mountainous northern areas—Chitral, Kaghan, Gilgit-Hunza, and Skardu—laterally with one another. This allows tourists traveling by road to switch from one to the other without having to travel back to and from main airports. We are now trying to publicize our potential to attract local and foreign tourists. I am glad to see a gradual increase in local interest in tourism. This will encourage other infrastructure facilities, particularly hotels and motels, to spring up and in turn attract a greater number of foreign tourists.

I have been a sportsman of a kind. I call myself a jack-of-all-trades but master of none. Pakistan has been a reasonably good sporting country at various points in its history, and we have been world-class in cricket, hockey, and squash, and even bridge and amateur billiards and snooker. Unquestionably the best bridge player in the world, Zia Mahmood, is from Pakistan. Hashim Khan, Jahangir Khan, and Jansher Khan are the best squash players the world has ever known, with Jahangir the best of the three. If Hollywood only knew his story of tragedy, grit, and determination, it would make another movie like *Chariots of Fire*. Many of those who know him consider him the best athlete who ever lived. We compete at a high level in Asian athletics. Sports can provide a recreation that relieves stressful societal pressures. But in 1999, our sports achievements were at a low ebb. I therefore launched a campaign to improve the situation.

The first thing we had to do was reorganize all the sports bodies, which had become hotbeds of fraud and cronyism. Accordingly, we restructured all the sports federations, introducing merit and efficiency into them. We then strategized and helped to encourage an interesting, participatory, and competitive sporting system for the country, at three levels: interschool and intercollege competitions, the regional and district level, and corporation-level competitions in the public and private sectors. We are also trying to encourage the private sector to sponsor events and sports teams. This, we hope, will attract national talent, expose people to competitive sports, and improve our overall national sporting standards while providing much-needed recreational activity to the entertainment-starved population of Pakistan.

• • •

Few people in the world know that Pakistan has a rich, diverse cultural heritage. We have the nearly prehistoric excavations at Mohenjo Daro and Harappa, the Mehrgarh civilizations, Alexander the Great, and the British raj. Both Alexander and Britain left indelible footprints in our land. The people of the Kalash tribe in the remote Kalash valley of Chitral are said to be descendants of Alexander's army, which turned back from here. Our landscape is replete with monuments of the Mughal era, shrines of Muslim Sufi mystics, and remnants of the British colonial era. The revered religious sites of Buddhism (in Taxila, Swabi, and Swat), of Hinduism (in Katas Raj), and of Sikhism (in Hassanabdal and Nankana Sahib) add color to our heritage. When you walk in our land, you walk alongside history. Every stone, every path and byway, every nook and cranny, and every peak of our mighty Himalayas, the Karakoram, and the Hindu Kush mountains will have a story to tell.

The four provinces of Pakistan have rich and distinct cultures. Music, dance, and art have flourished in our land for millennia. Ironically, all this has remained the best-kept secret of Pakistan. Worse, the forces of religious extremism and obscurantism reject this cultural activity as being un-Islamic. No previous government had the courage to tell them that they were wrong.

All this needed a drastic change. We had to bring normality and cultural harmony back into our national fabric. I started by revitalizing Pakistan's heritage. I asked the army to beautify the Quaid-e-Azam's mausoleum in Karachi and make it a fitting tribute to the father of the nation. Today, people by the thousands throng to admire the magnificence of its surroundings. We also erected an impressive national monument at Islamabad, dedicated to the people of Pakistan. It features an underground museum focusing on the Pakistan movement—our struggle for winning our homeland. An imposing monument at Walton, Lahore, which we call Bab-e-Pakistan ("Gateway to Pakistan"), is under construction at the exact site where the father of the nation first addressed over 100,000 refugees fleeing from India. In addition to these monuments, I launched an ambitious plan to create a National Heritage Museum in Islamabad, showing Pakistan's regional culture and traditions. This project has since been completed by Uxi Mufti. He is passionately involved in our art and culture and has done exemplary work on this project. The museum is now an attraction for many local and foreign visitors and dignitaries.

I also encouraged our performing arts, including music, theater, and dance. We opened a National Academy of the Performing Arts in Karachi, and I selected the renowned thespian Zia Mohyuddin to run it. We also opened a National Council of Arts with an art gallery in Islamabad. Both institutions are attracting a lot of young talent to the performing arts, particularly music.

Finally, as I mentioned earlier, many private television channels have opened since the liberalization of our media. We have to work hard to improve our image around the world, and we must proceed on all fronts simultaneously. We have to defeat terrorism and extremism, but at the same time we must also present a culturally rich, inviting, and economically vibrant alternative in its place. The media need to gear up to sell Pakistan abroad.

CHAPTER 32

LEADERSHIP ON TRIAL:
THE EARTHQUAKE

At eight fifty-two AM on October 8, 2005, the world literally fell apart for millions of Pakistanis. An earthquake measuring 7.6 on the Richter scale struck our mountainous, inaccessible northern region, affecting the North-West Frontier Province and Azad Kashmir, bringing death and destruction in a few seconds, and leaving complete havoc in its wake. It affected an area of nearly 12,000 square miles (30,000 square kilometers) and left 3.5 million homeless; 73,000 dead; 500,000 homes and buildings destroyed; most educational and health facilities obliterated; and all government structures demolished. Even our capital, Islamabad, was affected when a high-rise apartment building called Margalla Towers collapsed, killing many residents and burying hundreds under its rubble. The nation went into shock. As the news started trickling in, the magnitude of the disaster became clear to me, the government, the nation, and the entire world.

Initially, I had no information of what had happened in the North-West Frontier Province (NWFP) or Azad Kashmir. The only news I received was about the collapsed building in Islamabad. I visited the site immediately. But as soon as we started to hear reports from the mountains, I ordered the army's chief of general staff to fly over the area to assess the scale of the disaster.

The collapse of Margalla Towers made me realize how ill-equipped we were to carry out rescue operations. I must acknowledge with extreme gratitude the spontaneous response of Turkey and Britain in dispatching their well-equipped, well-trained rescue teams. Many people saved from the debris owe their lives to these valiant few and their sniffer dogs. These rescue teams also reached the NWFP and Azad Kashmir and did an equally impressive job there. We owe them a great deal of gratitude.

By about five PM the chief of general staff returned with the first group of casualties at the military hospitals in Rawalpindi. The magnitude of the calamity was now clear. I decided to visit the sites personally early the next morning, not only to assess the damage for myself but also to comfort the wounded, the homeless, and the bereaved. The army was swift to react. The few routes to the area had been closed by landslides. Army engineers were ordered to move immediately and open them up. Divisions totaling a strength of about 50,000 troops were sent from garrisons in the Punjab. The entire helicopter strength of our army and air force was mobilized for immediate relief and evacuation of casualties.

I left for the earthquake zone at nine thirty the next morning, October 9. We went to two places in the NWFP and three in Azad Kashmir. The town of Balakot in the NWFP had been completely destroyed. What I saw was heartrending. There was not a building left standing. The entire government of the town had been obliterated. Those left alive were standing around in shock. I could hardly bear to see their glazed eyes and traumatized expressions and the hopelessness etched on their faces. I could do no more than give words of solace and comfort and convey my resolve to help them through this catastrophe. Wherever I went I saw doctors at work—some civilian, most military—tending to patients in the open or in makeshift shelters. At Muzaffarabad, the capital of Azad Kashmir, I was surprised and pleased to see a Turkish medical team already at work. How had they gotten there before me? Knowing Turkish, I thanked them for their selfless devotion and love for our people. At Muzaffarabad, at about one PM, I was given the good news that the army engineers had opened one of the two roads leading to the city. They must have moved at night and worked in the darkness to complete the job. The other main arteries to other cities were also opened within two days. However, access to the remote mountain valleys took weeks to restore. Those areas depended on helicopter support.

Returning to my office, I took stock of the situation and decided to launch the President's Reconstruction Initiative (PRI). This effort involved four stages: rescue, relief, reconstruction, and rehabilitation. We first set up a Federal Relief Commissioner's Organization to manage the rescue and relief operation. We later created an Earthquake Reconstruction and Rehabilitation Authority to look after the third and fourth stages.

The rescue operation lasted for about a month. Pakistan was ill-equipped for it, lacking technical expertise and equipment. We shall always remain grateful for the fast response of Britain and Turkey in dispatching their rescue experts. They saved many lives.

Our main preoccupation was the relief operation, since so many millions were homeless and winter was approaching. This involved three distinct elements: bringing in food and water to prevent famine; mobilizing medical assistance, including essential lifesaving medicines and field hospitals; and providing shelter for the homeless. Pakistan is not like the wealthy western nations that have vast resources and well-organized social security nets. While the government does stock a certain amount of relief stores for unforeseen calamities, a vast network of private charities must share the burden and fill the gaps. The whole nation rose as one to help, with countless citizens and innumerable volunteer organizations donating, collecting, and transporting relief goods. Hundreds of doctors—local and expatriate Pakistanis and foreigners—streamed in to help. The generosity of Pakistanis as well as our friends abroad was as impressive as the disaster was unimaginable. The NGOs, UN organizations, and indeed the entire world community opened their hearts to us. The Pakistani nation can never forget their spontaneous generosity and empathy.

The role of my government in all this was coordination. We realized that if we did not control and regulate the huge flow of relief goods to the earthquake zone and maintain our overburdened telecommunication network, the whole system would become chaotic and collapse. The army was the only institution that could do this. Accordingly, we spread the army divisions, ten brigades and approximately fifty battalions, to various locations covering the length and breadth of the affected area. These locations we called nodes. Their telephone numbers and the names of the officers in charge were publicized through the media for access by anyone who needed assistance. The army thus regulated all the incoming and outgoing traffic and directed and distributed relief supplies on a most-needed basis. The nodes also acted as telecommunication hubs. We nominated two main relief air bases to receive relief goods, developed a sorting organization at these bases, laid down six forward bases in the mountains, and created an organization centered on the army nodes to carry the goods from these bases to the affected villages by helicopter, by airdrops, by mule, and on foot. I would be remiss if I did not make special mention of the contribution of the Chinook helicopters from the United States and Britain in transporting relief goods to the disaster areas. Time is of the essence in any rescue and relief operation, and we could not have succeeded without the Chinooks.

I must also mention the contribution not only of the governments but also of the people of Saudi Arabia and Turkey. They kept us supplied with relief goods such as tents, food, and medicines. Their governments launched special campaigns for generating public donations. The people of both countries opened their hearts to us. Most touching were the schoolchildren who donated their pocket money and the many poor people who came forward with their only valuable possessions.

Perhaps one of the wisest decisions I made, a few weeks into the relief operation, was to "monetize" the area. I saw that hundreds of thousands of people had been left penniless. Patients taken to field hospitals or to far-off main hospitals had no money to return home. All the small retail businesses in the earthquake zones had collapsed. There was not even a semblance of any commercial activity—there were no sellers and no buyers. We decided to distribute cash immediately to the next of kin of the dead or missing, to the wounded, and to all those who lost their homes. Approximately $350 million was distributed in about three months. This really did wonders. Commercial activity started up again, people commenced their own reconstruction effort, and one could see signs of economic life returning.

Cynics and pessimists predicted that tens of thousands of people would die of injuries, thousands of starvation, and thousands more of disease and in epidemics. None of this happened. They also predicted that tens of thousands would freeze to death in the merciless

Himalayan winter, which would soon be upon us. I call such people uninformed alarmists—feebleminded, feeble-hearted, and, not to put too fine a point on it, simply stupid. I knew all along that their predictions were wildly overblown.

Reconstruction is a more complex, long-term activity. We examined how it had been done around the world, particularly after the recent tsunami in south Asia and Hurricane Katrina in the United States. About 400,000 houses, schools, hospitals, and government structures needed to be built. For the houses, we thought it would be unwise and impractical to impose a solution from above. We therefore decided to follow an owner-driven strategy based on a fixed cash compensation for each house destroyed, together with a design for making new houses earthquake-resistant. For schools and hospitals we followed a need-based strategy whereby we worked out the optimum health and educational requirements of the area in the form of primary, middle, and high schools, colleges, and various categories of dispensaries and hospitals. As to the government infrastructure in Muzaffarabad, we decided to relocate it to create space for beautification of the city.

Rehabilitation involved caring for destitute women, orphaned children, and the physically impaired. We decided to open rehabilitation centers called *ashiana* around Islamabad, but later to shift them forward to their own areas in the NWFP and Azad Kashmir. One worry I had was the financial and "in kind" resources that we needed over the long term, to sustain the relief effort and to undertake the reconstruction and rehabilitation program. We launched a survey to evaluate the total damage in conjunction with the World Bank, the Asian Development Bank, UN organizations, and the government of Pakistan. We wanted everyone to agree on our needs from the start. The estimate produced was $5.2 billion: $1.6 billion for sustaining the relief operation for one year, $3.6 billion for reconstruction, and $100 million for rehabilitation. Armed with these data I decided to call a Donors' Conference in Islamabad to generate funds internationally. I also launched the President's Relief Fund. It made me proud to see the huge international response at the Donors' Conference. Seventy-six countries were represented, and in all they pledged $6.4 billion—$1.2 billion more than we had targeted—some in grants, some in soft loans. The entire Pakistani nation and I personally are grateful to the world for showing such generosity to Pakistan in its hour of need. The President's Relief Fund also received generous donations, mainly from local and expatriate Pakistani individuals and organizations. This fund had crossed $170 million in early 2006.

The earthquake was an act of God that caused tremendous pain and loss. Yet, the recovery effort—public and private, domestic and international, spontaneous and organized—is its own act of God, or perhaps thousands of His acts. With so much assistance and goodwill, the area and its people will recover, and we will all remain grateful.

REFLECTIONS

Sometimes when I reflect on the life I have led, from its beginning to its heights, I thank God for the mercies and kindnesses that He has showered on me. Born into a middle-class family and living in an elitist society, one should never, ordinarily, expect to reach the top.

Starting from the dangerous train journey during our migration from Delhi to Karachi, I have led a turbulent life. I did not demonstrate or even possess intellectual brilliance that would have predicted a bright future for me. In army service I was considered a casual, happy-go-lucky, confrontational officer, rather than a serious professional. I never took life too seriously. I landed myself in serious trouble for disciplinary reasons every now and then in the early part of my career. Seeing my overflowing record of indiscipline, you would never have expected me to have a great future.

God has always been kind to me. He protected me from certain death not only during the two wars in which I fought, but also in the face of assassins, air crashes, and one politically inspired hijacking. I wonder why.

My promotions from brigadier upward invariably faced obstacles—some political, some merely because I was competing against the elite, against officers born with a silver spoon in their mouth. Yet I kept moving up. That speaks volumes in favor of the promotion system in the army. My strength was my performance in wartime, my performance as a commander, my handling of troops on the ground, and most of all my relations with my bosses, my colleagues, and my subordinates. Along the way I raised my intellectual and professional acumen to a level where I was considered an able military tactician with a strong sense of strategy.

Whatever my weaknesses or strengths, my final step up to the position of army chief reinforced my belief in destiny. As a lieutenant general commanding the most prestigious strike corps, I had resigned myself to retiring gracefully. But Prime Minister Nawaz Sharif's decision to take the power of appointing service chiefs away from the president changed all that.

I firmly believe that success in one's life and career depends more on the wholesome development of personality than on mere intellectual brilliance. Everyone needs a healthy balance between intellectual development, moral development, physical development, and social development.

Your intellect keeps developing long after physical development stops. Each individual has a natural, inherent intellectual capacity, but personal efforts to sharpen it are essential.

Moral development forms your core personality. Honesty, truthfulness, contentment, and humility are the most important qualities of character. First, I have seen for myself that honesty—even under adversity, even when it could lead to a negative outcome—always disarms the other person. Second, truthfulness is a sine qua non of good character. Third, contentment with whatever I have possessed or achieved has kept me from greed or overambition. I was fortunate to rise as far as I did, but I would have been content if my fortunes were different. I have never lost sight of people who have been less privileged, and I remain thankful to God for His bounty. A person should be like a tree that can bend and sway even more as it grows higher. Fourth, being humble in greatness raises one's stature. One should never argue over one's qualities; instead, let others see these qualities for themselves. My character traits were instilled in me by my parents through direct teaching and personal example.

Leadership is inborn to a degree, but it can be acquired through effort. It is an art, not at all a science—or as my friend Colin Powell puts it beautifully, "It is the art of accomplishing more than the science of management says is possible." It is the art of interacting and talking with people; it is the art of reacting to situations; and it is the art of meeting challenges. What people like most in a leader, aside from his character, is decisiveness, as well as boldness and a cool temperament that remains unruffled in adversity.

A leader must understand his environment in all its intricacy. He must always have a finger on the pulse of the times.

Selecting a person for a critical position or a team is perhaps the most important duty of the leader. He has to be extremely circumspect and incisive. Loyalty, honesty, and uprightness are essential prerequisites in colleagues, but they are not all that is required. A person must have professional capabilities and the will to deliver in accordance with the leader's thoughts and ideas. Loyalty can be direct or indirect. Personal loyalty to you by your subordinate I call direct loyalty. But more than that, if a person is motivated by the same cause and believes in the same aims and objectives as you, and with conviction, he is bound to you more strongly.

Having grasped the environment and selected his team, a leader must evaluate the tasks ahead, prioritize them, and then evolve strategies for addressing them. This process has to be done in a manner that is embraced by the whole team. The best way to ensure this is through a democratic process, rather than having the leader work out strategies himself and dictate them to his team. A thorough debate of all pros and cons, in which everyone is encouraged to speak out, especially about the cons, is essential. The leader's task then is to make the final decision. This he must do efficiently—the earlier the better. A leader must never, as Richard Nixon says in his book *Leaders,* "suffer paralysis through analysis." I agree. Napoleon said that two-thirds of decision making is based on study, analysis, calculations, facts, and figures, but the other third is always a leap in the dark, based on one's gut. Anyone who increases that one-third is too impulsive. Anyone who increases the two-thirds lacks decisiveness and is no leader. I agree with this too. Of course it goes without saying that the leader must make the right decisions most of the time.

After the leader has strategized and made decisions, there remain two more aspects of leadership. First, decisions are final and the whole team must accept them—including anyone who may have voiced different ideas. There is no room for dissent after the final decision. Anyone not on board must quit the team. The leader must be cold and ruthless in firing a team member who refuses to accept the final decision. The second aspect is that the leader must delegate all authority of implementing his strategy to a subordinate, and back that subordinate up fully with all his strength and support. A leader must never get involved in micromanagement. He should only lay down the road map of what he wants to see at various stages and then monitor progress at the right intervals. Such monitoring is especially essential in Pakistan, because in any developing country there is always a big gap between formulation and implementation of policy.

No policy is ever 100 percent successful or perfect. I have come to the conclusion that while pushing for optimum results, you should accept partial success as long as you are moving in the right direction. A glass at least half full is a good thing. You can always add to it.

Leaders of nations have a much larger overall responsibility: to motivate their people and their nation, inspiring them, infusing confidence into them, and generating in them a spirit and urge to perform. This a leader can best do through personal example. The nation must see the leader perform up front. Only a man of real substance can be a true leader. A true leader will always be loved by his people. They will be prepared to follow him not because of his rank and position but because of their respect and esteem for him.

In fact, I strongly believe that while a leader must flow with the current of public opinion, a time and situation will always come when he will see that the flow of the current is wrong. It is at such times that true leadership qualities emerge, for the leader must change the course of the public current. The leader must have the will to change public opinion in the true national interest.

During the period that I have been at the helm of affairs, I have faced one crisis after another. I started with the biggest domestic challenge: having to steer the ship of state out of troubled waters before it sank. I crystallized the areas of focus in the form of a seven-point agenda and then identified my special areas of focus. Things were moving well domestically despite the external constraints being imposed on me by the West in its demand for "democracy." I fought my case, applying the logic of the essence of democracy that I wanted to introduce versus the artificial label of democracy that they were shouting about. I continued this struggle on the internal and external fronts for almost two years, quite successfully taking the country out of trouble and onto a path toward growth.

Then came 9/11 and its aftermath. The whole world changed. The world powers focused new attention on five areas of special concern: counterterrorism, nuclear proliferation, democracy, human rights, and narcotics. Pakistan sits at the center of each, and the external pressures are diametrically opposed to domestic sentiment. It is not that the majority of our public supports terror, or drugs, much less nuclear proliferation. Small factions support the first two, and even fewer people have been greedy enough to pursue the third. But a majority of Pakistanis do oppose our cooperation with the West in the war on terror. They opposed punishments aimed at Dr. A. Q. Khan. I believe my positions on all these issues are in our interest, and morally strong. But there are times when the behavior of our western allies undercuts our alliances.

This is particularly true of western counterterrorism policies. The West rejects militant struggles for freedom too broadly. The United States and Europe too often equate all militancy with terrorism; in particular, they equate the struggle for freedom in Indian-held Kashmir with terrorism. Pakistan has always rejected this broad-brush treatment. We demand that terrorism be seen "in all its forms and manifestations." This is a serious statement, because when states kill innocent civilians in an effort to crush struggles for freedom, we call it "state terrorism." I feel that the killing of innocent civilians, whether by a state or by any group, is terrorism. A state causing atrocities and killing civilians in violation of resolutions passed by the UN Security Council is certainly carrying out state terrorism. I differentiate between killing civilians as collateral damage in an attack on a military target on the one hand and targeting civilians intentionally on the other.

Pakistan's position becomes more difficult to sustain, however, when the mujahideen fighting for freedom in Indian-held Kashmir are guilty of involvement in terrorist activities in other parts of India and around the world. It is not just that one man's terrorist can be another man's freedom fighter; sometimes a man can be a legitimate freedom fighter in one context and a terrorist when he does something else. My efforts toward rapprochement with India and the significant thaw in our relations have saved Pakistan to a large extent from the blame of abetting what the world calls terrorism and we call a struggle for freedom in Indian-held Kashmir.

The issue of democracy is a recent, post–Cold War obsession of the West; and unfortunately this obsession clouds its vision. I have always believed in democracy, but I certainly oppose any fixed formula for all countries. If democracy is to be functional and sustainable, it has to be tailored to local conditions. I have traveled the world to present the case of Pakistan, and I have seen countries where democracy was failing because it did not meet local needs and dictates. Every nation must fulfill the basic principles of democracy: freedom of speech and expression through unfettered media; true empowerment of the people, including women and minorities; a guarantee of the vote for people to elect their own representatives; and, most important, a continuous and significant improvement in the human condition. Beyond this, the particulars of the system, the political and administrative institutions the people introduce, should be left to suit the national ethos. The sooner the West accepts this reality, instead of thrusting on every country ideas that may be alien to people's aspirations, the better it will be for global harmony. I still am struggling to convince the West that Pakistan is more democratic today than it ever was in the past. Ironically, to become so it needed me in uniform.

Ever since October 2002, when we held parliamentary national and provincial elections and I handed over governance to elected representatives, there have been complaints. I personally have been criticized for not ensuring a certain level of quality in our ministers and other government functionaries. I am even blamed, in some quarters, for forming a coalition with unscrupulous elements or a much-maligned political party. These accusations are true in many cases, but I prefer such "wrongs" to the alternatives.

Democracy in illiterate, feudal, tribal, and parochial societies has a serious downside. People are not elected on pure merit. They rise in the political hierarchy because of family connections and financial resources. From 1999 to 2002 I was selecting individuals purely on merit; now the people are electing them. If you want democracy, then you must also be responsible enough to vote for the right people. If you don't, then don't bellyache about the poor quality of parliamentarians and ministers.

Pakistan is accused of having a poor record on human rights. I agree that our record is nothing to be proud of, but I have always maintained that it is no worse than the record of most other developing countries and even of some developed countries. We have taken major strides to improve our record. We liberated the media, allowing freedom of speech and expression. We empowered women politically. We main-streamed minorities in political life by giving them a joint electorate sys-tem. We passed an ordinance banning honor killing. We are addressing the issue of child labor. We have introduced administrative measures to prevent the blatant misuse of the law against blasphemy. The most thorny issue of the Hudood law is being examined by a parliamentary committee. These are no mean achievements.

The drug trade is an international ill. Pakistan has been accused in the past of growing poppies and transporting drugs through carriers. We clamped down on poppy cultivation, reducing it to zero growth. We have strengthened the antinarcotics forces, and they are quite effective against drug carriers. We hope to continue improving our performance to the satisfaction of the world community.

In my first year in office—the year 2000—I put in over fifteen hours a day at work. I used to leave home about at nine AM, work the first shift till around six PM, return for a shower and a change of clothes, receive some working group or other at seven PM at home, continue with them till about ten PM (with or without dinner), and finally receive another working group at around eleven PM, to continue till around two AM. This routine remained constant for over a year. In these sessions, through sheer hard work, we evolved strategies for many elements of governance that had simply been nonexistent. I realized then how the state was being run on a day-to-day basis in a directionless manner. It was also through these laborious sessions that I learned all I did not know, especially about the economy.

There are innumerable things that have yet to be done. But I believe that one has to judge Pakistan's condition optimistically. Those who see every half-full glass as half empty tend toward cynicism, pessimism, and negativism. The alternative is to focus on the half that is full, and try hard to fill the rest. I remain ever conscious of what more must be done to sustain Pakistan on a path of progress and prosperity.

- We have to stabilize the North-West Frontier Province by defeating al Qaeda and checking the region's Talibanization.
- We have to suppress extremism and intolerance and eradicate them from our society.
- We have to sustain our huge economic growth through better irrigation and agriculture, increased foreign direct investment for industrial growth, and enhanced exports. We must convert Pakistan into a regional hub of trade and energy. All this has to be done while our fiscal deficit is kept in check.
- We have to transfer our economic gains to the people through alleviation of poverty, creation of jobs, and control of inflation. We have to improve the quality of life by providing everyone with access to electricity, clean drinking water, and natural gas.
- We have to concentrate all our energies on developing human resources through improved education and health facilities at every level.
- We have to consolidate our democracy and ensure the supremacy of the constitution.
- Last, but not least, we have to maintain and further enhance our international diplomatic stature.

Pakistan still has a long way to go. We have made great progress, but we cannot rest. With determination, persistence, and honest patriotic zeal, God willing, we will become a dynamic, progressive, and moderate Islamic state, and a useful member of the international comity of nations—a state that is a model to be emulated, not shunned.

INDEX